Beyond the Scoreboard

# Beyond the Scoreboard

Examining Teamwork, Tension, and
Triumph in High School Athletics

John P. Steltz

Mill City Press

Copyright © 2010 by John P. Steltz

Mill City Press, Inc.
212 3rd Avenue North, Suite 290
Minneapolis, MN 55401
612.455.2294
www.millcitypublishing.com

All rights reserved. No part of this publication may be reproduced, stored in a retrieval system, or transmitted, in any form or by any means, electronic, mechanical, photocopying, recording, or otherwise, without the prior written permission of the author.

Scripture taken from the HOLY BIBLE, NEW INTERNATIONAL VERSION®. Copyright © 1973, 1978, 1984 Biblica. Used by permission of Zondervan. All rights reserved

From the book *The Power of Now* Copyright © 1997 by Eckhart Tolle . Reprinted with permission of New World Library, Novato, CA  www.newworldlibrary.com.

Back Cover Photo provided by:
Steve Kemp, Photographer
Countryside Photographers
835 S. Main Street
Seymour WI 54165
920-833-6357.

ISBN - 978-1-936400-02-7
ISBN - 1-936400-02-2
LCCN - 2010931471

Cover Design & typeset by Nate Meyers
Cover Photo © 2010. All rights reserved - used with permission.

*Printed in the United States of America*

For my mother and father, Tom and Ginger, my siblings, Julie, Ellen, David, and Barbara, and my devoted wife, Desiree who have all inspired me and encouraged me to allow my light to shine and to share my God given talents.

# TABLE OF CONTENTS

### INTRODUCTION
The Heart of a Small Town ............................................................. xi

### GAME TIME
The Essence of the Game ................................................................ 2
Triumphs and Tensions ................................................................. 14

### THE INFLUENCE OF EGO
Emergence of the Destructive Ego ............................................... 23
Parents: The Ego's Engine ............................................................ 32
Coaches: The Ego's Vehicle .......................................................... 42
Student-Athletes: The Ego's Manifestation ................................ 53

### PURPOSE OF HIGH SCHOOL ATHLETICS
Winning and Life Lessons ............................................................. 60
Parents: Creating a Legacy .......................................................... 67
Coaches: Creating a Resume ....................................................... 78
Athletic Directors: Creating a Collaborative,
Healthy Environment .................................................................... 90
Student-Athletes: Creating a Positive Sense of Self-Worth .... 104

## HIGH SCHOOL ATHLETICS: A DEFINITION OF SUCCESS

High School Athletics:
The Education of the Whole Person..................................117
The Five Gifts of Successful Parents..................................121
The Foundation of Successful Coaches ...........................142
The Integrity of Successful Athletic Directors ....................162
The Visibility, Value, and Validation
of Successful Student-Athletes .........................................178

## EFFECT OF YOUTH SPORTS

A Hopeful Beginning........................................................197
Building a Strong Foundation ..........................................203
The Potential Destruction .................................................210

## BUILDING A MISSION STATEMENT

The Mission .....................................................................218

## CONCLUSION

The Spirit Within...............................................................230

## APPENDIX

Appendix A......................................................................236
Appendix B......................................................................245

## ACKNOWLEDGEMENTS

Acknowledgements .........................................................252

My Grandmama was a wise old soul,
took me by the hand not long ago,
said, "Son what's your hurry? Boy, slow it down.
Taste the wild honey. Listen to the sound
of the wind that's blowin' through the trees,
rivers flowin' to the sea.
Yeah, they're all headin' home just like you and me.
Life's for livin' child, can't you see that these are the days
    we will remember?
And these are the times that won't come again.
The highest of flames becomes an ember.
And you've got to live 'em while you can."
These are the days we will remember…
So take 'em by the hand, yours and mine.
Take 'em by the hand and live life.
Take 'em by the hand, don't let 'em all fly by.
Days go by just like a hand out the window wavin' in the
    wind as the cars go by.
These are the days….

*These Are The Days*  Keith Urban

# INTRODUCTION

# THE HEART OF A SMALL TOWN

    I live and work in a quiet quaint community. Desiree and I moved here for three reasons. First, I teach students High School English and we wanted to cut down on my commute time to spend more family time together. Second, Desiree and I believe that this is a wonderful community to raise a family. Finally, we wanted to be active participants in a community where people-helping-people was the tapestry of daily life. The heart of this town beats with pride and the blood that runs through its veins are the hard-working, mostly blue collar, kind-hearted people. During the cold and snowy winters my neighbor willingly clears the snow off my driveway with his four-wheeler. During the summer months I have willing students cut my lawn or clear the leaves. Our new hometown hosts the County Fair, car races on Sunday nights, and BurgerFest. Yes, our community is the Home of the Hamburger; I was born and raised in the town that owns stake as being the Home of the Ice Cream Sundae, and now I am raising my kids, proudly, in the Home of the Hamburger. All of these summer events showcase a family oriented community that counts on each other to come together to pitch-in any way possible. Desiree and I volunteer our time for BurgerFest, Vacation Bible School, and other community events.

    Our vision has come true in the sense that we are active members in our community, active in our church, and surrounded by positive people who share our values. We believe in deepening our faith, the importance of strong family structure, and quality education for our children. We get all that and more in our new hometown.

The premise of this book was born of a challenging predicament that I was in just two years ago. In 2008 I had the misfortune of being at the center of a high school coaching controversy in my community. Although I had led the varsity girls basketball team to the greatest success in the school's history, many parents who thirsted for a state championship second guessed game plans and play calls. My administration, who never defined what comprised a successful high school program, did not provide the structure I believed was effective for me to help kids and without that structure I found myself turning in my letter of resignation. I had prided myself on developing basketball skills but also fostering leadership, character, teamwork, honor, and sacrifice. Nevertheless, I was told by one of my administrators that such a holistic approach to coaching might fit better in a middle school than a high school setting.

My resignation set off a firestorm in the community resulting in over 150 posts on a local online sports blog and articles written in multiple newspapers. People on both sides of the issue passionately argued over whether pressuring me to resign in the pursuit of a gold ball was a misguided travesty or needed change. The whirlwind of conflict galvanized my belief that as educators, parents, and coaches we have to go beyond the scoreboard to build much needed life skills to make our student athletes viable, resilient, and successful in their future pursuits.

In support of the arguments presented in this book, I reveal glimpses of the aforementioned controversy and other triumphs and missteps of my 20 year coaching career; the foundation of the book is much broader and more philosophical. It challenges parents, coaches, and administrators to be proactive and collaborative in creating mission statements that will serve as a compass in times of tension and conflict that are an inevitable part of the high school sports landscape. Furthermore, it outlines the rights, roles, and responsibilities of coaches, administrators, parents, and student athletes. The myriad of real life scenarios that are weaved throughout the book challenge readers to develop their own philosophies and are sure to spark discussion among sports lovers regarding what defines success and what is the best way to handle various scenarios.

Beginning with the definition of ego and how the ego affects our reality the book dives into a faith driven movement to redefine the purpose of high school sports to include a holistic approach to co-curricular activities. The book outlines how the ego affects parents, coaches, athletic directors, and student-athletes. In addition, the book offers insight on how to overcome ego to allow the inner uniqueness of each person to surface.

I have identified the essential purpose of high school sports. These chapters, devoted to parents, coaches, athletic directors and student-athletes, focus on the common purpose of learning and gaining experiences that will promote success after high school. Furthermore, high school sports are a vehicle that must support the growth of a positive sense of self-worth for all student-athletes.

The book transitions from the purpose of high school athletics to providing definitions for success. I argue that success is in the learning and preparation, not entirely in the winning. Too often coaches are judged on their win-loss record, when what is really important is if that coach has been a teacher of life lessons where student-athletes gain valuable experience that will help them in the future.

The examination of the culture of high school athletics would be incomplete without a discussion of the effects of youth sports. I outline the benefits of youth sports and highlight how the world of sport can make a positive impact on children. Furthermore, I also outline the ways in which youth sports can prohibit emotional and psychological growth and, even worse, damage the sense of self-worth in our children.

Finally, this book provides suggestions for an athletic program mission statement. Throughout the book, there is a strong implication that high school athletic departments as well as individual high school sport programs need a mission statement. The section devoted to highlighting the mission statement provides guidelines to promote leadership, communication, and a positive sense of self-worth.

*Beyond the Scoreboard* highlights many personal experiences that give credence to the book's primary purpose. I do weave in a strong sense of spirituality as a foundation for realigning the values of high school athletics. At the very least, this book will provide great insight for high school teachers, coaches, administrators, student-athletes, and their parents as to the proper expectations and intended outcomes of high school athletics and challenges participants at all levels to confront their own priorities and philosophies, beyond the scoreboard.

*Part One*
# GAME TIME

# THE ESSENCE OF THE GAME

*The whole point of being alive is to evolve into the complete person you were intended to be.*
   *Oprah Winfrey*

It was a Tuesday night in late February 2008. The varsity girls basketball team that I was coaching was beginning play in the annual state tournament. This was the regional round of competition commencing over the entire state of Wisconsin. Every game held the same significance for each team: win or the season is over. We earned the fourth seed in our regional bracket of eight teams. This meant that we got to host the first round of the tournament and we faced the number five seed. From a public or fan perspective, the game was a toss-up in terms of picking a winner.

The team I was coaching this particular year had five sophomores starting on varsity. Our team included one senior who contributed on game night quite often. She had even started a few games her junior and senior year. Although, she was a tall girl with average basketball ability, she was a good athlete and she had been on the varsity basketball team since late in her freshmen year. She had earned an athletic scholarship for her prowess as a volleyball player to attend a Division 1 college.

## THE ESSENCE OF THE GAME

This particular season we had outscored our opponent 11 times out of 20 tries. We had been outscored by our opponent just nine times in that season. Our opponent on this particular night had a similar won-loss record. Their team was made up of players from several different grades. They did have more seniors make contributions that year than we did. One particular senior had outstanding skill as a basketball player. She also presented something that we did not always have an answer for; she was tall, strong, and could run the floor well.

The coaching staff knew we needed our solo senior to neutralize our opponent's standout senior. The coaching staff knew that both kids would play with a tremendous amount of passion because, at this point in the season, any game could be the last of their high school career. The coaching staff knew we needed our senior captain to meet the challenge of competition that night. Her team needed her to fulfill her role.

I felt confident that our team would be successful in this game. I believed that our kids were well prepared because of the lessons we had been learning all season long in our wins, losses, and practices. The group of sophomores that had been in the starting lineup had very high expectations from their group of parents, their peers, and themselves. It was no easy task to combine those expectations along with my own expectations of helping them grow into responsible, mature young ladies. Generally, public eyes and minds only understand wins and losses; some are only literate in terms of the scoreboard. However, there are so many more successes to be had in the world of high school athletics.

The game turned out to be an entertaining one for high school basketball fans to watch. There were many highs and lows throughout the course of the game for both teams. The lead changed on several different occasions. Our young, inexperienced varsity players were holding their own against a team that had a few more seniors with valuable game experience. As expected, the two teams were evenly matched and it would come down to who would respond to adversity the best. What a valuable life lesson for all of the student-athletes playing in this contest: how to respond to adversity while maintaining sportsmanship and respect for the experience.

As the fourth quarter began, our team was just about ready to put the game out of reach of our opponent. We had battled to gain almost a double digit advantage mid way through the fourth quarter. The senior standout on their team was held in check most of the night. Our senior captain fulfilled her role in helping her team defend the best player on the other team.

The best skilled players do extraordinary things when challenged. The senior standout from the other team decided to put her team on her back. She was a big factor in our opponent shaving the deficit down to one point. There was now just under a minute left in the game, and we had possession of the ball.

Our plan was to continue to look to score, but we knew we had to protect the ball with all our skill we could gather. We knew that their team would have to come after us hard, even trying to foul us, to get the ball back. The stage was set. It was win or season over.

The later the game got, the louder the modest crowd roared from both sides. By now, with time winding down to under 30 seconds, the noise was prohibiting any communication from the coaches to the court. The clock continued to tick down, now less than 20 seconds, as our team protected the ball and continued to look for avenues of scoring toward the basket.

With a narrow one point lead, our offense getting nearer and nearer to half court due to the defensive pressure applied by our opponent, and my assistants begging for me to use a timeout, our point guard dribbled herself into basketball hell. Any corner of the basketball floor could be considered basketball hell, especially when a team is applying intense pressure defense to get the ball back. The mid-court corner acts like two more defenders. A player cannot step out of bounds, or cross the half-court line without committing a turnover. Two defenders on a player in this situation is like having four defenders, two of which are the red lines on the floor.

## THE ESSENCE OF THE GAME

As our point guard tried like crazy to reverse her dribble to get herself out of hell, the tall senior standout on our opponent's team took the ball away. In two dribbles she was shooting an uncontested lay-up at her team's basket. The ball rolled around the rim and fell through the net. The gym exploded in a collective cheer on one side and a gasp on the other. The result was a one point lead for the other team with less than 10 seconds left in the game.

From the bench, I immediately signaled for our last time out. This stopped the clock and gave us the opportunity to talk about what we wanted to accomplish in our next possession, which was probably going to be our last. We talked about setting up the play we had been practicing all year for this exact situation. I knew that our student-athletes would understand exactly what was expected of them. I knew that they all understood their roles in the given situation.

We broke the huddle of our time-out by simultaneously saying "FINISH!" What transpired in the next few moments was absolutely exhilarating. Everyone in that gym experienced the essence of high school sports drama. Nothing makes coaches feel more alive than a moment such as this. Every possible emotion is felt throughout the entire body. This game, the length of our season, had come down to one last possession.

Down by one point, we had to inbound the ball under our opponent's basket. We had to get the ball down the entire length of the floor, get off a shot, and prepare for a rebound and put-back all under ten seconds. Our opponent continued to be aggressive in their defensive pressure. They, strategically, decided to play a full court defense on that last possession. So, not only did we have to get the ball the length of the floor, shoot, and score under 10 seconds, we had to do it against pressure defense the entire length of the floor.

First, disaster struck. In our attempt to inbound the ball, the inbounder's pass was just enough off target to create a bit of apprehension in the girl that caught it. Upon catching the pass, she turned to start dribbling down court, the defense, like bees to honey, went hard after the ball. The ball was knocked loose and rolled out of bounds. The referee blew his whistle. After a moment of deafening silence in the gym, he emphatically signaled that it was still our ball. Our opportunity still had potential.

Now we had yet another challenge facing us. We had to run our play from a side out of bounds situation which we did practice, but it was just a little different in its execution. In addition, we had to pass the ball inbounds right in front of our opponent's student fan section. The students believed that the ball had been last touched by our team, of course. They were loud in their support for their team. It was an intimidating situation for a group of inexperienced varsity basketball players. We had no time outs left and there was now just over six seconds remaining in the game.

As we slapped the ball to set the play in motion, our first option was covered and our second option was covered. A young lady, another sophomore, who had not started the game and who had been improving as the season went along came from deep in the front court to an open spot near the half-court line in the back court. Our inbounder noticed her at the very last second to pass the ball in (it is a violation to hold the ball longer than five seconds on an inbound play) and she made the uncontested pass to this young lady.

This was not how the play was meant to be run, but this young lady took advantage of her opportunity. She dribbled the remaining distance down the floor near the free throw line. She was never once fully defended until our opponent realized someone better track her down when she was approaching the free throw line. She avoided the defender with a short crossover dribble. Slightly off balance, she proceeded to shoot the ball. The ball softly hit the rim, fell through the net, and the buzzer sounded. The gym erupted one more time. The fans of our opponents this time gasped. Game over. We earned the right to play the next round. Our opponent's season was over.

Two days later we traveled to take on the number one seed in our regional bracket. They had won their first tournament game by over 50 points on the night we outscored our opponent by one on a last second shot attempt. They were one of the top five ranked teams in the state in our Division.

We played them in the tournament the year before and outscored them by one point in their gym. This particular year we had the same opportunity. The stakes weren't any different than the previous year, but they had a much improved team. Two of the players that made major contributions in last year's meeting from our team had graduated. They, on the other hand, had every one of their players back. We were two different teams than the year before.

There had been a lot of media hype about our opponent. They were the favorite to win our sectional which would earn them a bid to the final four of the state tournament. They had one player that was a phenomenal basketball talent. She was tall, strong, and could score from anywhere on the floor. To compliment this gal, they had another tall girl. The second of the tall girls was taller, but much weaker than the first. Both were seniors and both were on a mission to help their team win games. Our opponent was a tight, disciplined team. They played together, believed in each other, and respected each other's roles.

Our coaching staff had decided that we needed to present this game as a special opportunity for our team. I knew that our young team probably had some concerns about playing this team. If they didn't, then they did a good job of ignoring the hype and our team of coaches must have had them well prepared. The coaching staff decided that when we arrived at the gym that we would all walk in together. Normally, we would all filter off the bus, straggle in, and walk in a single-file line, chatting with people as we walked in. This time, we wanted our kids to be with each other. We are a team and we will walk in as a team because we are here to win this basketball game together. This is a business trip. We believe in ourselves and each other. We will exude confidence. We unloaded the bus, waited until everyone was off, and walked in as a huddled group of confident people.

This was a short trip from our school so I made sure that we arrived to this gym with just enough time to get dressed in our uniforms and take the floor for pre-game warm-ups. I did not want to show up too early and have too much down time in the gym before the game. The plan worked great. I was proud of how our team responded to the new routine. We were all business and focused on the task of the evening. The only thing left to do was play the game.

Much like the first tournament game, this game was a battle of attrition. It was close the entire game. The gym was packed with fans from both schools. It was hot, loud, and a fun atmosphere for a high school basketball game. In our scouting preparation for this team we noticed that they were not particularly good against effective zone defenses. They were not great perimeter shooters. Their goal on offense was to get the ball into the two tall girls, take high percentage shots, and score inside.

Our coaching staff believed it was in our team's best interest to play a zone defense that took the inside away from these two girls. We would allow them the perimeter shots. We believed they could not outscore our team if they continued to take perimeter shots. The plan worked. Our kids kept themselves in the game with great defense, rebounding, and some timely shooting. It was a physical game, just like the previous year, and our kids handled themselves well given the conditions.

Like the game two days ago, this game came down to the last possession. This time we were down by two points, with the ball, and we had just spent our last time out. We had gotten the ball back by one of our sophomores diving on the floor after a loose ball. We now had a chance to tie the game or take the lead. We had been doing a great job of getting the ball deep into our opponent's defense and scoring at short range or, at the very least, getting fouled and shooting free throws.

In the time out the coaching staff decided, like the other night, in our last possession that we should run a play that our student-athletes are used to running. We talked about the play we were going to run. In fact, we had run the exact same play at the end of the first half of this game and scored on it as time ran out. We talked about our roles and the various options of the play.

Like the other night, we broke the huddle of our time-out by simultaneously saying "FINISH!" We set up our final play of

# THE ESSENCE OF THE GAME

the game. Unlike the game two days prior where we had to go the distance of the floor on our last possession, here we had the ball out of bounds at half court, right near our player bench. Our opponent provided some pressure defense, but they did not want to overplay us too much and allow us an easy basket. So, they pressured the inbounds pass, but then backed off just a bit to keep every one of our players in front of them. The play looked as though it was developing the way we expected it to. Our guard with the ball in her hands had four different options after she had dribble penetrated the defense to get into the free throw lane. First option was for her to score on her own. The second option was to kick it out for a jump shot for our best perimeter shooter set up on the right hand side of the basket. The third option was to hit one of two players positioned right near the basket on either side. The fourth option was to kick it out the opposite direction of our best shooter to our next best shooter.

With just under nine seconds to go, our guard penetrated the defense, but did not get as far as the coaches wanted her to go. That was okay because she had other options. She then looked to her right where our ace shooter was, then came back left and found our second best shooter open. After skipping option three, the players near the basket, she chose option four. Ironically, the ball landed in the hands of the player who made the game winning shot against our previous opponent. She caught the ball in rhythm and made a three point shot attempt. The ball seemed to hang in the air forever. Then, suddenly, it hit the rim hard and caromed away and the buzzer sounded. The gym erupted in exhalation. One of the best teams in the state had survived a real scare to play another day.

Our opponent that evening outscored our team by two points in an exciting, hard-fought game. They would not face an opponent over the course of the next three games that would challenge them as much as our team did on that night. Our plan to be focused, take care of our own business, and display good sportsmanship worked. We were successful. Our opponent that night ended their season, five games later, as the state runner-up in our division.

In my coaching career, these two moments, and many more like them, define the passion of high school sports. Nothing in sports can make us feel more alive than moments like these, no matter what level. Student-athletes participate to be in moments like these. Coaches coach to prepare student-athletes to be successful in moments like these. Communities are filled with pride in moments like these.

I certainly believe that the arena of high school athletics is one of the most powerful learning environments for our youth. High school athletics brings our community together; it gives us all something to look forward to each week. Lessons that are learned on the field, court, track, swimming pool, or wrestling mat can be as powerful as anything learned in the classroom. In fact, there are certain lessons that can be learned in sport that cannot be replicated in the classroom. As a high school English teacher for 13 years and as a coach of student athletes for more than 15 years, I have come to appreciate the opportunities that both disciplines have given me to teach young people life lessons of success strategies.

*The Essence of the Game: High School athletics provides opportunity to grow by overcoming adversity and preparing to succeed.*

Most importantly, high school athletics present opportunities for student-athletes to grow as people. The valuable lessons of acceptance and accountability really help student-athletes investigate their inner uniqueness to share their strengths. This can only be done when the ego is shrunk to a controllable level. God has created a unique purpose in each and every one of us. It is our duty and responsibility to unleash that inner beauty. It is our obligation to share this inner passion with the universe. In discovering who we are we can develop a positive sense of self-worth that has long lasting effects on our confidence and the success of our future endeavors. The participation in high school athletics and a sense of spirituality will aid in the discovery of self.

# THE ESSENCE OF THE GAME

Athletics in high school, in several cases, has become the means people have used to feed their own egos. Parents, coaches, student-athletes, athletic directors, entire communities, and anyone associated with a high school sport have, increasingly, attached their identities to the success and failure of high school athletics. The problem with feeding our own egos with the success and failure of a high school athlete or team is that it is creating an identity within each of us that is grossly false and fleeting. Maybe it has been this way for years, but I do see a difference in the way things are today than the way they were 20 years ago when I was in high school.

Media has glorified high school sports and the student-athletes to levels we have never seen before. Today, there are so many vehicles like newspapers, high school sports TV shows, high school athletic events aired on TV, on the radio, and online, Internet articles, websites with rankings of players and teams, and Internet blogs. It is not the media's fault that high school athletics are popular and help sell advertising. There wouldn't be the same interest generated from math decathlon, Odyssey of the Mind, solo and ensemble, or forensics, all of which are extracurricular competitions.

High school athletics and the student-athletes that participate along with the coaches are in the eye of the public. In the midst of all the hype there are some very fundamental things that are swept under the carpet. The learning opportunities provided through high school athletics are numerous. The attention of winning should not be the emphasis for any people involved. Learning life lessons to maximize potential as human beings needs to be reestablished as the purpose of high school athletics.

I felt a calling to help kids grow and mature. I had a tremendous high school mentor. As my junior varsity basketball coach and my position coach in football, he taught me so much about life. So much of my discipline, accountability, and respect were developed by this man. He was also my freshmen English teacher. Coincidentally, I developed a passion for athletics and an even stronger passion to read and to write.

I began coaching right out of high school. I worked as an assistant football coach at the high school from which I graduated, working with the entire program, 9th grade to varsity. I did that my first two years out of high school while I was attending a two year college. My next coaching stint came at a Middle School in an affluent suburb of Milwaukee. There I began coaching football which led into girl's basketball. I finished my undergraduate degree at the University of Wisconsin-Milwaukee where I earned a Bachelor of Arts Degree in English. I then made my way to the University of Wisconsin-Green Bay to get certified to teach high school English. While earning my teaching license, I coached middle school football again and 9th grade girl's basketball in a rural town north of Green Bay. When I became certified to teach English on the secondary level, I landed my first, and only, teaching job just outside Green Bay at Seymour Community High School in Seymour, Wisconsin.

At Seymour, my first year I volunteered as a coach with the football program and I was the 9th grade boys basketball coach. In only my second year in Seymour I was given the responsibility to coach Junior Varsity football – and get paid – and I was asked to serve as the Varsity Assistant Boys Basketball coach. In my third year, I was given the responsibility of heading up the girls basketball program. I have had several experiences throughout my years as a coach that have allowed me to formulate some ideas on the significance of high school athletics. The values that have grounded high school athletics for so long have become somewhat misaligned.

As my wife, Desiree, and I watch our daughter, Brooklyn, and son, Dawson, grow we are examining the values that we believe are important for their maturity. In our reflections we find comfort in prayer and knowing that God has an intended purpose for all of us, including the children. The values I see being emphasized in high school athletics all the way down to youth sports is disturbing. We are living in a world where winning is expected and anything less is failure. This is wrong. There are lessons to be learned in losing. The kids who never have the opportunities to identify their own passion and who never develop a positive sense of self-worth are really the ones losing out on the experience of high school athletics.

As parents of two young children, Desiree and I believe that athletics are an important part in the social and emotional development of all children. We will never sacrifice learning life lessons for the purpose of winning. If our values are solely on winning, we have lost all perspective as to what is truly important. We must continue to have faith in our inner uniqueness and share it with the world. In our efforts to find peace within ourselves, we have to live a life absent of ego. We cannot allow the allure of winning or the greed of attention to define who we are so much that our true identity gets buried under the layers of a false self. Examining the values of our expectations will help us better understand the true purpose of high school athletics.

# TRIUMPHS AND TENSIONS

*If we are to go forward, we must go back and rediscover those precious values -- that all reality hinges on moral foundations and that all reality has spiritual control.*
   *Martin Luther King, Jr.*

Mid-December of 2001 marked my fourth full season in my tenure as head coach of the girls basketball program. Our team was emerging as a formidable, well respected group of student-athletes in our conference, in our region, and in our state. This was the dawn of a triumphant time that would span the next five years.

The group of student-athletes who I was coaching was on the brink of a special basketball season. In that season many wonderful moments occurred and the result was the best season of girls basketball, in terms of winning and losing, in school history. This group's uniqueness went way beyond the scoreboard and all of the winning. They were focused, disciplined, responsible student-athletes that worked well together. The defining moment came on one particular mid-December evening.

We were facing a conference opponent that had the same record our team had achieved at that point in the season. Both teams had yet to lose a game. Our opponent was extremely talented and well-coached; they were disciplined, focused, and worked well together. The game was evenly matched throughout.

Late in the final quarter of the game, our opponent was just about to put the finishing touches on our first loss of the season. With just under a minute to play in the game, our team was behind by six points. Our most talented player had just earned her fifth and final foul which forced her to leave the game. We had a mountain to overcome with not much time to do it.

There was a good crowd in our gym that night, a tremendous community atmosphere, due to the fact that both teams had been so successful up to that point of the season. I was really proud of how our student-athletes had represented themselves in this particular game. Our opponent was beginning to run offense as long as they could to take as much time off the clock as they could. We needed to foul them to stop the clock and get the ball back. The down side to fouling was that our opponent earned free throws; however, they needed to convert those free-throws to extend their six point lead. If not, we would have a chance at reeling them back in.

The first time our opponent went to the free throw line she missed and we rebounded. We then converted a two point shot to pull within four points. The pattern continued. We needed to foul them and we did. This time the player from our opponent made one out of two free throws. Now the lead was inflated to five points with under 30 seconds left.

In our next possession one of our players was fouled in the act of shooting which earned her two free throws. She made both free throws and now we had the deficit cut to just three points with 25 seconds remaining in the game. Upon inbounding the ball, our players immediately fouled our opponent forcing them to the free throw line with 23 seconds left. The gym was loud. Fans from both schools were cheering on their teams.

The player missed the free throw. The rebound was knocked around and the ball had landed out of bounds. The official blew his whistle and signaled that it was our possession. We had no time-outs remaining, our best player on the

# BEYOND THE SCOREBOARD

bench finished for the game, and the length of the floor to go to maybe tie the game.

In this moment our coaching staff quickly called on one of our sophomores. She was a three point specialist and one helluva an athlete. She was physically strong and emotionally mature beyond her years. The play we normally run for the student-athlete that was now on the bench was now being called for one of our youngest players.

Our senior point guard brought the ball down the floor. She made the entry pass to begin the play. The clock was winding down now under 15 seconds. Our young sophomore was making her way off of three staggered screens to the three point line. The crowd was loudly restless in eager anticipation.

She came off the screens clean. Her teammates had done an outstanding job of getting her open. The pass was right on time. She caught the ball in stride at the top of the free throw circle above the three point line, faced the rim, and launched a high arcing shot. It seemed as if time had stopped and everything was in slow motion. As the ball came down, it barely touched the net as it went through the rim to tie the game. The gym exploded in one of the loudest moments in a gym I can remember as a coach.

Our opponent's coach immediately signaled for a time out with just under nine seconds remaining in the game. They had possession of the ball and had one more chance to make a game winning shot. Their shot attempt went astray and the game headed to overtime.

We ended up outscoring our opponent by five points in most unorthodox fashion. Remember, we were losing by as many as six with less than one minute to play in regulation. Our conference opponent on this evening ended up winning the conference and finished the season with 22 wins and just two losses. This was a defining moment for our team, our program, and our school. Everyone had come together to create a positive energy that personified the essence of high school athletics.

By early January of 2005 the program that I was coaching had already established a reputation for good, fundamen-

*Triumph:*
*Working together, earning respect, and building a positive sense of self-worth.*

tal basketball. We were competing at a high level and had many "big wins" under our belt, and our program had been recognized as formidable in a challenging conference that was made up of Division 1 and Division 2 high schools. For three consecutive seasons, which would eventually stretch into six straight seasons, a student-athlete from the girls basketball program represented our school, community, and conference in the annual state senior all-star game. In the summers of 2000 and 2001 I was asked by some highly successful coaches to be a part of the Division 2 North All-Star coaching staff. In the summer of 2004 I was honored by being selected to be the head coach of this elite all-star team.

The 2004-2005 season was a pleasant surprise. This particular season we were really exceeding public expectations in terms of winning and losing. We had a starting line-up of two seniors, one junior, and two sophomores. We had outscored our opponent seven out of nine times in this season already. On this night we were facing a conference opponent in their gym who had yet to lose a game. Furthermore, our opponent was one of the most highly touted teams in the state of Wisconsin in regards to girls basketball. They were ranked number one in Division 1.

Many proclaimed our opponent as unbeatable. Quite frankly, our conference opponent was everything, and more, they were advertised to be. They had height, strength, quickness, and pretty decent team chemistry. They had not been challenged by any other team all season. Our opponent that night had been winning games all season by an average of nearly 20 points per game.

Our team had an entire week of preparation for this game. Because this team had so many offensive threats, the coaching staff agreed to make the preparation for this game extremely simple. We focused on four elements of the game that we believed were in our control. First, we had to box out and out rebound our opponent. Second, we had to take advantage of every shooting opportunity we had at close range, including being aggressive going to the basket, reaching the free throw line, and converting our free throw opportunities. Third, we needed to defend the best we could to limit our opponent's opportunities at easy baskets; we emphasized that we did not want to allow fast transition points that come from turnovers. Finally, we needed to believe in ourselves and each other. That was it. That was the entire game plan. It was simple and effective.

The coaching staff did not inundate the team with multiple defenses to puzzle our opponent. We decided not to show our team the multiple offensive sets our opponent utilized for fear of overwhelming our student-athletes. We focused merely on a single strength of each player from our opponent. Practice time was spent on emphasizing the simplicity of the game and taking advantage of this opportunity.

In a major upset, our team won the game that night by outscoring our opponent by just five points in their gym. The victory shocked many in the girls basketball community around the state. It was truly an amazing moment for my coaching staff. We were elated for our student-athletes to accomplish such a feat. Our team of players and coaches were honored to represent our school and community in such a positive way. The student-athletes on our team did the little things right and believed in each other and accomplished something no one else had that entire season. The opponent we outscored on that evening ended the season with 23 wins and just two losses. Our student-athletes earned respect from others and built a positive sense of self-worth. I know that student-athletes remember moments like these. By achieving the accomplishment after preparing hard that led to the satisfaction of success and the building of a positive sense of self-worth.

*Into each life some rain must fall, some days must be dark and dreary.*
   Henry Wadsworth Longfellow

    By the spring of 2008 my life was turned upside down. Like the merciless winter we had just experienced where all life had been suffocated by snow and layers of ice, my marriage too had suffered the wounds of countless hours of separation due to my passion of coaching. My two young children had never truly experienced me being totally present as their father, ever. Furthermore, I was beginning a difficult transition within the framework of my job.

    What I knew as warm was now cold, what I knew as peace was now anxiety, what I knew as happiness was now an utter empty sadness. There were moments prior to this wreckage that nudged me to one side or the other, but never fully flipped me. Maybe I resisted too much, maybe I was ignorant or naïve, maybe I was just too damn stubborn. When one finds himself looking up from the dirt we walk on, all he sees are ghoulish monsters. All those who surround him become larger than life and become distorted looking spirits of intimidation.

    The depths with which I plunged when I began to carefully examine every area of my life were beyond my wildest imagination. My head hurt. It wasn't a headache; it was a pressure; pressure that I could not make go away. I couldn't think straight, I was never in the same room my body was, my worth was diminished to something less than a finger nail clipping lying on top of the garbage – at least this was my perception. My entire existence was based on how I affected other people's lives: my children, my parents, my wife, my friends, my co-workers, my students. I feared failure more than I feared death and more than I trusted in God's love for me.

    God pushes and pulls us like the wind does the dandelion seeds; it is an orchestration of magnificent harmony. We have no idea how it all is supposed to end. In my slow ascension from the flip side, I have realized that that having genuine faith is all the purpose I need to rise each and every day. In that love I can ultimately fulfill my role as dad, husband,

> **Tension:**
> *Be steadfast in your beliefs; adversity challenges the core of your values.*

son, brother, teacher, and friend. Anything done with love will never fail.

I have accepted who I am and where it is I am going. I need help along the journey. My faith is as constant, now, as the lighthouse leading the fishing boats off the lake on a foggy night. I don't need to be validated through anything other than the trust I have in God's love for me and the love He has for all of us. The lessons I experienced as a high school student-athlete and those as coach, have helped me understand myself better, allowing my inner beauty to shine. Even more, the situations I was in as a result of participating in high school athletics in one way or another have provided the tools to face and overcome adversity.

When we find within ourselves that which was created especially for us, our "uniqueness," we can find peace in trusting that lead. There are many challenges punching me in the face on a daily basis that I don't understand at all. I often question, "What the hell?" Have faith. God will make good out of the bad choices we make. That doesn't make me free of the knucklehead things I do and their subsequent consequences, but it sure is comforting knowing that He will be there even when things don't go as we had planned. I know that I must accept the direction in which He guides the currents of my life. I know that I am forgiven and will receive help making good out of the destruction.

God is showing me the way to right side up. If I had never been turned on my head to see the world in such a different way, I would never have grown in my relationship with God. Furthermore, I would never have grown in my relationships with my family and friends. I must not have been ready until I was awakened. We were made to love and to be loved. Our spirits, that which makes us truly who we are, are connected to each other. God loves us as we love our own children... unconditionally. Trust in that love. We have all crossed paths for a reason. I believe that the people that have come and gone throughout the journey of my life have added much quality to my life and have brought me to better understand my inner self.

Through athletics I have had the joy of getting to know many people. One of the most special people I had come to know and love was a man who coached with me for eight years. He died at a very young age after a tumultuous battle with cancer. He understood. He personified what high school sports really meant by his vibrant enthusiasm, bright smile, and caring eyes. I sense his presence and spirit each and every day when faced with situations that disturb me about high school athletics. His spirit reminds me that there is value in athletics that go much further than winning and losing. He believed in me as a teacher, coach, and friend. He helped me define the true meaning of high school athletics. The student-athletes who participated under his leadership remember him fondly; those who come now will have missed the opportunity to learn so many life-long lessons from a true treasure of a man.

Participation in high school athletics provides many opportunities to develop a strong, positive sense of self-worth. It also provides many opportunities to experience lessons of life. It is essential that all co-curricular activities in high school be extensions of the classroom. It is the responsibility of all teachers, coaches, and administrators to provide a positive learning environment that educates the whole person. Athletics are only a part of what shapes our young adults in their transformation to becoming mature, responsible adults.

*Part Two*
# INFLUENCE OF EGO

# EMERGENCE OF THE DESTRUCTIVE EGO

*The ego believes that through negativity it can manipulate reality and get away with it.....whenever you are unhappy, there is the unconscious belief that the unhappiness "buys" you what you want. If "you"--the mind--did not believe that unhappiness works, why would you create it? The fact is, of course, that negativity does not work. Instead of attracting a desirable condition, it stops it from arising.....Its only "useful" function is that it strengthens the ego, and that is why the ego loves it.*
  Eckhart Tolle (The Power of the NOW p 156-7)

    We spend most of our lives comparing and contrasting ourselves. This is our measuring stick to our success. It is also our aide in strengthening our self-esteem. When we compare ourselves to others within our social circles, our colleagues, or any other part of our lives we are trying to measure up to those around us; we find ourselves trying to keep up with the neighbors or hoping our children are as successful in school as our friends' children. Not always does this leave us with a feeling of doing well. In fact, in comparison, we usually find things that we are failing at or we are highlighting our inadequacy.
    For many years, through my twenties and early thirties, I really tried to find enjoyment in the Green Bay Packers. I still love the Packers and really look at the NFL as a form of entertainment, but no longer do I so much associate as strongly with

the success and/or failure of the Packers so that my happiness is defined by a win or a loss. I have many friends who are true sports fanatics. Their escape of reality comes through the distraction of the professional sports teams they follow. Many sports fanatics love to compare how their teams are doing in comparison to other teams. Recently someone mentioned to me that the average NFL fan around the country looked at the dismal season of the 2008 Green Bay Packers as a direct result of letting Brett Favre become a New York Jet. I thought to myself, "Why do I care about the average NFL fan around the country?" I don't. People find it entertaining to compare. I wonder, does this develop a sense of superiority which, in turn, creates a false sense of happiness?

When we are contrasting ourselves to others it is usually in an attempt to make us feel better or superior to those in our circle. In this state of mind we are usually finding elements of someone's character in which we are better than or even as justification for our own actions. In turn we feel better about whom we are but only for a moment. For when we realize that we are talking about someone else's inadequacies we often raise our level of guilt in terms of celebrating in the failures of others.

I have coached high school sports for many years but have recently begun to pursue other interests. God wants me to do more with my life now that I know better. I was guilty many times throughout my teaching and coaching career of contrasting myself and the performance of my teaching and athletic teams to others in my particular field. I found a sense of enjoyment of hearing of other's failures especially when it might have made me look better. I felt that if I went to church and someone else didn't, I was a better person. I felt that if my team won, then I was a better coach than the coach whose team lost. I felt that if many students were interested in taking my classes and avoiding other teachers, I was the better teacher. This is wrong and unhealthy.

What has been true since the beginning of time is that we are all created by the same Hand, His Hand. Deep within us is a very unique Spirit that was only created for us. However, we were all created by that same Hand; therefore, we are all connected, no matter what we do. God accepts and loves all of us the same. Those of us who have been fortunate enough to have been gifted the presence of children can understand and appreciate God's love for all of us. He loves us like we love our own children. Even though my children make poor choices from time to time, I will never leave them. I love them unconditionally. And so God loves all of us. Because of this, I can forgive myself and those around me, which doesn't mean that I have to agree with or accept the hurtful actions of those who haven't had the same opportunities or awareness that I have had.

Our egos allow us to connect with the world on a very superficial, surface level. Our egos look to compare and contrast who we are to everything and everyone else in the world. We can gain an inflated sense of superiority, have a false sense of our own image as we are perceived by others, and begin to and maintain a belief that our "self" is more important than any other "self". I have become aware of these thoughts in my own mind and have become increasingly aware of the negative energy that my ego fabricates within me. The only sense of peace we can have is when we can hold back our ego by condemning thoughts of comparison to others and allow our "self" to simply be.

The failure of today's high school education and the role high school athletics play in the lives of the student-athletes is in part due to the unreasonable expectations of coaches, parents, and athletic directors. All three of these groups of people in high school settings can be victims of the ego. It might be argued that our egos are needed to fight, to win, but, in reality, what are we "winning"? It is true that, as educators and parents, we want our children to become independent through knowledge and experience. Furthermore, I believe that we should want our children to experience self-actualization. Our children need to learn about themselves. They need to know who they are at a deep level. They need to know what moves them in order to find their true purpose. It is the responsibility of teachers, coaches, and parents to assist children on this journey. How can we, as adults, do this if we continue to allow our own egos to control our realities?

When we become adults and take on the challenges of an adult world we are often faced with issues that handcuff us. The most demoralizing issues involve feelings of inadequacy or disappointing those closest to us. In an attempt to avenge these demons we feed our egos which make us feel like we are better than we really are. Our egos are very superficial – meaning, our egos harbor and promote only what we perceive to be good in ourselves. Our egos disappoint us. We begin to believe that we are superior to others because of how we allow our egos to control us. Coaches, parents, and athletic directors create, in themselves, this false sense in two different ways, either by seeking attention or playing the victim. Once we become aware that this is happening to us we must keep our egos in check. All of us are responsible for helping children. Being superior is not only unimportant, it is fleeting. Superiority can only last so long. In coaching and in athletics, we are only as good as our last game. In other words, if we were superior in the previous game by scoring more points than our opponent that does not mean we will be superior in the next contest by scoring more points than our opponent. Even further, because we do score more points than our opponent does that truly make us superior?

When we break down high school athletics, it is important to recognize that all winning truly means is that we have outscored our opponent. That's it! When we begin to attach our self-image to "winning," we have allowed ourselves to create a "false self" in that we believe that the perception others have of us is more important than the true peace we can find within. Coaches create a false sense of who they are by believing their win-loss record really matters. Coaches believe they are perceived as successful when they win games. Well, truly, it is the athletes who win games. Coaches are mere conductors of knowledge and strategy, some better than others.

Athletic directors have a false sense of who they are and how they are doing their jobs based on the successes of the athletics they direct. It is the athletes who have the successes. Athletic directors are mere vehicles of organization through scheduling and adhering to policy and procedure, some better than others.

The most obvious false sense of self comes from parents. The parents who believe somehow the success of their children in athletics makes them better parents or the notion that this allows them to be in a "higher" social circle than others is absolutely absurd. However, this is the reality surrounding the evolution of high school athletics.

In each of these scenarios there is a genuine need to maintain a "self" that is considered better than others. This is why so much conflict arises amongst parents, high school athletes, coaches, and athletic directors. It is utterly ridiculous to think that any one's identity should be hindered or manifested in the success or failure of high school athletics. With that said, it is the reality of the world we live in today that some adults do attach their identity to the success of high school athletics. Rather, we should be focusing on preparing our children for their futures. Most certainly there is a need for the lessons of sport, but not at the expense of a false sense of superiority.

What happens to the child whose mother has told him that he has done everything right? Reality hits hard when this child goes away from home for the first time to encounter people who are more gifted in some areas than they are. This is not fair to our children. Of course we want to build our children up and allow them to have a positive sense of self worth. What we must build is self-actualization and the connectedness of the inner soul, not the ego. My mother always encouraged me musically; as a result I am an adequate singer and a novice guitar player. Don't think I wasn't the least bit shattered when one of my band mates told me I was singing flat all the time. What?! Me?! That's not what my mom ever told me. The point is we need to be honest and be realistic with who we truly are. After all, God wants something from me. He created something in me that is unique to everyone else. I must connect to that uniqueness and share that gift with the world.

My father told me once that, shortly before I was born, he had a dream. His vision was one of a strapping young boy who grew up to be big and strong and a starting linebacker on a football team. When I was born shortly thereafter, my dad's vision was true in a sense. I was a boy and a big one at that, checking in at well over eight pounds. How did this dream my father had manifest itself in his upbringing of me? How did he perpetuate that image in his mind as I was growing up? Too often parents want more for their children than they had. This is good. We always want more for our children. It's just that we must decide what the "more" it is we want. Some parents see that "more" as recognition through fleeting moments of attention that high school athletics brings.

In my many conversations with parents of high school athletes I have sensed a palpable urgency regarding the athletic career of their child; it is a very short window of opportunity. They know, as the dew evaporates off the early morning grass, that their children are going to be in and out of high school within the blink of an eye. A rush of anxiety and urgency comes upon parents as they fear their children may not succeed or have the chance to be successful. I remember my mother and father telling me that high school was going to be the best time of my life. They remembered it as a simple time in their own lives, a time when things were easy, void of most responsibility that adult life brings. It is a "win now" mentality parents have for their high school student-athletes. There was never a time in my life when I felt that I needed to really take advantage of the time I had because this was going to be "it." These were going to be the best years of my life. The focus was then, as it is now, enjoy the social memories you make, enjoy the moments of high school athletics because these moments will pass. Never mind the idea of a "learn now" mentality that really should be the priority.

My parents were very supportive of school, as I am sure most parents are. But, it is my guess that my parents wanted to build me up; therefore, they were never overly concerned about my grades. As long as I was behaving, passing, and not making waves, then life was good. My dad always encouraged education beyond high school. I was an average student in high school, at best. My parents always told me that I needed to apply myself better, but that was it. I was an above average athlete. I was the quarterback of the football team and received a lot of attention because of it. My name was in the newspaper. My picture was in the newspaper. Therefore, my parents and siblings were proud. My point is that attention led me to define who I was through athletics. It was a short window of opportunity; it was only a four year stage of my life. My life has been defined and developed by so much more. How was I to know that as a teenager? I didn't see much past high school until I was a senior.

Outside of my parents my greatest role model was a coach I had in high school. Everything I did was to gain approval from these influential people in my life. That continued into my adult life. I became a teacher, which led me to coach, which led me to believe that I would make all of those influential people happy. That sounds absurd, but that's exactly what happened and still happens today. I am glad that I have had this awareness now so that I can help my children grow in their own awareness of who they truly are. Parents need to accept that their children are on their own journeys and cannot own the successes or failures of their children. It is our responsibility to give our children the tools of self examination and self awareness for them to reach their true potential, egoless.

Coaches and athletic directors, on the other hand, are not so much concerned with the here and now. They are more concerned with the legacy they are creating in their profession. In fact, most are more concerned about their legacy in the arena of their jobs than they are to the legacy they are creating for their own children and families. This is not only true of the teaching and coaching profession, but it is true of all professions. Adults tend to identify the success of their lives based on the success of their careers. What is lost in all of that is the spiritual reality that we are all connected in a simple, yet complex, way.

We must unlock our inner beauty to create our legacy and fulfill our destiny. The ego is potent. We cannot allow the nourishment of our ego to become our motivation. It is influential in the way people treat each other and it creates unrealistic expectations of self and others. Coaches and athletic directors must maintain some humility in their responsibility to children. They must act in the best interest of children and represent those children as adults are intended to do. High school coaches are not often trained to deal with the egos of parents or the egos of the children. However, high school coaches who are licensed teachers are trained in the development of the brain and the various ways in which children excel at learning. There can be a mighty explosion, however, when one person might represent two of those groups. In other words, when a coach or athletic director is a parent of a high school athlete, worlds could collide. Coaches and athletic directors believe success is gained if and when a career stands the test of time and maybe even if there is hardware in the trophy case.

*Ego:*
*Are you in control or is your ego manipulating you? You are in control if you practice 'we' not 'me' in collaboration.*

In order for high school student-athletes to receive a well-rounded experience, success in high school athletics must be defined. There must be a definitive blue print for success. School districts and the state and national government have bench marks set for teachers to meet in the classroom. There is a certain expectation of what the "finished product" of a high school student will be as they receive their diplomas. I believe that there needs to be a clear definition of the goals of high school athletics for each school as well. There needs to be a strong leader to monitor those goals and maintain consistency in encouraging all varsity sports, their coaches, athletes, and parents to create an action plan to achieve those goals.

As classroom teachers and administrators are held to certain standards, all high school sports and their coaches should be held to set standards and bench marks. These objectives must be set by a committee of people that include parents, athletes, coaches, and administrators. Finally, these objectives must be met and maintained from year to year. Close monitoring of the mission statement for athletics is essential for high school athletics to act as function and supplement to the extended classroom. School districts continue to struggle in finding and keeping good, strong coaches. Like teachers, coaches must be educated on the nuances of dealing with people, namely parents and their children. We must starve our egos to allow our personal strengths and gifts to shine. Conflicts will be limited when coaches, athletic directors, and parents can help the children grow physically, emotionally, and spiritually. It is surprising (and somewhat shocking) to me that when faced with pressure from the community, we find it difficult to support good coaches who do what is in the best interest of student-athletes. We must maintain our belief system, when that is truly defined, and maintain the integrity of our values even when a few are unhappy without just-cause. Believing that there is good in all people and acknowledging that we are all created by the same Hand will lead to defeating the poison the ego excretes on the true happiness of our souls.

# PARENTS: THE EGO'S ENGINE

*In opening our hearts, we hope this might promote greater awareness of this condition. Perhaps it will encourage a clearer understanding of the individuals and families who are affected by it.*
   *Ronald Reagan*

In my teaching and coaching career I have had many conversations with parents regarding their children; consequently, I have developed many close relationships with various parents of either students or players. I have also had disagreements with parents. In most cases the relationships have been rewarding; at the very least, the conversations and encounters I have had with parents over the years has been educational for me.

I have always felt that parents fell into different categories depending upon the motivation for their child. I also suspected that parents fell into different groupings based on what they thought the purpose was of the teacher or coach. In addition, I have always believed that, while parents always have the best interest of their own child in their mind, some had a purpose of their own. I never took the time to really consider naming the groups or even processing the idea passed the surface level of my consciousness. I just knew there were some distinctive differences in the minds of parents.

# PARENTS: THE EGO'S ENGINE

In a conversation I was having with one of my closest colleagues recently, I came upon some interesting discoveries. This teaching colleague of mine worked with me in coaching as well. He and I both worked on the same high school football staff for several years. We worked so well together that we both agreed that it would be a good idea if he assisted me in the girls basketball program. He continues to serve as an assistant football coach. We have a special relationship in that we can talk about many things with each other. He was an awesome assistant coach too. He knew how to challenge me as a head coach, speak his peace, and we continue to grow closer together as the years pass.

He is the father of three boys, and all three of his sons are involved in athletics all year round. His oldest boy is in high school, his middle child is in middle school, and the youngest son is in the late stages of elementary school. As parents, he and his wife are in the middle of all the fun, the drama, and the grueling schedule that comes with having multiple children involved in athletics.

As he and I were having our conversation, I asked him what his impression was of parents with high school aged children. I knew I could ask him this and he would provide good insight for two reasons. First being that he was a parent of a high school student-athlete and experiences conversations with parents in the same situation. Secondly, I knew his insight would be interesting because he is a coach. The enlightening part of our conversation helped me to better understand the motivations of parents and that there are actually "sub-groups" for parents of high school athletes.

From this conversation I decided on four crude "sub-groups" for parents of high school athletes. Under the large heading of "parents of high school athletes" fall the following "sub-group" headings: social, vicarious, casual, and supportive. This grouping may not be exhaustive as there might be other "sub-groups" out there. But from our conversation these are the ones that stood out for me and seemed fairly representative. I have witnessed each of these in action either during my time as a high school athlete, during my time as a teacher, or during my time as a coach.

The two most dangerous "sub-groups" are the social and vicarious parents. These parents are driven by an active ego that is constantly hungry for attention. Casual parents are, to a certain degree, less dangerous than those who fall into the first two "sub-groups." They are less dangerous because being casual implies some level of apathy; however, a high level of apathy can be harmful. The safest, most reliable, and healthiest group of parents is the supportive "sub-group."

The parents that adhere to the mission statement of the school's athletic department, the mission statement of the coach, and the importance of high school athletics as an extension of the classroom are those who support. These parents are supportive of the school administration, the coaching staff, and, most of all, their children. The supportive group of parents has experienced an awareness of how the ego can negatively affect the soul.

Typically, supportive parents are in a state of acceptance. They will accept "the law" as written by the school's board of education and managed from the superintendent right down to the building principal and ultimately the individual coach. From time to time, these parents might question policy if it is somehow negatively affecting the self-worth of their child. However, when questioning, they will never do it belligerently, in public, or in an accusatory fashion. The questions are just that, intended to gain knowledge to help their child succeed under the guidelines set forth by the school district. Indeed, this group of parents may disagree, but they see the forest for the trees; they understand the purpose driving the policy.

These same parents will support the coaches of their children. There is an appreciation of the time and effort a coach takes away from his "real" job of teaching – for those who are teachers – and the time away from his own family. There is an understanding that the coach has many student-athletes and their parents to manage all in the effort of extending the classroom to athletics. Finally, these parents will hold their child accountable to the mission statement decreed by the coaching staff.

I have had the opportunity to build relationships with many such parents. One set of parents in particular had a concern in regards to their child on the basketball team. They referred to the mission statement I handed out to them at the beginning of the season. Early on in my coaching career a coaching colleague of mine and good friend gave me the invaluable idea of creating a mission statement for the basketball program which, in turn, has become a prevailing theme of this book. Each year, the coaching staff and I would agree upon a mission statement to be handed out to all athletes and parents of the program. It was used as a guide to addressing concerns and outlining expectations.

This set of parents referred to the mission statement to understand what my expectations were in regards to addressing concerns and problem solving. To this day, this set of parents lets me know how helpful the mission statement was for their situation. Parents like these handle concerns behind closed doors with the coach and the student-athlete.

The best, and most powerful, attribute the supportive parents have is the foundation they have built for their own children. These parents are models in gifting their children humility, belief, and faith. They acknowledge to their children the importance of following the authority

of the people in charge. They also support the independence of their children, give them confidence in who they are, and love them for who they are as people, not as athletes, students, or whatever other role their children play. These children quickly reach a maturation of self-worth much quicker than others. These parents are reliable people who develop and maintain a healthy home environment for their children. These student-athletes have the appropriate perspective because their parents have the appropriate perspective.

Casual parents have some perspective but at the core of their interest lies the affect, or the emotional impact and inward disposition, high school athletics is having on their child. The simplicity of this idea is deceiving. While it may be true that casual parents may literally be

## High School Athletics: Sub-Groups of Parents

| Sub-Group | Description |
| --- | --- |
| **Social** | *driven by ego, feel pressure to involve their children due to addiction to social status or popularity.* |
| **Vicarious** | *driven by ego, children feel obligation to live up to unreasonable expectations of parent; children take burden of inadequacy on behalf of parent to make them proud and gain them attention.* |
| **Casual** | *interested in affect (attitude, self-concept, and behavior) of their child rather than the strategic or competitive level of high school athletics* |
| **Supportive** | *adhere to mission statement of school's athletic department* |

unaware of the strategic level of athletics, in contrast, they may be oversensitive to the attitude, self-concept, and behavior of their maturing child. On the other hand some parents might be casual observers because they are distant, withdrawn, and have waning interest in the development of their child.

It is unfortunate when parents reach a breaking point and lack the energy or focus to assist their child's development. There can be several causes for this behavior including divorce, substance abuse, or depression. In extreme instances, parents have seemingly given up on their children. Children with this background might show characteristics of being emotionally unstable, not responsive to authority, or acting out for the attention they are lacking at home.

In my experience the student-athletes that have come from similar situations have, at times, resisted discipline. These student-athletes, themselves, become withdrawn, angry, and develop a negative self-concept. The ego is fed by playing the role of victim. These children want someone to care, someone not to be indifferent, but any time someone tries to get close they put up tougher barriers. These children have a tendency to lose faith in adult leadership of any kind. They lose trust. Often times these children will begin to believe they are unworthy of being loved.

The parents that are casual observers to the strategic level of athletics can be described otherwise as myopic. Their concern is focused only on the contentment and well-being of their child, not necessarily the athletic activity itself. Innocently, some parents have never been exposed to athletics. They must quickly learn the rules of the game; they must become aware of the idiosyncrasies of the particular sport. Furthermore, they must form an understanding of the group dynamics of team sport. The one thing casual parents do understand, much like that of the general public, is the scoreboard. That is, they can come to understand that one team wins and one team loses; the team with the most points at the end of the contest is declared the winner.

Parents who are casually observers simply have not been exposed enough to the sport their child has taken an interest in. It is all as new to them as it might be to the child at the beginning of the interest. Usually, these parents won't be too challenging to the system and their egos are fed from different sources. In other words, they will support the emotional and intellectual growth of their children rather than the activity or the institution.

The two most dangerous "sub-groups" of parents are the ones who are seeking social status and the ones who are living vicariously through their own children. These parents have either lost all perspective or have never had proper perspective. Priorities and expectations are usually not aligned with spirituality and the well-being of their children. These parents are driven by ego. It is a challenge to be present for their children. It is a challenge to love themselves or their children for just who they are. It is a challenge, in most cases not worth fighting, to help their children identify and accentuate their true talents, that which God created by His own Hand.

A lethal combination of a starving ego and the need for a higher social status is a recipe for a dysfunctional situation. This takes me back to listening to stories from my parents. I attended public school until the eighth grade. Then my parents sent me to a parochial high school. The school was even in a different city. I was new to this group of students, friends, and families. My parents had told me stories of how there were even cliques among parents. My mom and dad were blue-collar people amidst many white-collar folk. Although my parents had a unique ability to fit in and get along with most people, they came to find out that wasn't the case with everyone else; not everyone was welcomed by the same group.

My parents naturally made acquaintances with parents of the student-athletes who were on teams with me and befriended me. The friendships my parents made crossed a gigantic range of economic and social status. They quickly learned, though, that the already established "blue-collars" of the group weren't so accepted. They also learned that the various Catholic grade schools feeding this high school were not viewed as socially equal. My parents also sensed that people were attracted to them because of my athletic ability. A shallow place to dwell is the ego. The new "friends" my parents were making personified the superficial justification that provided no purpose other than to be able to "move up" in social status in developing friendships. These parents weren't interested in knowing the inner soul, the inner beauty.

I see this happening today. Parents of the best student-athletes become magnets for parents who are seeking to bask in the glow of arrogance. The ego is fed by being able to say "I sat by so-and-so", or "so-and-so invited us to the post track meet party." They feel the pressure to keep their children involved in high school athletics because of the addiction they have to the newly gained social status. They begin to compare their children to the children of the other parents in their new social groups. That, in turn, then applies pressure to the children to do things they are not capable of or have no interest in doing.

None of this is helping the child develop a positive sense of self-worth. In fact, it is having quite the opposite effect. While the child might truly enjoy hanging out with the children of the "elite" parents, they may begin to withdraw from that group because of the parent pressure. Children often see a side of their parents that no one else sees. When a child sees that her parents are beginning to hang with a different social class but act completely different at home, the child becomes confused and, at times, angry. The dynamics may change in the family structure. Priorities change and perspective is lost. The ego is not only damaging the adults, it begins to emerge in the children as a survival technique.

Because the ego helps the child to survive, the child begins to identify closer with the ego rather than her inner uniqueness. When this begins to happen it is time to gain proper perspective and answer, what is the purpose of high school athletics? It is up to adults who have had an awareness to help these children realign the values that are important.

For parents, the purpose of high school athletics can never be to undo what they did or didn't do in high school. Parents who fall into the vicarious "sub-group" are the most dangerous. They may yell at officials. They may yell at the coach. They may even yell at the players on the team, and worse yet, they may yell at their own child.

The display of frustration and anger may be a result of themselves feeling inadequate. Maybe something is stirring a negative memory of a high school moment that they felt powerless to control. Now, as an adult, they are exhibiting their power by yelling and making vicious attacks on people with no justification. These parents also put a tremendous amount of pressure on their children. Often times, these parents will compare their child to other children or even themselves.

The child then feels a sense of obligation to live up to the unreasonable expectations of the parent. The child begins to develop a negative self-concept of not being good enough or not being able to ever do anything right. Even though it may be difficult for children to articulate, they begin to feel shameful for what their own parent's lack. They take on the burden of inadequacy for their parents and want to make them proud.

This is the wrong motivation to participate in high school athletics. If this is happening in high school, it will for certain continue to happen into adulthood. Parents who are attempting to live out dead dreams of days gone by through their children are doing the children a huge disservice. The irony is these parents don't often realize what they are doing to their child.

Parents need to rid themselves of the influence of their ego. Hiding behind the accomplishments of their children is a disastrous relationship. High school students already have so many decisions to make with so much pressure applied from so many different areas. They are expected to graduate from high school, make decisions about their future, and adhere to the rules and regulations of their parents. If parents continue to add pressure to their children to perform athletically to benefit the parent in any way, the child will likely overheat.

Keeping proper perspective on high school athletics by understanding its purpose will help parents visualize the big picture. We have heard so many times that high school students need to take advantage of high school because it will be the best days of their lives. I must confess that the longer I teach, the more I see the absolute distress high school students face each and every day. I am not sure who coined the idea that high school was to be the best years of our lives. Maybe that came out of the '50's when it seemed like they truly were "happy days."

Parents must know that high school athletics is not about them. In fact, it is not even about the student-athletes. High school athletics is designed to be an extension of the classroom. In high school athletics, student-athletes should learn lessons they can apply to their lives. The supportive parents are helping in their child's growth. The casual parents, at times are helping, but, at other times are destroying the opportunities for emotional growth. The vicarious and social status groups are setting their children up for hurtful moments. Keeping in mind that the high school experience is a very short time of our life, student-athletes need to gain as much as they can educationally from their experience. Parents of high school athletes must support their children's effort in the education of the whole. Like high school athletics, parents can supplement the education of their children by being supportive and grounding their whole families in spirituality not ego.

# COACHES: THE EGO'S VEHICLE

*The wise skeptic does not teach doubt but how to look for the permanent in the mutable and fleeting.*
   *Ralph Waldo Emerson*

   In my experiences coaching I have noticed that there are many fundamental differences between coaches that go beyond strategy, motivation, and preparation. God has gifted each person with unique talents and coaches ignite these talents with differing energy forces. The force of energy drives the motivation of these coaches. At a very simplistic level, coaches, like parents, fall into sub-groups. These sub-groups include, but are not limited to, "The Man", "old-school", "new-school", and "balanced".
   The "balanced" coach has proper perspective with every element of life in reasonable order. This coach can be recognized as giving equal time to family, spirituality, and a profession. Student-athletes will have the best opportunities to learn life lessons under this sub-group of coaches because they will completely understand expectations. Discipline and order are of utmost importance and student-athletes develop a growing awareness of the good and bad consequences of their behaviors.
   The "new-school" coach is developing his own awareness of appropriate behavior. These coaches are often

## COACHES: THE EGO'S VEHICLE

inexperienced, energetic, and, at times, overly enthusiastic. This sub-group of coaches is driven to compete at a high level without always having priorities in order. "New-school" coaches are often liked by the student-athletes, but not always respected, not yet anyway. These coaches are consciously working hard at gaining entry into the sub-group of "balanced".

The final two sub-groups are the most disturbing. Coaches driven by ego do not always have the best interest of student-athletes in mind. Ego masks the true strengths of these coaches never fully allowing them to blossom. The most dangerous coaches fall into the sub-group "The Man".

I have been told by young high school coaches who have been assistants in one sport or another that they want the chance at being "The Man." The implication here is that a young coach with the drive and compassion to be a high school head coach wants the opportunity to be in charge, to be in control. There is good and bad embedded in this implication. Being "The Man" indicates that a person might need to feed his ego with the role of head coach. The attention a head coach receives is only because of the position, not because of who he is as a person. The irony is that when you no longer have the title of "head coach" the attention seems to drift up in smoke. This happens, especially, to those who are not built with substance, the substance being the awareness of the inner spirit that is void of ego. Before taking on such positions of leadership, one must have his values aligned properly.

There are really two ways to look at how ego affects high school coaches. Some may argue that successful college or professional coaches have, historically, had inflated egos. Examining the presence of ego regarding college or professional coaches who earn a lot of money for their responsibilities is the subject of another book. First there is the coach who attaches his identity to the attention, good and bad, he gets from coaching his team. The second example is the coach who continually looks to connect with people, creating a false sense of self to gain respect through both successes and failures. In examining the attention seeking ego, this coach really sets aside all other responsibilities to make a name for himself as a coach. Coaches who feed off the attention they receive from their position as coach typically neglect their families and their responsibilities as a teacher, if, in fact, they are a licensed teacher. I have seen an increasing number of non-teachers taking coaching positions in high school. I am sure this is due mainly to the increasing amount of responsibility on teachers and the demands of the profession of teaching. Coaching is an "extra" activity where coaches are meagerly compensated. Some will argue that a coach must put everything else aside, namely family and all responsibilities that envelope that role, to be successful. Meaning, coaches who are successful win and in order to win the priority must be on that sport and those athletes. Coincidentally, coaches who feed on this attention most often spend more time with and develop better relationships with their athletes rather than their own children.

This, however, goes against everything those coaches teach to the athletes they coach and to their families. Coaches will often be adamant about building relationships and team chemistry. They will talk, at length, about teamwork and respecting each other, coaches, and the opponent. These types of coaches will often give the appearance of having a healthy family with supporting children and spouse. I would argue, however, that, although appearing healthy and together from the outside looking in, these families are no more functional than the family that has gone through a bitter divorce. Coaches have a tendency to be distant in their homes. Often times the physical body is present but the mind is off somewhere deliberating the next opponent, team issues, or trying to find the time to watch game film to assess the performance of the team or future opponents. Of course there are exceptions to this.

There are some "old-school" coaches who can balance their attention quite well between their family and their athletes and their hobby of coaching. These coaches are the most successful and stand the test of time. "Old-school" coaches have thick skin that can withstand criticism and are not led by an overzealous ego. Furthermore, these coaches do not attach their identity to the roller coaster of attention they receive from their position as a coach and teacher of high school athletes. Most of these coaches will give obvious evidence of putting their job as teacher first. These coaches will be recognized by their peers throughout their school district and state as being highly effective teachers; undoubtedly, these teachers may have awards of recognition and a long list of students who provide convincing testimonials to the success as role of classroom teacher first.

There will also be evidence of a well rounded family life. You won't find the children in the gym or at football practice every single day after school. The children play the piano, paint pictures, sing in the church choir, and participate in 4-H. The families participate in things outside of the sports arena. Typically, these families will be involved in their church and active in their community. With these coaches, most often, there is a genuine sense of happiness and purpose in all that they do in all facets of their lives. Even when put in front of TV cameras or interviewed for a news feature in the local newspaper's sports section, these coaches will be models of integrity without pretending to be someone or something else.

The individual coaches who feed their starving egos with the fleeting attention they get from coaching high school sports will often appear humble in media sound bites. Deep down, though, what motivates them and inspires them is feeding their ego as it identifies with the attention received in their role as coach. They look for opportunities to be in front of a camera to talk about their team or their individual success. They might even contact a news reporter personally to promote some personal feat or a particular success of a player only to showcase his own agenda. I was guilty of this when I was a young coach. I believed that who I was would be validated through the success and public recognition of my team, and this would define my success. Maybe I was trying to prove something to my parents, my siblings, my spouse, or my peers. Whatever the reason, it wasn't the right one. I often justified this publicity as being for kids. I believed this. Some coaches use their athletes to get the publicity.

I believe that I was more humble than others though. I remember seeing in the headlines of the newspapers coaches who earned their 100$^{th}$ win or 200$^{th}$ win and so on. Every time I saw this I pondered on all of the athletes who really won all of those games. When the record of the teams I coached reached the milestone of 100 I made it known to my assistants at the time that there was no need to make this public. It wasn't about me. I wasn't alone in that accomplishment. Don't get me wrong, I believe that it is quite an accomplishment to stand the test of time to achieve such accomplishments and weather the storm of emotional children and parents, but it is important to recognize that coaches don't do it alone.

Often these coaches become icons in their communities. Sometimes these coaches even become well regarded amongst their peers in their state or even region. Do we really know these people in their private lives? Are they good parents? Are they good spouses? Are they good role models for the student-athletes they coach? I have seen too many coaches who are too self-consumed to even appreciate the fact that the athletes they are coaching need guidance. Do they have a faith in the Lord and do they give thanks for the grace God has given them? As a result of the success, notoriety and attention there is an "untouchable" aura that surrounds some of these individuals. Administrators welcome the attention that comes to the school district due to the success of a certain athletic program. What other choice do they have, right? Some parents want their children to participate in these programs to be recognized as being a part of something "special." It is dangerous practice to allow individuals to be placed on pedestals made of such seemingly strong stone. The perspective is lost in the intoxicating aura of attention.

Some coaches act in a responsible way when it comes to the power they receive, but others abuse their power. The abuse of power is, at times, not even a conscious effort by these individuals. A former school lawyer once told me that administrators have the obligation to look at where the power lies within the school district when decisions are being made.

The source of power doesn't always see the big picture; this is the responsibility of the administration. In other words, some of these coaches or teachers are given the authority to make decisions they are not trained to make.

It may never be admitted by any administrators, but, in fact, there is truth to the notion that the more successful a coach is and the more aggressive his personality is, the more power they will have within their school district. All teachers and coaches within a school district, are under the same contract and obligation as any other teacher in that district. There should be no preferential treatment given to one individual over another. Now I am aware that some teachers are more gifted than others, some are great leaders amongst their peers, and certainly administrators may seek input from these people. However, administrators must weigh the significance of the input regarding the big picture namely, curriculum, personnel, and mission statements. No one person is bigger than the team. I was told by one of my administrators once that it is plausible that some teachers may have more pull or have a longer leash than others. Like it or lump it, certain teachers have more power in the school and community than others. They have influence in what happens. I am not an administrator, nor do I pretend to be, but this made me wonder, does allowing one teacher more influence than the rest show a weakness amongst an administrative team? There is nothing, in my mind, that should give credence or could possibly justify this comment. Everyone should be held to the same standards and expectations. In order for that to occur, the standards and expectations must be made clear to all people involved.

The abuse of power by the ego of a coach is dangerous. This most certainly leads to the manipulation of student-athletes, administrators, and colleagues. Winning at the high school level, or any level for that matter, is simply an opportunity to help students grow as people; it is an opportunity to help students prepare for the demands of college and the work force.

## High School Athletics: Sub-Groups of Coaches

| Sub-Group | Description |
| --- | --- |
| **The Man** | *driven by ego, attention seeking, attaches identity to role as coach, driven to win at all cost* |
| **Old-School** | *some driven by ego, stand the test of time, 'teacher-first' mentality, balanced lifestyle* |
| **New-School** | *some driven by ego, inexperienced, energetic, enthusiastic, driven to win, evolution is in infant stages* |
| **Balanced** | *proper perspective, in control of ego, divides time-equally-between family, spirituality, and profession, recognizes discipline and order as significant* |

Any time a coach thinks himself superior he is allowing his ego to take over. The bottom line is that each coach has an obligation to extend the classroom to the wrestling mat, the basketball court, the football field, and the swimming pool. Coaches need to teach students how to become adults. Coaching shouldn't be about building of a legacy for a coach that is only fleeting and will not make them a better person or bring them closer to God.

In theory, the athletic directors are trained to make decisions about coaching personnel, athletic programs, and to provide leadership. The leadership must be strong, consistent and representative of the entire school. A strong mission statement must be in place for equal opportunity for all programs. After all, if all programs are treated fairly, then all kids who choose to participate in high school athletics will have the opportunity to learn and succeed in a supplement fashion to the classroom. I was always under the impression that the athletic director and the administrators of the school really had the best interest of the coaches and athletes in mind when making decisions. Most often I would defer to

## COACHES: THE EGO'S VEHICLE

my athletic director for guidance and for proper procedure when it came to enforcing codes of conduct and even just working cooperatively with fellow coaches. I learned, the hard way, that some coaches have more influence with the athletic director than other coaches. There might be one or two coaches within a school district who possess "the power" because of success and status within the community, therefore giving them unjustified, in my opinion, pull in the athletic director's office. Again, this is an example of feeding the ego of a person who is coaching for himself rather than for the honor of the school.

In my tenure as a head coach I often consulted with the athletic director in terms of scheduling, team building, academics, athletic code violations and enforcement, and all other issues that might be controversial or scrutinized. I was fortunate to coach student-athletes over one particular four year span that were close and well motivated. When I began the challenge of being a head high school basketball coach, I had four very talented freshmen. The two classes that followed that group were talented as well. There was a little lull in the commitment of the following group, but the last group of this four year span was special. They were not the most gifted from a basketball skills standpoint, but they bought into the program and they believed in the coaching staff and worked extremely hard.

When this group had become seniors, the program was in the midst of reaching the regional final of the state tournament for the sixth straight year. This group was not expected to do much in terms of winning or out scoring their opponents. Two seniors started along with one junior and two sophomores. There was one senior, who had been a starter as a sophomore and a junior, who decided not to come out for her senior year. She had even received recognition as an All-Conference player her junior year. This team began the year with five wins against no losses.

On a day we were preparing to play in our sixth game of the year, I came to school that morning to begin my day teaching and found a note left on my desk. On the ripped piece of notebook paper there was a scribbled declaration in a funky marker color, "Steltz, I wanna play ball." She signed her name to the scrap paper note. Many thoughts swirled through my head. We were having an incredible season and I knew this child would help, if her heart was in it. I also knew that we had great chemistry with this team that wasn't expected to win many games. Furthermore, I knew this child had a younger sister who was an incredible basketball talent who hadn't yet gotten to high school. Nevertheless, we had trouble with the commitment and motivation of this young lady for two years. She was a great person with a sensitive personality. She was driven by her parents who wanted her to play basketball. However, she wasn't always motivated for her own reasons. Furthermore, I knew her parents were not always supportive of me and the coaching staff. I really didn't mind the fact that her parents weren't always supportive; I always knew that if I could get her to buy in, as with any athlete, and I could get her to believe in herself, her teammates, and coaches I would be satisfied and everything else would work itself out.

When I finally got my thoughts together I called my assistant to inform him about the surprise I found on my desk that morning. I then set up a meeting with my athletic director to discuss our options. Being in a public school, it is important to give all children who want to participate in an athletic program the opportunity. I expressed all of my concerns with my athletic director and asked for his input. After all, I knew that he and I needed to be on the same page because I knew that this was going to be a polarizing situation in our locker room. The athletic director and I, privately, decided that she did have the opportunity to "go out" for the team at the beginning of the season. The course of action that we (my assistant, my athletic director and I) had decided upon was to present this situation to the team and have a team vote. We also agreed that it needed to be a unanimous vote because if there was any dissent at all it would tear apart the fabric of our team.

I presented this issue to the team the next day. We were now undefeated with six wins and things were looking really good. We had made huge strides and our team was now

## COACHES: THE EGO'S VEHICLE

competing for the conference championship in the early part of the season. The team voted and it was not a unanimous "yes, we want her back on the team" vote. That answered the question in terms of allowing this child back on to the team. Sure, it can be argued that there could have been a better way to do it; in fact, I am sure there is a better way to do it. At the time, I did what I thought was best with the help of my athletic director and assistant coaches. The bottom line is that athletic directors and coaches must present a unified vision in the face of controversy.

At the end of that basketball season I found myself in a meeting with my Athletic Director and the father of the girl who wanted to join the team five games into the season. The father had a laundry list of things he was concerned about. The Athletic Director only sat quietly and allowed me the opportunity to fend for myself. When the meeting was over my Athletic Director explained that this meeting was necessary to appease the parent. In effect, he was trying to put a bandage on a problem that should never have even been raised to that level. The lesson learned is when coaches trust their Athletic Director enough to include them on team issues, which all coaches should do, the Athletic Director needs to protect the coach's back.

As we all know, the ego is a fleeting thought or feeling. The ego really masks what is real inside all of us, our inner being. Our insecurities are often hidden behind our ego. As coaches, we can hide easily behind the identity we create as the role we play as a public figure. I used to tell my assistant and close friend that I really didn't like the spot light to be shining on me in my role as head coach. He would vehemently argue with me that, yes in a sense there might be some truth to that, but in the end something in me really did like that attention otherwise I would not have chosen to be a head coach. I now accept his argument because I can recognize that my ego needed to be fed. It found nourishment in the attention I received from fellow coaches, my own players and their parents, my fellow teachers, my students, and the media.

As a high school athlete I really didn't like that attention, positive or negative. I know it had a lot to do with the dynamics of my family. I have a brother who is eight years older than me. We share a lot of laughs now and have a very good relationship. However, there was a time in my life when I remember being embarrassed by the attention I received from being an athlete because I thought that it would make him feel bad. He was not gifted with the same athletic talents I was given. He has a remarkable gift of creative intelligence. He can construct a home in his mind, then make that vision real by physically constructing it. It is poetry in motion: his creative mind and his physical ability acting in concert. I have been gifted, somewhat, musically and athletically. It seems as though, as children, there is more attention given to those who are athletic rather than to those that are gifted with their hands that create things. Look at the dynamics of our schools now. The athletes receive much more attention than the students in auto club, shop class, band, choir, or drama. There are never any blogs created or news features about students building garages or replacing the brakes on their English teacher's ride. We learn at a very early age that we can gain attention, whether we like it or not, from athletics. This feeds our egos which, in turn, creates an identity that is fleeting; one that is truly not who we really are.

The dangerous sub-groups of "The Man" and "new-school" often feed their ego off the attention, good or bad, gained by being involved in athletics. Coaches that model a positive work ethic, are moved by the Spirit, and advocate on behalf of the best interest for all student-athletes have the best opportunity to survive void of ego. It is coaches that are "balanced" that need to be a model for all coaches. Coaching high school athletics can be very demanding, but, if priorities are in order, coaching at this level can be extremely rewarding for everyone involved.

# STUDENT-ATHLETES: THE EGO'S MANIFESTATION

*Thomas said to him, "Lord, we don't know where you are going, so how can we know the way?" Jesus answered, "I am the way and the truth and the life. No one comes to the Father except through me. If you really knew me, you would know my Father as well. From now on, you do know him and have seen him."*
John 14:5-7

The influence of ego on the high school athlete is detrimental to their state of mental health. Teenagers are in the midst of figuring out who they are and what role it is they are expected to play relevant to the world. In the process of this development, the ego casts an impending shadow onto the inner uniqueness of each child. Influential adults must help these young people with their awareness of the negative effects of the ego. I would suggest that these adults, be them parents, family elders, teachers, or coaches give high school age children the weapons to battle, even destroy, the ego.

I am not certain that any of us, especially young adults, have the capacity to ultimately destroy the ego; however, we can equip ourselves and our children to keep it at bay. The first tool is to recognize the forces that keep the ego alive and allow it to survive in all of us. Attention, positive or negative, will allow the ego to maintain its own heartbeat. Improper perspective will allow the ego to breathe. In other words, ranking attention higher on the scale than one's own spirituality will lead to a perspective focused on the fleeting values of the world. Those fleeting values might include (but are not limited to) how others perceive us, the amount of money we make, or the amount of times our name is in the newspaper. These types of things don't feed our spirituality; instead, they allow our inner uniqueness to lay dormant.

Reversing this process, in essence, allowing spirituality to triumph over the ego, we must encourage our children to seek out their uniqueness. High school co-curricular activities, as their fundamental function, should accomplish two things. First, these activities must be structured to be an extension of the classroom. Through involvement in extracurricular activities, students should gain valuable experiences and learn lessons that will help them in their quest for success. Secondly, as a fundamental function of high school co-curricular activities, students must build a positive sense of self-worth by revealing their inner uniqueness, their special gifts and talents which ultimately will quench the red hot coals of the ego.

The development of a positive sense of self-worth can be mistaken as ego. There is a lesson for teenagers to learn about self-worth and how it relates to ego. Self-worth is grounded in our spirit. It is who we are. In contrast, the ego is the mask we wear to the ball, hiding our natural beauty, our God created beauty. Self-worth blossoms from within. Ego is a parasite that grows only on the nutrients provided by some external energy force. Self-worth will suffocate the ego but it will never kill it. Enriching self-worth is a necessity in nurturing its growth and controlling the ego. As a result, high school students must be given the tools to care for their self-worth.

There are several tools that, when used, lends to a sense of a high school student feeling valued. The strategy of goal setting, building an action plan, and achieving goals is essential in the growth of self-worth. Given a role within a group and emerging as an integral part in any type of collaboration is one such tool used in the development of self-worth. From this comes a sense of usefulness and validation. The strategy of sharing our talents also fits in to the concept of a growing self-worth and will undermine the ego. From this comes a sense of selflessness and visibility. All of these ideas make up the foundation of the arsenal to limit the ego's power. Finally, this foundation will allow the positive sense of self-worth to grow and, eventually, overcome the ego.

Goal setting should be included somewhere in the high school curriculum. In addition, goal setting can be an effective tool to use in high school athletics. Student-athletes who can utilize goal setting as a success strategy are able to build upon this foundation from which self-worth blossoms. Goal setting is really a four step process. First, a goal has to be set. Second, an action plan must be developed to achieve the set goal. Next, achieving the goal occurs. The final step in the goal setting process is to set the next goal and continue the process.

Writing the goals down on paper motivates the goal setter. Posting the goals in a place where it is visualized each day is powerful in continuing the action plan to achieve the goal. Once the goal has been reached, it is important to start the process all over again. Those who look to continue raising their own self-set standard will find comfort in achieving a goal, yet it is healthy to be somewhat unsatisfied. The lack of satisfaction will be the motivation to set the next more formidable goal. It is important to celebrate the hard work of achieving a goal, then moving on to the next level of accomplishment.

Student-athletes who experience personal accomplishment in goal setting, and they will if it is practiced correctly, will inevitably begin to grow their sense of self-worth. Reaching goals successfully, with the right practice, provides internal motivation for future endeavors. This inner drive begins to diminish the external forces feeding the ego.

Internal motivation leads to a growing confidence in self. The inner uniqueness begins to emerge when there is confidence in who we are at our spiritual roots. When student-athletes become aware of their ability to independently achieve goals through a goal setting process, it

## Function of High School Athletics to Enhance Self-Worth

1. Structure resembling classroom with teachers and learners.

2. Building a strong, positive foundation of self-worth through:

       - goal setting

       - planning action

       - attainable goal achievement

       - collaboration

       - sharing talents

leads to a willingness to participate in collaboration. The escalating confidence and feedback of any kind in collaboration shrinks the ego and enlarges the positive sense of self-worth.

Feedback, when properly processed, will increase the positive sense of self-worth. Feedback that might be considered negative gives us the opportunity to improve ourselves. Nourishment of our soul through feedback is healthy. It allows us to understand better where it is our strengths lie. Positive feedback will reinforce our growing positive sense of self-worth and give us the confidence to strengthen our weaknesses and enhance our gifts.

Being involved as an integral part of a collaborative group gives a feeling of usefulness to a student-athlete. Therefore, the student-athlete who makes contributions in practice to make the team better but sees limited playing time on game nights will still feel useful and part of the team. Another example of this is, often times, when student-athletes become injured and cannot physically participate, they will contribute in other ways. These student-athletes support the team verbally or become an emotional inspiration for the others still able to compete. This act of selflessness is a form of sacrifice that nourishes the inner spirit and chokes the ego.

Considering our usefulness and actually being useful are important in our efforts to limiting our ego to control our lives. When we feel as though our strengths are useful to others it gives us validation for letting our inner uniqueness shine. The validation is not external however. This sense of usefulness comes from deep within our soul. It is the experience of knowing that our spirit is alive and accepted on the surface.

Thus, our positive sense of self-worth is defined by how well we can limit the destructive power of the ego. The ego is diminished by the emerging inner uniqueness. Being who God intended us to be will occur when the gates of insecurity that fence in our spirit are unlocked. The key holder is the self, within that which is form. Our physical form houses the Spirit that has purpose in the external world; the purpose for each is defined by God.

As long as our spirit, our inner uniqueness, is validated from within we will project our naturally crafted talents to the outside world. Sharing our talents willingly is evidence that our positive sense of self-worth has blossomed. Having the need to share our gifts and meeting that need is a selfless act. This action makes us visible, memorable. As our Spirit becomes action, it is the personification of God's love for us.

The selflessness in sharing our gifts and talents in a calling for stewardship is the quintessential act of showing love. By allowing ourselves to be transparent to the world by exposing our inner uniqueness, we become vulnerable. This vulnerability shows that we are willing to trust God and the love He has for all of us. If we give of ourselves wanting nothing in return, abundance shall be provided.

Giving without want or need of receiving is the ultimate sacrifice and shows control of ego. The ego will never die, but it can be kept out of harm's way. Letting go of our insecurities and finding internal validation will overpower the ego. The Spirit will rise above the destructive ego when a positive sense of self-worth is nurtured. Proper maturation through the guidance of influential adults will help kids, student-athletes, become aware of the beauty within. This awareness will build and maintain a positive sense of self-worth based on substance, not the immaterial perceptions of our external world.

Student-athletes who can learn the lessons of goal setting, the usefulness in collaboration with others, and the selflessness of talent sharing will own a positive sense of self –worth. Their lives will be richly rewarding from an internal mechanism that the inner uniqueness, the Spirit, will flow through swiftly and freely. The only blockage to such freedom is the ego. The ego's presence will be but a shadow when awareness of self and all of its beauty is greater than the need for attention from external forces. The ego is born of the mind; our Spirit is born of God and, thus, has greater power, greater energy, and greater lasting strength than anything else in our world of form, material, and substance. God has created beauty within all of us with His hand, it is our obligation to search for it so that it can be released and shared in fulfilling our purpose.

*Part Three*
# PURPOSE OF HIGH SCHOOL ATHLETICS

# WINNING AND LIFE LESSONS

*Let your light so shine before men, that they may see your good works, and glorify your Father which is in heaven.*
   *Matthew 5:16*

In the late nineteenth century and early twentieth century it was a common belief that children that were involved in interscholastic athletics would be prevented from getting into "trouble." Furthermore, it was a common notion that interscholastic athletics had a unifying effect. The students of the school, their parents, and the community would often come together to celebrate the successes of their youth. In addition, small communities viewed high school athletics as a form of entertainment. For this very reason, it can be assumed, that the media found an interest from its customers in covering high school athletics.

J. Thomas Jable in an article, "High School Athletics: Evolution and Cultural Implications," published in the *Organization of American Historians Magazine of History 7 (Summer 1992)*, prepares lessons that address the historical and contemporary settings of high school athletics. Furthermore, Jable identities the implications high school athletics has on our society. Jable sites that Joel Spring, professor of education at the New School University, theorized that the competiveness of high school athletics helped students prepare better for the tedious manufacturing jobs in their futures. Jable further sites Tim O'Hanlon who argued that the unbalanced structure of high school athletics prepared student-athletes for a future of jobs and salary that were not equal.

Like many people who have theorized before on the implications of high school athletics, I believe there are major benefits to participation in co-curricular activities. For high school athletics to be beneficial, however, they must be administered and managed appropriately. In an article written by Amy Donaldson, "Chance of Prep Making it as College Athlete Tiny," published in May of 2006 in the *Deseret News* (Salt Lake City, UT), Steve Hodson, a local high school girls basketball coach stated, "The point is to make the most out of the high school experience…I hope they learn life lessons, like what you get, you earn, team work, unselfishness…"

In the same article by Donaldson, two other points were made in regards to the goals of athletics and the lessons that can be learned. In her research for the article, she interviewed the Assistant Director of the Utah High School Activities Association, Dave Wilkey. He stated that the number one goal of high school athletics is to "increase participation opportunities, and ensure those involved have meaningful experiences." Participation opportunities are important as long as the experiences are teaching life lessons that will have long lasting effects on the student-athletes.

In Donaldson's interview of a high school junior it was stated that "…the best thing I've learned is just to be a good person and work hard…Everyone loves to be a part of a team and feel needed…I wouldn't be anywhere without all of the teams I've played on." When student-athletes walk away from a high school athletic program with the tools to be successful after high school, it has certainly been a positive experience.

The purpose of high school athletics in its form and function is to supplement the experiences our student-athletes have in the classroom. In its most basic form, high school athletics are meant to provide opportunities for students to participate in competitive activities within a set of rules. In other words, the activities are monitored and under surveillance to promote physical fitness, sportsmanship, and, in most cases, teamwork. There are some sports, such as track and field, swimming, cross country, wrestling, golf, and gymnastics that might be more focused on individual performance, but all in all there is some cooperative dynamic being taught and experienced. I would argue that, beyond the life lessons taught through high school athletics, these programs provide student-athletes to develop positive relationships with their peers and to develop a nurturing connection with adults. A fundamental outline and mission of high school athletics is quintessential to provide a school district's justification for funding such programs. The absence of a mission statement as a compass for high school athletics will lead to a chaotic, dysfunctional environment.

School districts often refer to these activities and programs as "extracurricular." In its simplistic definition, this term, "extracurricular," implies anything that takes place outside of the core curriculum offered by each school district. In addition to language arts, math, science, and social studies, students are provided "extra" opportunities to learn. Yes, to learn. Learning how to prepare, learning how to compete, and learning such intangible strategies for success such as responsibility, accountability, cooperation, and integrity. All of these things are promoted during the regular school day in the classroom, but the activities provide supplemental opportunities for children to further enhance these skills and strategies. In recent years, the term "extracurricular" has been changed to "co-curricular" in many school districts to emphasize the partnership between the classroom and all other activities. Learning is not only taking place in the classroom, it is embedded into these "extra" activities as well.

There are several programs beyond athletics that schools support and promote. Some of those may include, but are not limited to, forensics, concert choir, band, cheerleading, dance, FBLA, and FFA. High school athletics provide just another opportunity for students to enhance their learning. Inherently, high school athletics and other such "extracurricular" programs are about making memories for the students that choose to participate.

Participation alone does not encompass the creation of the long lasting memories. Interestingly and maybe obvious to some, coaches, athletic directors, and parents are enormous variables in the making of those memories for student-athletes. The memories can be good and bad. The bad memories are a direct result of the influx and domination of ego. The good memories are not necessarily void of ego, but there is a certain acceptance to the experience gained in such activities. Memories that might register as bad stem from an individual, student or parent, feeling invisible in the midst of the attention seeking ego of others. On the other hand, positive memories registered stem from a "feel good" moment that the individual, student or parent, had during the short window of participation in high school athletics.

Students will carry the pleasant and unpleasant memories into adulthood. If the individual does not process the experience and place it in its proper place in the memory bank, the degree of satisfaction and the degree of detriment will continue to manifest within the ego and

**High School Co-curricular Activities Provide Opportunities for Growth**

The experience of high school athletics will help student-athletes learn:

1. Proper Preparation

2. Healthy Competition

3. Responsibility

4. Accountability

5. Cooperation

6. Integrity

multiply in intensity with age. I am coming upon my 20th anniversary of my high school graduation, and I have many positive memories from my participation in high school athletics. I know of some classmates who did not have the same positive memories I have had. When I see these people again, we will assume our roles as if 20 years ago was yesterday. In years past my ego may have swollen by listening to those who will validate me because of my prowess as a high school athlete. Others will support their ego by pointing out negative aspects of my personality as a high school student. Maybe I was arrogant in their perception, or maybe I received too much attention for athletics. Desiree, my wife, and I graduated from the same high school. She graduated one year behind me, and we never knew each other in high school. She knew of me and did consider me to be a bit arrogant because I was a jock. She really didn't know me at all; what she knew was only a perception.

I was an average student. Some of my classmates who went on to higher education and esteemed institutions maybe were not recognized for their talent. Their names were not in the newspaper and they probably didn't receive any awards that anyone heard about or acknowledged beyond their immediate families. Regardless of how the ego will be fed, it is a completely useless state of mind because of how quickly it evaporates and finds the need to refuel itself.

Juxtaposing these two experiences is quite interesting. I have an adult friend and colleague who has bitter feelings inside about high school athletics because he never felt as though he was a valued contributor to his team. Being somewhat undersized and less talented in comparison to others as a high school athlete, he was often times left behind or not even acknowledged. He is a teacher now and provides good balance for the athletes in our school, giving the athletes with the most attention insight to how someone might feel who is really trying and wanting to participate but who is not being accepted or valued. That is the feeling of invisibility. This friend of mine has empathy for those students who really struggle to find their place in the social status of high school athletics. Clearly, at an age when people are so vulnerable, a high school student needs to feel as though they are visible, talented, and valued.

Another behavior I have seen in adult coaches who felt invisible or undervalued as athletes is one that can be very disturbing and often interpreted as immature. This coach will belittle his athletes by telling them they are no good and really shouldn't even be on the field, court, or mat. This coach falsely perceives this is a motivational technique. Tearing a high school athlete down verbally can be motivational if, and only if, the student-athlete is built up through encouragement and a shower of positive feedback and affirmation. These coaches are seldom successful over a long period of time. The worst part about being exposed to this type of coach, because of the negative high school experiences that have resonated in his memory bank, is how detrimental the experience is to the psychological development of the children. The pattern continues, however. The same feelings of invisibility and worthlessness the coach harbors as an adult is perpetuated with the athletes he coaches. The sense of self worth is absent and the child feels like a failure which can even lead to severe depression in some cases. As a result of this, the child may respond to other adults in unrelated situations in a destructive way. This ball gets rolling early in life and continues to grow into adulthood.

    I, contrastingly, had mostly positive memories. I believed I was visible, special, and valued. My ego was fed constantly by seeing my name and picture in the paper, by winning awards, and by parents who were supportive and sensitive. I have high regard for the significance of high school athletics and their impact on teenagers. Now I understand that the impact can be both negative and positive. Furthermore, I now understand the importance of inner peace and not allowing the ego to be distorted or in control of my feelings and behavior. This is the purpose that needs to be included in defining the role of high school athletics in our schools. We must adhere to strategies that help students find their inner purpose and their role in our world that is void of ego.

    The polarized experiences of the starving ego searching for visibility and the self perception of invisibility manifesting itself in a negative sense of self-worth do not truly define the purpose of high school athletics. It is unhealthy for adults to assume that the sole purpose of high school athletics is to make student-athletes visible or to perpetuate invisibility through negative motivation. As teachers know and as coaches should know, we never really can measure the impact of our words or actions on the children we teach and coach. As hard as we try and as diligent as we are in choosing our words and monitoring our own actions, something can be completely misunderstood leading to a spiraling chain reaction of negativity that affects a child momentarily or, in worst case scenario, forever. We must practice what we preach. In other words, we must be models of positive behavior and choices. Coaches and athletic directors must be advocates for the future success of the high school student-athletes. Furthermore, coaches and athletic directors must completely understand and embrace the privilege they have earned to be some of the most influential people in the lives of children.

# PARENTS: CREATING A LEGACY

*You are the bows from which your children as living arrows are sent forth.*
   *Kahlil Gibran*

    My parents were very supportive of me and my four siblings. They continuously encouraged us. In fact, I remember my father always telling us that we can do and be anything we want to be. All of us tried athletics at some point. I may be the only one of the five who had positive experiences that I can remember. My parents did not understand the mixed messages we were getting at very vulnerable times in our lives. They were telling us we were good enough to do anything. The world was telling us that maybe we weren't quite good enough.
    My parents believed in their vision. They really wanted us to know that we should try everything and that, within reason, we had the right to do whatever it is we wanted. The part that was missing was truly helping us in identifying exactly what it was that God intended for each of us. They believed they were doing that by letting us explore and discover our strengths on our own, like they had to do. We lived on perceptions and stereotypes that weren't real. Their continued support of us continued to feed our egos, but, in reality, we were not truly finding our gifts. It was only a moment of time

in our lives that went by in a heartbeat, but the lasting effects on all of us were a bit damaging to our self-image. We are better now and understand our purpose much better. Even though our parents made us believe that we were important, special, and unique within our home, to the rest of the world, though, we were just people.

As we know now, we are people of God and my parents instilled in all of us a deep sense of faith and spirituality. I can't thank them enough for that. My parents showed me how faith is always there for us as long as we are willing to accept it and utilize it. My parents still wanted us to try anything we wanted because it was our right and it was good to be involved.

My oldest sister Julie was involved in athletics. There is a legendary story that surfaces occasionally at family gatherings about a track meet she was in during her middle school years. She was running the 400 meter dash which is a one lap race around the track. Legend has it that she took off as if she were shot out of a cannon. She led the way for the first 200 meters. At the 200 meter spot, the track wrapped around a set of bleachers. Spectators watching the event from the opposite side of the track saw the runners disappear behind the bleachers.

As the group of runners disappeared behind the bleachers, my sister was in the lead by a good length. As the runners emerged from behind the bleachers my sister was no longer in front. The bleachers are maybe the length of one hundred meters. In that length of track she had fallen off the pace and was rapidly slowing down. It wasn't as if she had a piano on her back, it was more like a ten story building. Julie struggled to finish the race, but she did finish. It is in our blood to finish what we start. The attention she received from this event wasn't necessarily positive. Of course people, including her parents, thought it was humorous the way she crashed and burned in this episode. Needless to say, her lasting memory of this moment did not help to create a positive sense of self-worth because to her it wasn't funny but embarrassing.

One other experience Julie had that devastated her had to do with cheerleading. In high school, she decided to get involved with cheerleading rather than athletics. She liked to dance and was a good cheerleader. In the spring of her junior year, after being a varsity cheerleader for two years, she did not make the cheerleading squad for her senior year. For whatever reason, she was not included on the final roster. This was a turbulent time in her life, a vulnerable time and she needed guidance from her parents. She needed to be pointed in another direction as opposed to wallowing in misery and shame because playing the role of victim never allows our inner light to shine.

My sister Ellen's athletic involvement is somewhat vague to me. I remember stories of her being involved in track and field, namely the field events of shot and discus. She did not have much athletic ability and was a bit awkward. Her physical development was much like mine. She was ahead of the girls her age physically. She struggled in the shadow of her older sister Julie who was just one year older. She often heard comments like "Why can't you do it like your sister Julie?" or "Why can't you just listen like Julie?" Ellen wanted to venture to realms outside of athletics. She wanted to prove her talent elsewhere.

Ellen's talents lie in the domestic arena. I remember her being an excellent baker. She also had a magical gift in the realm of arts and crafts so at Christmas the gifts she gave were beautifully wrapped with colorful paper topped off with delicate ribbons. She could tickle the keys of a piano to make it sing wonderful melodies. Her gift is creativity. She needed the guidance to recognize it and appreciate it.

The relationship I had with my brother David growing up continued to affect me as an adult. I received a lot of attention as an athlete. His gift is in the realm of spatial and conceptual design. I write more about my brother's athletic experiences in "The Athlete's Purpose."

David's gift is one I have been envious of. He can create things in his mind that he then makes a reality with his hands. He is a tremendous plumber, carpenter, and man of reason. I am a misfit in these areas.

Finally, my sister Barbara followed. Barbara competed with her two older sisters in everything. She was pretty, like a princess. She excelled in dance, music, and athletics. She was gifted many of the same things I had been given by God. I remember watching her play basketball in middle school. She was good. If my recollection serves me well, I remember her being quite an effective runner and hurdler during her first two years of high school, but she sustained an injury and her interest began to wane. As a result, Barbara went down a bit of a different path, the path less traveled let's say. Barbara wanted to free herself from the restraints of the family and the world to be independent.

My parents did the best they could in raising their children. I know my mother prayed for all of us. My mother would frequently pray the Rosary, meditating on the well-being of her children. My father's role was to maintain discipline with the children. Today, as adults, all of my siblings are wonderful, faith-filled contributing members of our world. I am proud of all of them and appreciate the gifts each has given me.

The purpose of parents in high school athletics provides the foundation for support in times when everything might seem to be in despair. Within the foundation of this purpose, parents also must model the celebration of success. Allow the inner beauty to be alive in our souls and activated in our thoughts, words, and actions; personifying in the smile on our faces, our movements of dance to the magical music of life. Exposing our children to multiple opportunities of experience will allow them to discover their gifts. After all, the gifts we were given by God are intended to be shared with all.

Desiree and I want our children, Brooklyn, Dawson, Faith, and Hope to have the opportunities to have fun with children their own age and meet new friends. For this to happen and with their permission, we have signed them up for things like dance class, Girl Scouts, soccer, basketball, tee-ball, and softball. As we know with child development, ages 0-4 are important years in terms of proper brain development. Children between the ages of 5-10 begin to develop their passion. During this stage of development, the ego has not yet taken over completely and the inner beauty begins to radiate as each child learns where it is they find peace and happiness.

The passion for every child, for every person is different. There are areas of exploration that each of us have to venture into in order to know what it is God has intended for us. The vastness of this exploration can be intimidating. It is up to Desiree and I, as parents, to help our children process information and thoughts so, in their minds, they can organize the world. Areas such as music, arts and crafts, dance, and sports of all kinds (i.e., hunting, fishing, basketball, soccer, skiing, etc.) are just a few activities explored by our children.

Some of you have been parents a lot longer than I have, so you may be much more of an expert than I am on raising children. However, I believe that our children, like us, are on their own paths, their own journeys. I cannot own their successes or failures. I can be proud of who they are and what they do, and I might even be disappointed from time to time. I know that I have my own inner peace to make with God and have to continue to focus on that. If I spend my energy owning Brooklyn's sensitive, always concerned personality, or Dawson's fear of the dark I might feel the pain for them and want to take it on as well. All I can do is help them to organize the world in their own minds; I can't take their pain away. The discomfort they experience is between them and God. The good they experience is between them and God.

*The Prophet*, written by Kahlil Gibran, is a collection of visions and insights articulated through poetry. Upon the birth of my first child, my mother had gifted me a copy of *The Prophet*. It was a book that my mother always had around the house as I grew up, and she felt compelled for Desiree and me to have our own copy.

Recently, as a father, I have found Gibran's chapter "On Children" quite compelling and profound. The thought that our children are present in our lives but belong to God is powerfully inspirational in a spiritual sense. I have reflected on this many times and as a result make every effort for my children to know God. We pray before bed and we pray at our evening meal. We don't pray for anything in particular other than to give thanks and ask for God's grace and presence in our lives. Some time ago, at our evening meal, I was trying to explain to Brooklyn and Dawson Jesus' parable of the multiplication of bread loaves. I tried to explain how Jesus fed 5,000 men, not counting women and children (so there possibly could have been close to 15,000 mouths fed) on two loaves of bread and a few fish. The men Jesus was with tried to talk him into dispersing that crowd because there would be no way they all would be satisfied. To the amazement of all, Jesus miraculously satisfied all of them and there were 12 baskets of leftovers. The point is that with God and Jesus at the center of our lives, we will be abundantly satisfied beyond even our own expectations.

Literature and history can also provide us with great examples of parenting. There have been numerous examples throughout literature that show the appropriate relationship between parent and child. In the literary genealogy of fiction, it can be argued that the family tree – the mother and father – begins with Homer's *The Illiad* and *The Odyssey*. I use *The Odyssey* each year as a teaching tool in my classroom for ninth grade English students. The master mariner, Odysseus, was absent from his son's life for the first twenty years. Even in pagan worship there was something to be said about our children not being our own. Upon Odysseus' arrival home after his long journey from The War of Troy, Odysseus showed Telemachus, his son, how to control his anger. He showed Telemachus how to be a true and honest man without owning him or making Telemachus exactly like himself.

As parents of high school athletes, it is not our purpose to live vicariously through the successes of our children. Too much pressure is laid upon the fragile ego of a child when there is continuous comparison to others. If high school student-athletes are motivated to succeed because they want to validate themselves through their parent's approval, then they will have a difficult time succeeding at all. This type of motivation, if not processed and placed in the correct place of the brain's memory, will have long lasting affects and hinder the development of this child as an adult. The child will continue to go through adulthood trying to please his or her parents. The irony is that the child will never fully please his parents and rarely will this individual find peace in life.

Throughout my coaching career, I often had casual conversations with parents who enjoyed telling me about their past experiences in high school athletics. Some would even go as far as telling me how proud they were of their son or daughter for wearing their old high school number. I know these types of conversations went on at home as well. I believe, mostly, that these conversations are not inspired with spiteful intentions, however the psychological affects on the child fester; the thought process continues to find ways to make Mom and Dad happy.

Parents who use their high school aged children to identify with and increase their social status, in extreme cases, are really committing a form of abuse. If we, as parents, feel so insecure about our own abilities to connect with people that we need the success of our children to support our ego, then we create a turbulent atmosphere in our homes where there is social competition between the children and the parents. In other words, when parents attach their egos to the success of their child they will continue to feed their egos through their child. As a result, the expectations grow for that child and when that child fails or when that child is no longer interested in the athletic competition, the parent's status then begins to fall. Conflict then arises from the parents who insist that their children keep participating because it will publicly make the parent look better and it will continue to feed their ego.

Sure, the argument can be made that parents need to keep their children in line, demand excellence, and never quit. However, are these things for the parent or for the child? Some parents who live off their ego may even claim they are demanding of their children for "the child's own good." If in fact this is true then there is healthy parenting taking place. However, if the parent is pushing the child because the parent is addicted to the attention and fears losing the social status, then it is an extremely ill thing. This is an intoxicating, fleeting behavior. The price is too costly.

I read an article recently published in one of the local newspapers. There was a family that was hit a devastating blow when they found out several months prior that the mother had brain cancer. I was familiar with this family through coaching; the family was a member of another school district that our school district competed against. There were some outstanding girls basketball players from this family who always presented a challenge to the girls I was coaching. The youngest two daughters of four are still in high school. The mother died just before Christmas. The article pointed out how the student-athletes on the basketball team rallied to support the two youngest girls. The most interesting point of the article, I found, was how the parents, past and present, rallied around to support the mother in her final days and the father who is now left alone to parent his children. It represented the true essence of high school athletics at work: kids learning the heart wrenching lesson of loss, parents understanding the need to support a peer in the devastation of losing a life partner. Pure in its purpose, this is really an example of the good high school athletics offers.

It is obvious to me that parents have the responsibility to help their children grow through high school athletics. These activities present athletes multiple learning opportunities and teachable moments for parents. Take advantage of those moments. Resist the idea of getting lost in the shallow, fleeting world of the ego; instead help to ignite the passion that God created deep within us. Adults need to help the high school athletes see the depth of their souls, easier said than done.

I remember coming home shortly after beginning my freshmen year of high school football and telling my father that I wasn't good enough to be the quarterback of the football team. I believed that the "other guy" was better. I know now that I was trying to feed my ego through my father's affirmation of me. I was playing the victim. I wanted sympathy from my parents to boost my poor self-image. Because it was hard work to compete, maybe I was looking for a way out. My dad did not provide me the opportunity to quit. Finish what I start. A lesson I learned at age 14 that continues to resonate with me today.

The source of fuel for my ego at such a vulnerable age was my parents. They were there every single day. They always believed in me. Jim Valvano, the former college basketball coach who reached a high level of success when the team he coached, North Carolina State, defeated Houston and won the national championship in 1983, in a motivational speech long after, discussed the significance of the role his father played in his life. He talked about "the gift his father gave him." It was the gift of belief. Valvano felt valued and loved for who he was, not for anything his father wanted him to be. He mentioned that when he didn't measure up as a father, son, brother, or husband his father would tell him that he was going to "make it." There is nothing more we can give our children than the belief in them as people. It is not feeding the ego of the child. It is a show of support to allow the inner beauty to blossom on the outside.

Soon after this motivational speech, Valvano died from a long bout with cancer. His legacy lives on today as a result of the furious fight he gave in attempting to defeat cancer. Throughout his treatment and his battle with this demon, he remained a positive public figure and provided inspiration for many. The foundation of this inspiration came from "the gift his father gave him," the gift of belief.

In believing in their children, parents have fulfilled the most important role as parent: celebrating the successes of their children and allowing them to embrace their uniqueness. I remember talking with my father when I would get home from football games or basketball games in high school. Typically, I would hang out with my friends after the games and get home a little later on a Friday or Saturday night. My dad would always be waiting up for me. He would help me process my performance and that of the team. He always wanted to know where I was at mentally and emotionally. He always wanted to celebrate team victories with me and be a pillar of support when the team lost.

My father always had words of encouragement for me. As an adult, my father still gives me support when things aren't going so well for me or shares in the celebration of success with me. I have made many close friendships with parents of student-athletes I have coached over the years. The ones I have been closest to really bought into the same philosophies that I had. I remember as I was into my third and fourth year coaching, parents began to rally together to celebrate and support. During these years, the student-athletes who I coached had tremendous learning opportunities in basketball. There were strong relationships being built between parents, athletes, and coaches. It was a healthy atmosphere. I was not yet aware of how my own ego was affecting my behavior and decisions so I was not able to sustain the goodness of those moments. As the program became more successful in terms of outscoring our opponent and given the turnover of athletes and parents in the program, the expectations continued to grow for more success in terms of winning.

Parents began to focus on the elation of winning and the celebrating that ensued and forgot to support when we were outscored by our opponent. Finger pointing becomes the norm because everyone wants to blame someone else for the lack of athletic improvement or the lack of winning. In the end, blaming others for our shortcomings is wrong. Most of the good and bad that happens to us usually is brought on by our own actions. Student-athletes that begin to level off in skill sometimes stop working at the sport because they think they are good enough or have lost interest. When the lesson of work ethic is nonexistent and avoided, then the team may not do as well in outscoring their opponent.

*Parents:*

*Celebrate the success of your children; allow your children to embrace their uniqueness.*

Overall, the purpose of parents in high school athletics is to show support of coaches and athletes in times of need. Furthermore, a parent's purpose is to celebrate the gifts that God has given their children. Whether it is in football, swimming, art, or music, it is incumbent upon parents to help their children accentuate their strengths. Parents need to be aware of the effect of their own ego and diminish it to see things in the proper perspective. Then parents are willing to accept the God given talents of their children, help their children see the world for what it really is, and where their strengths can be fully utilized. Learning to blame others for our weaknesses is the wrong message. Take responsibility for the proper development of your child, believe in the child, and celebrate with the child the miracle God created.

# COACHES: CREATING A RESUME

*The key is not the will to win... everybody has that. It is the will to prepare to win that is important.*
    *Bobby Knight*

Shortly after I began my tenure as a high school head coach I adopted the philosophy that I wanted the student athletes who participated in the sport I coached to gain a strong sense of self-worth. I needed to understand my purpose as a coach beyond winning and losing. I realized early on that I was a significant part of the lives of the student-athletes I coached. I spent a lot of time with them. I began to know players and their families on a very different level than I had with the students in my classroom. I knew I had a responsibility beyond winning and losing to help these children develop into adults.

In theory, building a sense of self-worth is a tremendous idea; I just didn't always have the insight to apply the theory. I would often get lost in the need to fill my own ego with meaningless attention. I believe that, as part of defining what makes a high school athletic program successful, we need to include the notion of building self-worth in our student-athletes. Don't mistake this concept with feeding the ego. Self-worth comes from the understanding of who we are deep down, beyond the surface personality of our ego.

I have a very strong spiritual faith. My faith is stronger now than it was when I began coaching. I wanted to share my faith with my athletes, but teaching and coaching in a public school prohibits this type of connection. I learned, early on though, that the Spirit moved me to share in subtle ways. Random acts of kindness, listening with an empathetic ear, helping kids with academics, assisting in choosing education beyond high school, developing leadership skills, and helping students to process relationship issues with peers and family were all ways I could share my faith. To me, this helped me define my purpose in high school athletics beyond the fleeting results of winning and losing.

Early on in my head coaching tenure, the father of one of the best players I was fortunate to coach was in the hospital due to complications with diabetes. I sensed this was bothering her. This athlete was somewhat introverted and not always willing to open up. She was a dynamic athlete and a highly motivated student with a very reserved personality. I made an effort to help her process her thoughts and offered her an open ear any time. I made the time to take a trip to the hospital to check in with her father and the rest of her family to let them know that my family and I were praying for them and we were there to offer our support.

The purpose of high school athletics for coaches is to model building relationships through listening and support. This young lady has earned her undergraduate degree in business and has a good job with big plans for the future. My family has been close to this family ever since. It has been a beautiful relationship and connection that has been nurtured and maintained for many years.

Another one of the athletes I coached was in conflict with her parents. She had a highly successful career in high school athletics and academics. She was one of the best female athletes our school has ever seen pass through its gym doors. This athlete was humble, yet slightly immature because of how young she was within her class. She had an athletic code violation the summer following her sophomore year. The news of this violation came to me first. I was shocked, in denial, and somewhat disappointed. I had to inform her parents of the information I had gained. The suspicions of her bad decision were proven through a conversation with her father. I then had to inform our athletic director for proper action to be administered. As much as it hurt me to turn in a good kid from a good family who had made a mistake, she had to face the consequences of her actions. Her parents were extremely supportive in this action and, at the same time, disappointed – as would be most parents. This athlete was able to serve her suspension during the volleyball season, the first athletic season of the new school year.

She was an outstanding athlete and her parents were active in the community. She was close with her father. Her father had always been a good sounding board for her. He would listen without casting judgment, but at this time of her life she didn't always see eye-to-eye with her mother as is very common with mothers and teenage daughters. This particular student-athlete saw a different side of her mother, that side that every mother has, challenging their children to be the best they can be. As we all do, we see our parents very differently than the rest of the world might perceive them. This athlete did not understand the difference between her mother's public persona versus the matriarch persona. I did my best to listen and give sound advice to continue to nurture her relationship with her mother. The purpose of high school athletics for coaches is to support parents in raising their children in emphasizing communication and making proper choices. This young lady earned a college scholarship to play basketball, earned her undergraduate degree, master's degree and now makes more money than my wife and I combined. She has been successful and will continue to be. Her connection with her mother and father is stronger today than it ever has been, and it continues to grow. The relationship my wife and I have with her and her whole family continues today and we are thankful God has allowed us to cross paths with them.

In my most exciting season of coaching I had a senior athlete who challenged me every day. She was a good athlete. A typical three sport athlete who was above average in all sports she participated in because of her God given talent.

She worked hard, was strong, and had a very unique personality. However, she wasn't the most dedicated student. I always felt that she was the type of child who came to school to play sports and not to advance her education. She bent the rules daily. She was an intelligent young lady, but didn't always apply her strengths to academics. She wasn't mean or ill-spirited, she just felt like no one would notice, that is until I came along. We did have a good relationship. She was honest, a true credit to her parents. She was a starter on a team that wasn't expected to do much. She hardly played her junior year, but she was really needed by her teammates during this particular season, her senior year. Her grades were average or below. I can remember talking with her and really trying to stress the importance of academics as I did with all of the athletes I coached. I checked her grades weekly. Because her attendance was sporadic, I checked her attendance hourly.

On my prep period one morning, the day of a game, I was at the local grocery store getting Gatorade for the team to take on the long bus ride we had later that day. It was 11:00am and I ran into this child in the junk food aisle. I asked her what she was doing there. She responded by telling me that she had a doctor's appointment earlier that morning and was on her way to school after she picked up lunch. I was a little confused because I did not know that she was ill or injured and needed the attention of a doctor. I didn't pry too much.

I informed her that she needed to be in school at least half of the academic day if she planned on participating in the game that evening. When I arrived back at school I immediately checked with the attendance secretary to see if this young lady had been "called in" by her parents. Her answer made my stomach turn. Our attendance secretary told me that she had not been called in and that she was considered truant at the moment. Not only was the student skipping school on her own, she lied to me. I felt horrible because of all the hard work and time I had put forth with this young lady. I didn't take it personally at all; I was just disappointed. I felt bad for her because of the inner conflict she must have been having in trying like hell to make good choices but just kept coming up short.

I immediately got on the phone with her mother who was working. I asked if the child was at the doctor. Her mother told me that her daughter was tired and was just going to sleep in and come to school late. I explained the circumstances to her mother that I had just run into her daughter at the grocery store and this may have ramifications in regards to the game that night. The mother understood and was supportive of any policy that had to be followed by the school and the team.

My next move was to make sure that she was in school and in her classes. Once I was assured of that, I went to my athletic director. I told him what had happened and told him that I didn't think she earned the right to compete in the game that night because of the poor decision she made. He told me that because of school policy she really couldn't play under those circumstances. In the same breath, he told me that he might be able to find a loop hole. Maybe it was an honest mistake. It is not in my make up to play that kind of game. The purpose of high school athletics is not to find loop holes. The purpose is to help kids learn. This was a golden opportunity. Did the team need her to win the game? Absolutely. She put herself above the team when she decided to take the morning off and that type of attitude is detrimental to the team.

She traveled with the team that night but was not allowed to suit up for the game. I talked with her on the bus ride to the game explaining that I did not want to see her feeling sorry for herself or attempting to gain sympathy from her teammates. That wasn't fair to the team. They had a right to be upset; her teammates were counting on her. She admitted her mistake to the team and I asked her to apologize to them right before the game as well. We won the game by three points. The team rallied to put on a good performance without one of their friends, teammates, and starters.

I took the opportunity to have a conversation with her on the bus ride home about how people need to act when others are counting on them. She also was good about the conversation we had on the bus ride to the game. She understood and she learned something more that day than she would have in playing in that game that night. The relationship my wife and I have with her and her family continues today and we are thankful God has allowed us to cross paths with them.

Another positive relationship that came out of my most exciting season of coaching was with a player who had missed most of her junior year due to an ACL injury of her knee. She hurt her knee playing summer basketball prior to her junior year. She and her family had high expectations for their daughter, but they were realistic about her ability. She was a captain on the team her senior year. As a leader she was strong; she spoke her mind and never let things get out of control in the locker room. She was honest with me and worked extremely hard each and every day.

The rehab for her knee went well and she was able to begin playing in January of her junior year. She wasn't the same player, though, that she had been her sophomore year. She struggled in her comeback. In retrospect, maybe she rushed herself back too early. In any case, her senior year was one to remember. She was a blessing.

This player had a great summer of basketball prior to her senior year and her knee was fully recovered. I had high expectations of her. I remember being at a summer tournament with the team and having a great conversation with her about leadership. I talked with her about the importance of being a strong leader and what was all involved in that. We talked about being honest, communicating, and holding others accountable. Her basketball season started out a little shaky. In fact, in the third game of the season I had to pull her from a game we were playing because she was not performing to her potential at all. My assistants and I agreed to make a change at half time of that game and she did not start the second half. In the fourth quarter of that game the light went on for her. In the same game that one of our starters could not suit up because of the poor choice she made in not coming to school; the newly motivated senior who sported a heavy knee brace really emerged as a potent part of our team. She dominated rebounding, scoring, and defending to help lead our team to a narrow three point win.

My purpose as coach was twofold with this athlete. First, I had to help in her rehabilitation and, second, I had to help her realize her significance to her team. Her rehabilitation was not easy. In the fall of her junior year – this was my first year not coaching football – I remember being in the weight room with her after school helping her stick to her rehab schedule. We were holding each other accountable. We were sharing an experience of hard work, teacher and student. The basketball season had begun and she was not ready to begin participating yet because her rehab had not yet been complete.

I had an encounter with her mother who had a prestigious job with a local hospital. Her mother had contacted me to set up a time when I could meet with her, her daughter, and the rehabilitation therapist to check the progress her daughter was making. We decided this meeting should take place after a late practice. It was early in the season and we had been struggling a little in terms of wins and losses. The girls basketball program had just come off of three consecutive seasons of winning many games.

The timing of this meeting was my mistake. I had a 21 month old daughter at home and a three month old son. I had been gone all day and the night before due to a basketball game, my teaching job, and basketball practice. I was tired and wanted to get home. I was short in my patience with this meeting. As I watched the athlete perform for all three of us, it was obvious to me that she wasn't ready to play at 100% yet. She was very weak in her one leg. The muscle atrophy hadn't yet been conquered.

The next day I received a passionate email from her mother. The mom claimed that I appeared to be distant, somewhat annoyed, and short in my patience. She explained to me that her daughter had worked very hard to get to the point of playing again and it seemed like I didn't care. I felt horrible about this situation. I responded to the email by apologizing. There was not much else I could do other than explain my situation. It was a poor excuse, but I was honest. Mother and I eventually talked via telephone; we worked things out and all was forgiven. The point is that my purpose here was to recognize the work this child had done for me, for her team, and for herself. It was an opportunity for me to emphasize that hard work results in positive gain and is worth the agony and pain of the journey. The athlete had, through her determination and commitment, built up her own self-worth; there is nothing more I could have ever asked of her.

During her senior year, I found my purpose was to help this athlete realize her full potential and responsibility to her team. She had a tendency to take breaks on the court, and she didn't have the kind of ability that allowed her to do that and still be effective to help her team. She also had to be our leader. Going back to that conversation she and I had during the summer, she had to hold herself accountable to hold her teammates accountable. She had to lead by example. It took some stubbornness on my part, but we were able to accomplish this feat.

This young lady is well on her way to being a leader in her adult life. She is strong, mentally and emotionally. She is going to be a teacher and wants to coach. She has had positive memories from participating in high school athletics beyond winning and losing. I suspect that she is going to be a master teacher in time and a coach who I would want for my own children. The relationship my wife and I have with her and her whole family continues today and we are thankful God has allowed us to cross paths with them as well.

I have had players from broken homes. Some children are much better adjusted than others. I can't imagine what it is like to try to raise children in the absence of one parent. I can't pretend to know what it is like for the child to be torn between the two sources of their life. I have been raised by two loving parents with four other siblings, a 'charmed' life some might say. My wife is from a broken home and has always been a good resource whenever I have faced the challenge of a student-athlete who suffered the pain of this situation.

The particular player who challenged me most was one who was extremely talented in regards to basketball. I noticed that during the holidays this player's demeanor would change. She became agitated, moody, and would even withdraw at practice. She had a bright personality and was a successful student. She was well-liked by her teammates, but she and I struggled to get on the same page. I finally accepted that all I could do was be there for her in support if needed.

By the time she was a senior, we began to understand each other better. One day, about mid-basketball season, she came to see me with a couple of concerns. The first was a family issue and the second concern involved one of her teammates, one of her best friends. I often sensed through conversations with this athlete and my own observations that the more attention she received as an athlete, the more her father wanted to be involved in her life. Having parents desire to be more involved in the life of their children is admirable. Her father was a self-proclaimed knowledgeable person when it came to basketball. She was on the brink of earning a college scholarship to play basketball, but her dad wanted her to fulfill her lifelong dream. Her dad wanted her to play for Tennessee. Yes, Tennessee, probably the most storied women's college basketball program in the country. The issue she had with her friend concerned making good decisions outside of school and basketball.

*Coaches:*
1. *Listen with an empathetic ear*
2. *Help with academics*
3. *Assist with post-high school plans*
4. *Develop leadership skills*
5. *Promote faith, family, and friendship*

In an instant I needed to address two very sensitive issues. This athlete confided in me about her best friend without her best friend knowing she was telling me anything. This was the most important issue to handle at the moment; I would get to her father later. This best friend and athlete on the team played a very important role. She was a leader and a role model to all of the younger players on the team. This young lady had a terrific personality, always happy and willing to help out with anything. This student-athlete was also sensitive to the needs of others and really poured her heart and soul into all that she did. Although she had many interests and basketball was probably at the bottom of her list, which never stopped her from being an integral part of the team.

I had a meeting with her and explained to her that her best friend was concerned about the choices she was making. At first, she was angry. She was angry at me and at her best friend. I knew that she felt as though she had disappointed me and that she was "outed" by her lifelong friend. I explained that it was good that her friend was concerned, that her friend was looking out for her best interest. I also gave her the benefit of the doubt by telling her that making mistakes is really a part of who we all are. Nobody is perfect. The most important part of this conversation was the teachable moment that I needed to take advantage of because this was my purpose. I told her that mistakes are good. Errors give us a chance to learn and improve. However, if we fail to learn anything and if we fail to improve, the choices we make after this learning experience then there truly would be a problem.

*Coaches: Make the most of teachable moments.*

I set up a meeting between these two friends, these two teammates. I had "coached" each of them separately on how to handle this conversation. I trusted that they could and should resolve this issue on their own. They talked. They cried with each other, laughed with each other, maybe even yelled at each other, but, in the end, they listened to each other with their hearts. When it was all said and done, they came out of that meeting together bonded a little closer and better people. High school athletics provides a purpose to learn valuable lessons of communication and acceptance.

The next meeting I had to schedule was one with this player and her father. Her father believed this young lady could play for Tennessee. He told me this was a dream of hers since she was a little girl and he believed that dream would come true. In all honesty, she had good basketball skills to go along with many natural, God given tools to perform at a high level. She was an excellent student as well. However, her basketball skills were not a match for a Division I college like Tennessee. Before her father came in to meet with me I had made a list of every area girls basketball player I thought had the potential to be a college level athlete. Included in that list were players from the previous two years that had earned scholarships at either Division I or Division II schools. The particular player in question really fit well into the category of the previous athletes that had signed Division II scholarships. The player and I were on the same page. She understood the level of her talent and accepted where she was at from a physical standpoint. I did the best I could to advise her father without damaging his ego. He accepted, not necessarily willingly, what I had to say after I had given him the proof in the list of other players. Prior to her high school senior season, she signed a letter of intent and earned a scholarship to play basketball at a Division II school far from home. She was happy and it was not a surprise to me that she accepted playing such a long distance from home. My purpose in this situation was to help guide this parent and athlete to make wise decisions for the child's future and to have reasonable expectations of her. Posing objective questions, I have helped several players answer the question of where to attend college. I have always reminded athletes that, when choosing a college, they must like what the college has to offer academically. They must be happy at the school they choose without the sport in question. Too many things can happen where that sport can be taken away and all that is left is the campus and the academic side of the experience, which, by no coincidence, is the most important part of their future.

In my final season of coaching girls basketball I had a senior athlete who was voted captain of the team. She hardly played at all, but was well liked and respected by her teammates. She and I were able to communicate on a very honest, up front level. It was a disruptive season in regards to the amount of parent involvement. Parents were vocal about their concerns in terms of the direction of the team. In her senior English class, this student chose to write an essay about the role parents should have in the high school athletic experience of their children. The essay made it to the local newspaper and in the newspaper's online blog. Comments on the blog were very much in support of her commentary on the state of high school athletics and the over involvement of parents. My purpose was to assist this athlete find the passion of honesty and the acceptance of the consequences of honesty. I was somewhat surprised and encouraged when I noticed how supportive her teammates were of her essay and the fact that it was a public story. As a team, we celebrated her accomplishments and supported her in the attention she did receive for her thoughts. She felt vulnerable, but through the support of her team, coaches, and her parents she gained strength.

    Beyond winning and losing the role of high school coaches are many. My underlying mission as a high school coach was to help high school athletes to build a positive sense of self-worth. I found it a necessity to listen without being judgmental, but, rather, supportive. Furthermore, it is essential for coaches to give their time without expecting the same in return. In building this foundation of self-worth, I believe the process has to include helping student-athletes find inner peace by processing conflict, minimizing the influence of the ego, and by recognizing each athlete's special talent and potential. If coaches can help student-athletes learn the lessons of their mistakes and continue to encourage hard work for positive gain, these students will be enriched beyond the classroom. Coaches must find the time to guide parents and their children to have realistic expectations and to set attainable goals. Furthermore, the attention of being a high school athlete, good or bad, must be processed and placed outside the reach of the ego and the end result will be a functional, well-rounded student prepared to enter life after high school. Ultimately, these things define success for any high school coach.

# ATHLETIC DIRECTORS: CREATING A COLLABORATIVE ENVIRONMENT

*Leadership and learning are indispensable to each other.*
    *John F. Kennedy*

The purpose of high school athletics is invariably different for coaches, athletic directors, and parents. Conflict arises within the framework of these groups because the purpose for each is different. Promoted as being a unified purpose for all involved, there lies underneath the political rhetoric from coaches, athletic directors, and the school districts a fundamental difference of purpose. The purpose of the Athletic Director in high school athletics is much different than that of the coach. While some purpose may overlap, the responsibilities of the athletic director are integral to the appropriate functioning of high school athletic programs.

The Athletic Director has an enormous job that includes scheduling, organizing events, monitoring and helping coaches, overseeing the distribution of the athletic budget, overseeing the appropriate policies and procedures as mandated by the school and the state governing athletic association, and dealing with the challenges of parents and their student athletes. There are some school districts that require the Athletic Director to split their duties either teaching in the classroom or in some other administrative way, such as dealing with discipline or truancy issues. Given the magnitude of the responsibilities an Athletic Director has directing co-curricular activities, the argument can justifiably be made that this job not be split with any other duties of the school. If school districts want to have an effective co-curricular program, it may be best to have a well organized person be in charge of this area, and only this area, of the high school.

Among the many jobs of an Athletic Director, supporting coaches must be a priority. Teachers who are coaches know that they are more often criticized by the public or community for their job as coach rather than their job as teacher. Generally, teachers are criticized publically as a group much more often than they are criticized individually. Teachers are perceived as more protected than coaches, so there isn't always an attack on individual teachers as a result, and sadly many parents place more value on sports than education. In addition, coaching is more visible and parents often have less of an idea of what truly is going on in the classroom. Coaches are much more vulnerable in their positions. Coaches and the athletes they coach are often recognized in the newspaper, on TV, within the school, and within the community. There is a spotlight that shines on coaches brighter in the realm of athletics than it does as their role as teacher. Clearly, this is a great example of the misaligned values that exist in high school athletics.

Parents and community members identify with and have a high degree of passion for high school athletics. Because coaches are under such scrutiny, coaches must be supported, publicly, by the Athletic Director. There must be an unwavering acknowledgment by the Athletic Director, as the immediate supervisor of all head coaches, that he supports the coach, his methods, and his interest in the success of student-athletes. Furthermore, it is the responsibility of the coach to be teacher first. Athletics provides the opportunity to teach outside of the classroom.

Athletic Directors must make the time to meet regularly with the head coaches in their schools. In order for the Athletic Director to support the coaches, there must be a clear understanding of the objectives and goals of each coach. Furthermore, the Athletic Director must know how the coach is going about attaining those objectives and goals. What methods and strategies is the coach using to inspire student-athletes and extend the classroom to the arena of high school athletics? The role of the Athletic Director is to listen, understand, and support the coach and his plan. The role does not include attempts at micromanaging the athletic programs. Instead, the coaches must be allowed to do their jobs. When there is just cause to disagree with the objectives or the action plan to achieve the goals of the program, the Athletic Director must discriminate between the expectations of the athletic program and the validity of the coach's vision. However, if the coach is meeting the expectations of the athletic department's mission statement, if the coach continues to treat student-athletes appropriately, relating to them in a positive manner, and if the coach is fielding a consistently competitive team, then the athletic director's support is, not only necessary, it is imperative. Privately and publicly, coaches must be supported by their immediate supervisors for the mission statement of the athletic department to be carried out.

Being an advocate for the coaches includes getting the appropriate equipment and funds the coach feels is necessary to help his student-athletes reach their potential. As with any good administrator, teachers are given the tools they request to allow them to do the best job they can for all students. Athletic Directors must act in the same way. Of course, there are some limitations in terms of budget. However, if a request is reasonable and the funds are available, there is no reason why a coach shouldn't be able to get whatever is needed to nurture the growth of student-athletes. It has been my experience as a teacher that the most effective administrators are the ones who do what they can to get the teachers what they need and then allow those teachers to be creative, given the appropriate resources, within their classroom. There is usually very little meddling. I believe the most affective athletic directors work in the same way. Get the coaches what they need and leave them alone. It is not the purpose of the Athletic Director to coach the athletes, instead coach the coaches and model appropriate relationship building skills.

All of this can be difficult for some Athletic Directors who identify with and attach their ego to the success of high school athletics.

Another problem of logistics often occurs in receiving the appropriate materials on time. Receiving requested items must be timely. For teachers, all budget requests usually arrive sometime over the summer months so that teachers can make use of it in their classrooms in the fall. The same urgency must be made for athletic programs. Equipment that is ordered through the Athletic Director must arrive prior to the season's beginning. This requires a well organized Athletic Director along with the assistance of effective support staff.

For the most part, my budgetary items were always on time, prior to the season. There have been a few exceptions to this, however. There were several seasons in which we began without the ordered practice gear for the players. What message is sent to the student-athletes if their equipment is not timely? The perception is that those particular athletes aren't important enough to have their equipment on time, especially in light of other programs within the same season that have their items on time.

In the final season I was head coach, we received our practice jerseys over two weeks late. Even worse, shortly after we had began using the jerseys, the numbers and letters began peeling off. To make matters worse, some of the jerseys began to rip, shred. When I reported this to my Athletic Director and showed him the examples of the ripped jerseys, he promised me he would "get on it." The vendor did come in to see the damaged goods and vowed to either replace them or give a credit to next season's purchase. It is now more than a year later and, to my knowledge, the jerseys have never been replaced. I have not been involved at all with the program since I resigned but was asked earlier in the school year by our athletic secretary if the defective jerseys had been replaced or if I even knew where the old jerseys were. Hopefully they have been taken care of and the issue has been resolved over the course of the past year and a half. In all due respect to our athletic department, I would assume that this problem has been resolved. I do know that it was not resolved, though, in a timely fashion.

I know that the Athletic Director has to address equipment requests from all sports. Therefore I have empathy in regards to balancing time and organizing priorities. Along with all of this, the Athletic Director is responsible for the scheduling of games and practice facilities. In our school district, the Athletic Director is responsible for scheduling practice facilities for many groups beyond the high school programs. I am empathetic to that as well. The Athletic Director has to manage a plethora of different groups while maintaining equity amongst the high school programs.

There are many variables that affect the use of practice facilities. The number of athletes in a particular sport, timing (i.e., which team has a game approaching sooner than another team), and level of team (i.e., freshmen, junior varsity, varsity) are just a few of the elements that affect the decisions of who gets what practice facility and when. A well organized person and one who can delegate responsibility is most effective in this role. It is not easy, in fact it is terribly challenging.

While supporting coaches must be a priority for Athletic Directors, so, too, does guiding parents and nurturing that relationship as a liaison between the school and the community. Proper practice for dealing with concerns in a proactive approach would be to have a meeting with parents of all high school athletes at the beginning of each school year. This meeting could address many topics including athletic codes and the consequences of violations, support of coaches, proper channels of communication for athletes and their parents, the acknowledgement of the importance of academics, and emphasizing the mission statement of the athletic department.

I also believe that it is important that Athletic Directors be present in sport specific meetings. In nearly every year that I was head coach, our varsity basketball team would host a "tip off meal." This gathering presented the opportunity for all athletes participating in the high school program to share in a meal, socialize, and share in the mission statement of the program with their parents and families. Not once did an administrator attend, just to make an appearance, in support of the athletes and the coaches despite the fact that each year they had been invited. Yes, I did invite them. I know it would be another night out of their busy lives to attend yet another activity. I am empathetic to that. I am not sure that a short appearance to open the evening would be too much of a commitment even if it was not feasible every year. How far would that appearance go in terms of the purpose of showing support for the program and being the liaison between the school and community?

Most high school athletic programs that I am aware of have season ending banquets and award ceremonies. I have heard of different ways of doing this. Some schools have an "all sports" banquet for each athletic season, fall, winter, and spring. For example, the "winter all sports banquet" would include boys basketball, girls basketball, and wrestling. All programs and their families dine together, and then might split up to give out sport specific awards. At the school where I was head coach, we had our own banquet for the specific sport we coached. In ten years of being head coach of this program, not once was the Athletic Director or any other administrator present.

I am not being critical of administrators who don't have the time or make the time to do these types of things; I am arguing that actions in these cases would go a long way in building strong, positive relationships between the school athletic programs and the community. This also further supports the argument for having Athletic Directors limit their responsibilities to serve their purpose within the framework of high school athletics. I would conclude by saying that Athletic Directors should make it a priority to attend all of these banquets, at the very least just to make an appearance. I can hear some administrators balking at this because of the time constraint issue. However, if we understand the true purpose of high school athletics and the roles of each "player" (i.e., coaches, athletic directors, etc.), then there would be no question as to the significance of the appropriate actions of an Athletic Director.

The most important element of being an Athletic Director in a high school setting might come in the role of being the ultimate advocate for the student-athletes. All sports, boys' and girls', deserve equity and recognition within the school. The one person who can make this happen is the Athletic Director. Recognition means to be viewed as equally important among all of the activities, including band, the musical, FFA, and any other co-curricular programs a school has to offer. Recognizing the importance each activity has on the education of the whole person. Recognition does not mean attention or valuing an activity more than the educational experience.

Balancing the egos of coaches, parents, and student-athletes is not easy. Most high school coaches take their sport and themselves too seriously. Given that, Athletic Directors have to maintain equity among all of the sports. All extracurricular activities must be governed by one person, void of ego, who fights for the best interest of student-athletes and the whole experience of high school education.

When coaches are not meeting the expectations required of them within the mission statement of the athletic department, and when the ego of coaches has gone too far and taken over their behaviors, a change needs to occur. The change might be in the coach's ego first. In order for this to happen, the Athletic Director himself must have an awareness of his own ego. If the supervisor of the coaches understands what feeds the ego, then he will have the capability to see the manifestation of ego in himself and in others. At that point a positive, working relationship results between the coach and the Athletic Director. They work together for the best interest of the experience of the student-athletes in their school, one not being superior to the other. Each learns from each other, and each works with each other in the common interest of the success of extracurricular activities, beyond winning and losing.

In the public eye, Athletic Directors look bad when school teams lose games consistently. On the other hand, Athletic Directors look good when school teams win consistently. Keep in mind that by "winning" I mean outscoring an opponent from another high school. Negligent Athletic Directors attach their identities to the winning programs and appear at their meetings

**High School Athletic Directors Have a Plethora of Responsibilities**

| |
|---|
| 1. Manage a number of groups while maintaining equity |
| 2. Guiding parents as a liaison between school and community |
| 3. Delegate responsibility |
| 4. Develop proactive plan to manage concerns from coaches, parents, and athletes |
| 5. Attending athletic events and many other co-curricular activities |
| 6. Be the #1 advocate for student-athletes |

and their banquets. You might even find them quoted in the newspaper or on TV concerning the success of one or more of the athletic programs. The ego begins to promote unhealthy, fleeting thoughts of superiority. This sense of superiority develops a lack of trust and can lead to unrealistic expectations. In faith, we must recognize that not one of the "players" in all of this is superior to the next, coaches, Athletic Directors, parents, and student-athletes. Added to this destructive model of misaligned values is the comparison of other programs that are losing within the school to the programs that are winning.

I was the head coach of a girls basketball program that coexisted alongside an extremely successful, record-setting boys basketball program. In the ten years that I was head coach of the girls program, the boys teams had been to the final four of the state tournament eight consecutive years. In a word: amazing! The student-athletes of this program were committed to achieving excellence led by a good team of coaches. The girls basketball teams were often compared, almost naturally, and never really did measure up despite the fact that in that same time period, the girls reached the division 2 regional final of the state tournament seven out of eight years and finished second in a predominantly division 1 conference two straight years.

This is where in lies the ego. Do I write about reaching the regional final to prove the success of the program that I coached in support of my ego? Those reading this that scoff at the idea that what the girls did during that decade was inferior to what the boys did might be feeding their own egos. In either case, it is unhealthy at all to compare one against the other. I argue that defining success by winning and losing is dangerous. In fact, winning and losing doesn't matter. The winning success or lack thereof does not measure the true success of the experience of the student-athletes. I know that there is an argument for both the positive and negative experiences of the athletes in each of these programs. One student-athlete, one coach, one parent is not any different or superior to anyone else. Some have different opportunities than others, but we have all been created by the same Hand and one responsibility we have is to share our uniqueness with those around us.

Our Athletic Director, uncharacteristically, showed up on my door step one week before the season began; the season that, at the time I didn't know it, would be my last. He held a six pack of beer under his arm and said he needed to talk. I invited him in. We talked. He was trying awfully hard to be subtle, to show his empathy and support (I think) by bringing the beer that he chugged as I sipped. But he was questioning the qualifications of my coaching staff and questioning what it would take to get "to the next level." At that point in time I knew that there was a comparison being made between the girls basketball program and the boys basketball program, from, of all people, the Athletic Director.

The Athletic Director often looked for affirmation from all coaches in the district regarding the decisions he made. There were errors made, nothing major, but it was like a nagging injury that never quite healed. In his attempt to make everyone happy, he was unsuccessful. His thoughts often wavered as the wind switches directions. Although he attempted to share his allegiance with all sports and all coaches, this was not always the perception. He needed to be more consistent to earn the trust of all coaches. Consistent support creates a productive professional relationship between a supervisor and his subordinates. The problem was not him. I honestly believe that our Athletic Director is a good person and honest in his intentions. However, he needed a vision and mission statement that would bind him to consistency for all activity programs in our school.

When he began to share his thoughts with me, I knew these thoughts did not originate in his mind because of the history of support he had given me. The source of this concern was coming from somewhere else. I had my suspicions, but couldn't get anyone to really give me honest feedback. The point of this example is to show that I, as coach, and the program I was providing for athletes was under some "special" surveillance. In comparison to other girls sports in our school, girls basketball was as successful, and in some cases much more successful than, any of the other programs over that course of time. Nevertheless, the Athletic Director was at my door, in my house, and sitting on my furniture. I don't mean to point the finger to inflate my ego. It is fact. I believe, too, that I would not have any problem with my daughter participating in any of the other athletic programs in our school as long as she was enhancing her learning experience in high school, as long as her whole person was being educated. Let's face it, if a high school coach is treating the student-athletes well, creating a competitive team, and preparing athletes to be successful participants in life, then that coach is doing a stellar job.

I demanded, from our team of administrators, to know what the expectations were of our athletic programs. I had even posed this question, in my letter of resignation, to our school board. My Athletic Director told me that all sports need to be at the sectional level of play in the tournament. He had mentioned that, with the athletes in our school, there is no reason we shouldn't be competing at that level of competition in every sport in every year. Is that really what the expectations and purpose of high school athletics should be? The *only* program in our school district that has done that in the 13 years I have been teaching here has been the boys basketball program. There was no mention of learning the important lessons of discipline, work ethic, or teamwork. In fact, one of my administrators told me in a meeting shortly after my final season concluded that maybe my expectations of athletes would be better served in a middle school setting. I do believe that my expectations would serve middle school students well. However, I believe that high school athletes need to be held to the same standards when it came to character building. This administrator didn't really want to meddle with the athletic department. He, too, however seemed to be influenced by something or someone outside. So, if those are truly the expectations, to reach sectional level of play, what of the other coaches and the other programs? Are they being looked at under the same microscope?

The point is that the purpose of the Athletic Director begins with his need to be strong in his own "self." The self that truly defines who he is, absent of the ego. He needs to know his "self." If he can allow himself to be vulnerable enough to stand for something real and believe in the people he works with, the results will be a positive high school experience in the education of the whole person. In knowing his "self," he will then have the ability to know others. Know others on an intimate level, students, parents, and coaches.

It was my suspicion that our Athletic Director was being influenced by outside forces. The uncertainty of beliefs and expectations are a result of trying to feed his own ego by seeking affirmation from too many sources. I was told once by my Superintendent that it was important to listen and then discriminate what was pertinent from the given information. I am sure that my Athletic Director received this same advice. However, we must always filter the crud to get to the reality or to what is important. Fundamentally, it is imperative that Athletic Directors listen, first, to all of their head coaches who are working directly with the student-athletes. Furthermore, Athletic Directors must be total advocates for the students participating in co-curricular activities.

In the early years of my teaching career, one of our history teachers and head football coach of some 30 years was retiring from teaching. This dedicated coach and teacher had received numerous accolades and prestigious awards throughout his career in both teaching and coaching. Furthermore, he was well respected in both the school and the community. He wanted to continue to coach and really had, in his mind, earned the right to that option. Being influenced by many, our Athletic Director, who had coached with this head football coach for many years and was a high school athlete under this head coach, had decided that the school and athletic department would be better off to move forward with a younger coach. The irony in this situation was that our Athletic Director had sculpted his own philosophy from the foundation given him by the highly acclaimed head coach he was now escorting out of the position.

I know that there was justification in the minds of our administrators to go forth with someone new. Maybe there was a power struggle, maybe there was a conflict of interest, and maybe there was a sense that his message wasn't being heard anymore. I coached for this man and knew that he still was making a difference with high school athletes. He was a driven man, passionate about being a teacher first, contributing greatly to the wealth of knowledge and experience of the student-athletes he coached. Given the history of the Athletic Director's relationship with this head coach, we all speculated that his motivation to find another coach for this position was not of his own thought process. How could it have been? He believed in this head coach more than anyone. He acts like him, talks like him, and personified the values he learned under this head coach. What the rest of us coaches were hoping for was our Athletic Director to think for himself and build a strong foundation of definitive expectations.

This happens as a result of not having a mission statement and not having honest, realistic, and measurable expectations. What are realistic expectations? It is imperative that our students learn to read, write and do math among other things. As teachers, parents, and administrators we certainly have the expectations that when our students graduate from high school they will have the tools needed to continue their education or become directly involved in the work force. The question is, how will participation in high school athletics enhance the experience of the student to help better prepare them for life after high school? The answer to this question exclusively comes from the mission statement of each school's athletic department. I would argue further that, regardless of how many contests are won by simply scoring more points than an opponent from another high school, the realistic expectations lie beyond winning and losing.

How will these expectations be measured? The answer herein lies, again, exclusively in the mission statement of each school's athletic department. Once realistic expectations are defined, then the ways in which they are measured can be developed. For instance, if a realistic expectation is to provide student-athletes with the opportunity to learn the value of working cooperatively, then a measurement of that can be made in the performance of the team as a cooperative unit. Now in this measurement, the term "performance" might jump out. I am not suggesting a performance based on winning or losing. I am suggesting that a team's performance can be measured by how they function together through respect and trust, neither of which have anything to do with winning. Of course, the teams that respect and trust each other most certainly do increase their odds of winning and winning certainly can be factored in as one component of success, but a team's record cannot fully define them. Even grounded, well rounded coaches and student-athletes void of ego have the desire to win and define part of their success on winning. However, if these student-athletes gain and give respect and trust and never win a game, they will still have had a valuable learning experience; kudos to the coach that can bring that together.

I believe that the mission statement is the key to success for all high school athletic programs. The mission statement goes beyond the athletic code of conduct, but certainly, the code can be included in the mission statement. The mission statement is definitive and has depth. Some may argue that, as with all "rules," a mission statement that is too definitive might put an administrator in a corner with no way out. While that may be true on occasion, I believe the positive, lasting value of such a mission statement far outweighs the sporadic situations of being caught between a rock and a hard place. If nothing else, a mission statement can offer some consistency for Athletic Directors to carry out their purpose.

I believe the mission statement should be conceived from the minds of select parents, coaches, and athletic directors. For each school the mission statement might be different given the variety of demographics for each district. A committee of parents, all head coaches, and the Athletic Director meet to share ideas and concerns in regards to what is expected from high school athletics. I would suggest that there be a mediator in this meeting. Maybe the Athletic Director could be this mediator. If not, there needs to be an objective person who will not allow one person or group to dominate. In other words, the mediator must be void of ego, able to recognize when ego is taking over the ideologies of the plan, and help maintain the committee's focus on the reality and significance of high school athletics; which is only a part of the educational experience of the whole individual.

# STUDENT-ATHLETES: CREATING A POSITIVE SENSE OF SELF-WORTH

*Just play. Have fun. Enjoy the game.*
    Michael Jordan

The number of high school student-athletes who actually earn an athletic scholarship to Universities or Colleges is less than one percent. In my ten years as head girls basketball coach, there were only two female student-athletes in our school who earned an athletic scholarship to play basketball. In my 13 years as a teacher, I know of only two other female student-athletes from our school to earn an athletic scholarship, one in track, the other in volleyball. Furthermore, in my 13 years of teaching there have been only six male student-athletes who have earned college athletic scholarships. On average, our school has graduated approximately 200 students each year. Over the course of 13 years, that amounts to roughly 2,600 graduates. Ten out of those approximate 2,600 high school graduates earned an athletic college scholarship; that is only .0038% of all students.

The numbers across the country might be slightly higher, but the chances of earning an athletic college scholarship are remote, at best. Student-athletes and their parents better have a purpose to participate in high school athletics beyond earning an athletic scholarship. Can student-athletes participate in athletics beyond high school without the benefit of an athletic scholarship? Absolutely. There are many opportunities for student-athletes who excel in high school athletics to pursue their interest beyond high school. However, the purpose of high school athletics must focus on the development of the whole person: to prepare each child for life beyond athletics. That is the reality.

It has been many years since I participated in high school athletics. On reflecting upon the motivation I had to be involved in high school athletics and based on the experiences I have had as a coach in the high school setting, I believe there are several elements to the athlete's purpose. As I watch my children through elementary school, I see their motivation as well. The purpose of a high school athlete is not too far from that of a first grader. The evolution of an athlete's purpose is intriguing to examine.

In the beginning, a child gets involved in organized sports at a very young age at a parent's urging. As a parent of young children, I can admit that Desiree and I want our children to take advantage of any opportunity presented to discover their true inner strengths and beauty. Organized sports are only a part of the mural of activities that our children are exposed to. Our daughter, Brooklyn, has participated in soccer, tee-ball, softball, and basketball at an organized level all before the age of six. The purpose of her involvement is a result of her parents signing her up for participation and because she likes to have fun. At the heart of all sport is the notion that the sport, or game, is fun. When the experience of participating in these activities becomes increasingly less fun, the child begins to withdraw from the sport. It is important for parents and other adults to recognize this transformation in the children. Finding out what exactly is at the root of the lack of enjoyment is essential in helping the child transition to another activity. Working through the issue to help them overcome the growing insecurity or conflict they may have within themselves prepares the student-athletes to problem solve.

Brooklyn enjoys participating in all of these activities, so far. She has never resisted being involved and seems to find a simplistic satisfaction in the experience. Brooklyn has yet to have a negative, painful experience. She often asks us about her performance, already looking for affirmation and wanting to do well for mom and dad. We encourage her and try to give her the best advice we can in terms of her strengths and weaknesses. Most of all, she has fun playing with kids her own age; the social element of meeting new friends through these experiences cannot be underestimated.

At this stage of the child's development, I believe it is important to emphasize the operative word "playing" as opposed to "competing." I know that my first grader and her friends, when asked about their favorite part of the school day, always choose recess over most anything, with the exception of snack time, as their favorite activity at school. Children learn at a very young age how to play and have fun. The introduction of organized sports in their lives is based on this idea that kids like to run around, kick a ball, and shout "GO TEAM!!"

As time goes on, kids start to abandon some of the activities they are involved in as a result of waning interest in one area and, possibly, an increase of interest in another area. For instance, for the first time during the summer between kindergarten and first grade, Brooklyn had the choice to participate in coed tee-ball or girls softball. She chose softball because she felt more comfortable with her friends and she lost interest in competing with the boys in tee-ball. Further examples include athletes who grow physically at different rates and show prowess in one sport over another. A young man that is 6'5, 180 pounds as a freshman in high school may choose to play basketball and abandon his pursuit of the sport of wrestling.

Another possibility of the abandonment might be caused by peer pressure. The peer pressure can work in two ways. First, the level of competitiveness increases between children as they grow in physical size and in emotional maturity. A child may begin to notice that they lack motivation to compete because of their lack of success or attention or, possibly they realize that some kids are "passing them by." A second type of peer pressure comes as a result of kids pushing kids to join or stick with an athletic program. Peer pressure can be good, but it can also work against the foundation of athletics if it causes kids to lose interest and diminish their sense of self-worth. Friendship groups that help each other stay involved in positive, drug and alcohol free activities are excellent examples of positive peer pressure. Friendship groups that work to disassociate a member of the group for self serving reasons is an example of negative peer pressure.

A popular team building activity among high school basketball teams is to have a "lock in" on New Year's Eve. Certainly a coach has to set this up and be willing to participate himself, but the student-athletes have to put pressure on each other to attend. When I was an assistant high school football coach I heard our head coach address the team on several occasions on the issue of drugs and alcohol. He had told the team that a popular excuse for teenagers was, "well, everyone's doing it." His rhetorical comment delivered in his commanding voice to this was that, and he would point his finger at the kids individually and look them square in the eye, "if you're not doing it, and you're not doing it, and you're not doing it, then EVERYONE'S NOT doing it." A simple message each one of those athletes could take with them and remind each other about in when confronted with making good decisions.

I was in the habit, and still am as a father and teacher, to remind my athletes to make good decisions. Each season I would say this phrase numerous times a week. It was a reminder that there are options out there, some good and some bad. I wanted the athletes to hold themselves and each other accountable. As each season wore on, I heard the athletes saying it before I did, especially when there were rumors of a party going on that weekend. All of these are examples of how peer pressure can have a positive effect on student-athletes.

Recently I had heard an interesting development occur in regards to negative peer pressure on a girls basketball team. A young lady had decided to try out for basketball as a junior after taking her sophomore year off. It was speculated that the girl took her sophomore year off because she had a poor self image in terms of basketball in comparison to the other talented girls in her class. When she decided to return to the team her junior year, within the first week of practice, two girls who had been on the team the previous year felt threatened by the presence of this girl. The threat, I suppose, was due to playing time being lost to someone who might contribute to the team. These two girls, it had been reported, had encouraged the "new" girl to quit so she could focus on volleyball. Granted, this young lady is an outstanding volleyball player, but she is a good athlete and could significantly contribute to the success of the team.

Consequently, the girl quit. After her mother talked with coach and explained the reason her daughter quit was because of two girls on the team pressuring her to do so, the coach took the situation to the team. He used it as a teaching tool and learning opportunity. He made the entire team run and run and run. The coach made the team run until the two girls responsible for this negative peer pressure admitted their wrong doing, were willing to apologize, and welcome the girl back with open arms. The coach's technique worked marvelously. The girl was back and the team had learned a valuable lesson of cooperation, honesty, and accountability, not to mention humility. This is truly an example of the essence of high school athletics in its pure purpose and function.

In sport, the shift from being fun to becoming challenging and more and more competitive tends to occur right around fifth or sixth grade for most children. I remember being consumed by every sport as a child. During the spring and summer seasons my favorite sport was baseball, during the fall I loved football, and during the winter months I enjoyed basketball. The first organized opportunities in sport that I can remember in the early 80's was basketball. I recall my parents had me try wrestling, but that didn't take. I remember joining basketball in fifth grade. During sixth grade I was introduced to organized football. I joined football, after the season began, due to peer pressure. My ego was active and I believed my friends who told me I would be awesome. My love was basketball, but I tried football. I was successful at football and basketball and, by middle school, my identity was being attached to my success in sports, particularly basketball and football.

# STUDENT-ATHLETES:
## CREATING A POSITIVE SENSE OF SELF-WORTH

In contrast, I had friends that had begun to withdraw completely from these activities. I remember a middle school friend by the name of Troy. His father coached our sixth and seventh grade football team. He played basketball with us during seventh and eighth grade. He was a good athlete and a good guy. Something changed though. He went in another direction. He didn't get the same attention for sports as I did. I am sure he felt pressure to be better. Instead of attaching his identity to the attention of athletics, he tried to escape it. He began smoking pot and cigarettes regularly in seventh grade. In high school, he got himself in trouble several times for using drugs and being truant. Why does that happen? There are a lot of factors that contribute to the fading interest. I would argue that, along with the starving ego, the high degree of importance that is placed upon athletics lacks the vision of a truly successful future which can lead to a negative self image and misinterpretation of reality.

In our world today, kids have many more opportunities than my generation did to be involved in organized activities well before middle school. In fact, parents of high school athletes who I talk with today claim that they felt the pressure to place their children in organized sports programs very early on due to the fierce competitive nature of it at the high school level. They believed that their children would not have the opportunity to even be a part of the team, much less be an active contributor, if they hadn't gotten involved early in grade school. In fact, I know of someone who inquired about signing up her six year old for youth hockey and was told that if her daughter didn't have hockey experience already, it was too late to start her in the sport. This pressure is a frightening reality and a great example of the misaligned values that have evolved throughout the history of high school athletics, making the association with these activities almost toxic.

My ego had been activated by middle school. I felt visible and valued because of the attention I received athletically. As I see it now as an adult, I find it absurd to write. I don't know if I was "good" or not, what I do know is that I got attention for being involved as an athlete. I was a huge fan of sports. I loved to watch them on TV. Now I was able to put on a uniform, be coached by a real coach, and watch the scoreboard to measure my success. At this stage of development kids need adults to help keep it all in perspective. However, if the adults don't have the perspective, how can we expect the kids to have it?

As the athlete's purpose continues to evolve from having fun through learning something new in the midst of the social element of meeting new friends, it moves toward the challenge presented by the sport. In the late stages of elementary school and throughout middle school, athletes become aware of the nuances of each sport. There are certain challenges to learning new things and perfecting wrestling moves, jump shots, swimming strokes and any other sport specific techniques. The challenge of a sport is intriguing to the human soul. We are all wired with a sense of adventure and challenge, and sports give us the opportunity to explore that inner passion.

In the latter stages of high school student-athletes become challenged by their sport. They have an opportunity to be good at something and feel moved to explore that opportunity. The purpose of an athlete then becomes to improve the skills they have gained. This is a challenge. This is such an important stage of a child's development emotionally, physically, and psychologically. Athletes learn the success strategy of setting goals and creating an action plan to achieve those goals. This is a critical time of development. Children need guidance to not allow their ego to control their attitude and behavior. There needs to be a discussion on the idea of acceptance. I am not saying that we should teach our children to be content and not look to improve. On the contrary, I am saying that at a certain point in life we have to recognize our strengths and accentuate them. Furthermore, we must acknowledge our weaknesses and accept them. This is difficult.

My older brother was the first born son in my family. He is my only brother. Our stages of physical development were almost polar opposites. He was tall and thin as a young adult. I, on the other hand, was a bit chunkier (5'10, 140 pounds in sixth grade). I am not sure my brother reached 140 pounds until he was a junior or senior in high school. My brother played high school football his freshmen year. He found that participating in athletics just wasn't his most inspired passion. I suppose that, being the first born son, he wanted to prove his ability, or athletic prowess, to my father in the early years of high school. He liked sports, and still does, in fact he successfully participated in softball leagues and basketball leagues after he graduated from high school. To his credit, he knew his strengths were in other areas while he was in high school.

Following two sisters with one behind him and a little brother, I am sure my brother felt pressure to succeed. I am sure that pressure mounted when he wanted to pursue other interests like woodworking and earning money. I think that at the time my dad competed in high school athletics most young men relied purely on their natural ability and strength. There wasn't much weight training going on in the mid 1950's for high school athletes, at least not in my father's case. That is what my father knew: natural strength and internal motivation to compete. My brother's strengths were not in kinesthetic in nature as a young adult; his strengths lie elsewhere.

My brother is gifted with creativity. He is a master with building and creating things with his hands. As a kid, he loved erector sets and working with our grandfathers on car engines or plumbing. The function and purpose of high school athletics helped him identify his strengths and creativity in other areas of his life. He can now put high school athletics into a healthy perspective for his own children. If my parents better understood the effect of their own ego, maybe they could have offered my brother and my other siblings clearer direction at finding in their soul God's true gift for them.

I am not being critical of my parents. It is not their fault. They only did what they knew was best and really did try to encourage all of us. Their attention did boost our egos, but, in reality, our egos were being hammered by the outside world. We were receiving a different message from the world. Our view within our home wasn't measuring up to the reality of the world.

I have heard student-athletes tell me that nothing they do is "good enough." I question *who* it is they want to be good enough for and *what* it is they want to be good enough at. The origination of this mentality comes from a few different areas. First, student-athletes want to be "good enough" for their parents; they want to prove that they can be good at something their parents have passion about and strongly identify with. Second, student-athletes might feel the pressure to be "good enough" in comparison to an older sibling or cousin or, in some cases, a parent. There is pressure to carry on the family name, to make the family proud. I know that I was told by my mother that I needed to represent my family well. Finally, student-athletes might consider themselves "good enough" in relationship to other athletes who have gone before them in their particular sport. Sure, it is good to have goals and to set them high. But, are they reachable goals?

A close friend of mine in middle school attempted suicide during the spring of our freshmen year of high school. He was an outstanding athlete. His ego, like mine, was addicted to the attention he received from athletics. Like me, he was the "baby" of a large family and had lived in the shadow of his older brothers who were good high school athletes. We lost touch with each other over time because we had gone to different high schools. I don't know this for sure, but, as I grew older, I began to believe that his suicide attempt was a result of the pressure he felt from his parents and family. Maybe it was just perceived pressure. In other words, maybe it was in his own mind to live up to the successes of his brothers and father. In any case, he was in a deep depression willing to take his own life. He survived the attempt and lives to tell about it today.

The student-athletes that use the motivation of proving something to their parents as their purpose for participating in athletics will fail. Children want to make their parents happy. I see that in my daughter Brooklyn. She wants to make her parents proud because her parents are the ones, right now anyway, who give her that affirmation. Maybe a son of an aggressive father might want to prove his manhood through success in wrestling or football. Maybe a daughter feels the same kind of pressure to make her dad proud of her. Any way you slice it, motivation originating from the desire to fulfill a parent's dream is unhealthy.

Following in the footsteps of a brother who was the star quarterback three years ago is an extremely tall mountain to climb for any sibling. When a younger sibling is constantly compared to the older sibling it is detrimental to the mental health of that child. Not only will this child's self-image be negative, there will be little chance of developing a positive sense of self-worth until that younger sibling can get out of the dark cloud of a successful sibling.

An athlete's purpose to be involved and succeed because of the legendary tales of the high school athletes that went before them is not always with good reason. Sometimes this can provide good motivation. This situation does provide a great opportunity for goal setting and the success of others can be a good measuring stick. The question is, are these reasonable and realistic expectations for the child with this motivation? An adult, void of ego, must step in to help this child keep his wits about him.

At this very critical time in the lives of these children, in the maturation of their personalities, and in the discovering of strengths and passions these kids need adult guidance. The influential people in their lives need to understand the active ego and give these kids the tools to manage their egos, the tools to let their inside passion shine. The underlying purpose for student-athletes being involved in high school athletics should never result from trying to prove something to their parents, result from peer pressure, or result from an unending need of attention. As adults, we have the responsibility to help them with this awareness. As adults, we have the responsibility to recognize these things happening in our students. All of these destructive purposes are external motivators and will only lead to a negative experience and worse, a negative self-image as they get older.

Students who are interested in competing in high school athletics must be helped to understand appropriate purpose for participating. The healthy purpose includes the challenge to improve their whole "self" and the desire to compete. Both of these motivators will enhance the overall educational experience for the student-athlete. The purpose for a high school student to

**Healthy Purpose of High School Athletics for the Student Athlete**

---
1. Improve whole 'self'

2. Develop a healthy passion to compete outside of classroom

3. Build a foundation of leadership and cooperative skills

4. Grow emotional maturity

5. Work with a group toward a unified vision

---

take U.S. History is to learn about all of the things that have happened that affect our world today. That foundation of knowledge can be used throughout their lives so that we can repeat the good and extinguish the bad. The same idea holds true with high school athletics. Define the purpose with them. Be sure that it is a healthy purpose and keep it in perspective, meaning, keep the ego in check to know really what the experience of high school athletics is about.

The student-athlete's ego takes an enormous hit when all of the attention getting days of high school athletics transform into days gone by. The negative experiences and the positive experiences turn into memories of the same kind that children turned adults associate themselves with. Their self-image is directly correlated to how they were treated at age 17 as well as to the attention, or lack thereof, they received.

I have met too many adults in their mid twenties, starting their professional careers or starting their families that are confused because of the attention they received as high school athletes. This attention is fleeting. When you are 28, nobody cares that you started 18 varsity football games at quarterback. Nobody cares about how many games your team won or lost or even if you broke school records. In fact, you are measured by a whole different set of criteria. What did you learn in athletics and the preparation to compete that you can apply to your professional career? What did you learn about working cooperatively with people in relationships that you can apply to your marriage? Learning to manage the ego and keep the importance of high school athletics in perspective, results in the former student-athletes associating the lessons they learned through the activities valuable.

The bottom line is the purpose of high school athletics for the student-athlete allows them to grow emotionally, compete at an intense level outside of the classroom, and be supported by a group of people with a common vision. All of these things last a lifetime and will aide each student-athlete in their quest for success. In the journey of our lives we can be sure of two things: We all have the capability and desire to release our uniqueness; and God guides us into and out of situations that help each one of us discover our intimate relationship with Him and share the talents He crafted within us.

*Part Four*
# HIGH SCHOOL ATHLETICS: A DEFINITION OF SUCCESS

# HIGH SCHOOL ATHLETICS: EDUCATION OF THE WHOLE PERSON

*To me, there are three things we all should do every day. We should do this every day of our lives. Number one is laugh. You should laugh every day. Number two is think. You should spend some time in thought. And number three is, you should have your emotions moved to tears, could be happiness or joy. But think about it. If you laugh, you think, and you cry, that's a full day. That's a heck of a day. You do that seven days a week, you're going to have something special.*
    Jim Valvano

    The definitions of success for high school coaches, athletic directors, parents, and athletes are ambiguous. The definition that makes the most sense is probably not the most popular. I would suggest that in high school athletics success is accomplished when it helps adolescents grow into young adults. There are lessons to be learned in winning. Similarly, there are lessons to be learned in losing and lessons to be learned in the preparation. As parents we all have visions of what we want our children to learn before they leave the nest, before they graduate from high school. If parents don't have some expectations of what they want their child to learn, it's never too late to start.

    Beyond the math, science, and language arts our children are learning in the classroom; we want our children to be independent, disciplined individuals that know how to work hard for the goals they set. Winning football games, wrestling matches, or the state volleyball championship are not truly the means to achieve the independence, discipline, or work ethic that will aide our children's success beyond high school. The "winning" will not help our children believe in themselves, be humble, or become leaders. The preparation for competition and all of the experiences that encompass being a high school athlete are much closer to the reality that children need to help their maturation.

The preparation takes place in many different environments. First, and foremost, is the home. Children must be guided by their parents or parental figure in the home. The support of learning and discovering the true essence of "self" comes from the development children have in the family household. Some children are raised by extended families, grandparents, aunts, uncles, or God parents. Wherever or whatever a child calls home is where the most important models of development occur.

Probably the second most influential environment is school. Learning to prepare for exams in algebra, chemistry, and American literature are essential to post high school success. In these cases, the most effective teachers prepare our students for the work force or education beyond high school. Embedded in the high school experience is that of co-curricular activities. Learning to compete encompasses skills that are essential to the future success of high school students.

Parents' view of high school success should mirror the definition for success for coaches and athletic directors. In theory, if the coaches are successful in teaching life lessons to student-athletes, the parents must be satisfied with the progress of growth in their high school student. A unified vision of all involved in high school athletics and the education of high school students will foster the healthiest atmosphere to learn. A school district utilizes a school board made up of community members to oversee the well-being of the students. The board works hard to create policy and apply that policy which is intended for the best interest of the students. In the same way, athletics should be managed. Under the large umbrella of responsibilities of the school board, the management of athletics is contained. However, if we looked at a pie chart that showed the amount of time and concern a school board puts on athletics, I would argue the slice might only provide a small meal for a field mouse.

An effective school board keeps the value of high school education in its proper place. The most important aspects of high school education, the biggest pieces of the pie, are how effective the teachers are helping their students reach the benchmarks provided by the state and nation. This may be the most normal part of the educational system. Kudos to the school boards that do, in fact, act in the best interest of the child's education, develop a mission statement, and hold their staff accountable to the expectations of that mission statement.

The definition of success in high school athletics goes way beyond the societal boundaries we identify as winning and losing. In fact, if parents can identify with and support the life lessons that coaches void of ego are teaching high school athletes, then parents can do their job as parents to prepare their children for life after high school. As we know, there are many variables that help student-athletes achieve success beyond high school. Parents and coaches are two significant elements in the development of the children.

There are times when I have sensed parents pointing the finger of responsibility at teachers, coaches, even clergy when it comes to the maturation of their child's development. Parents have the best opportunity to help their children. Whether or not high school athletics is fun for student-athletes can highly depend upon the attitude of the parent. Whether or not high school athletes get the most out of the whole of the high school experience highly depends upon the parents' attitude of acceptance. If the ego is controlling the behavior and attitude of the parent, it is certain that the experience of the student-athlete will be significantly less than the experience of the child whose parent supports him and is in total acceptance. Success for the student-athlete needs to be anchored in self-worth and a love for the game. "Playing" and having fun is at the root of the student-athlete's purpose. Together, the four entities (coaches, athletic directors, parents, and athletes) can make the short experience of high school athletics a positive, memorable one.

Making positive memories occurs when student-athletes experience an all encompassing education. As a result of the education of the whole person, a positive sense of self-worth emerges. When a positive self image surfaces we will see students who have allowed their inner passion to come out and have learned that experiencing life through their ego may be a dangerous way to perceive themselves and the world. God has created uniqueness in each one of us that is part of the spirit of all living things. At some point in our lives we have to locate that within us and allow it to be shared. Certainly, students will be successful beyond high school if their values are harbored within the good they can do, within their strengths, for their communities and the world. Success in high school athletics is only a part of the development of the purity of self.

# THE FIVE GIFTS OF SUCCESSFUL PARENTS

*That day when evening came, he said to his disciples, "Let us go over to the other side." Leaving the crowd behind, they took him along, just as he was, in the boat. There were also other boats with him. A furious squall came up, and the waves broke over the boat, so that it was nearly swamped. Jesus was in the stern, sleeping on a cushion. The disciples woke him and said to him, "Teacher, don't you care if we drown?" He got up, rebuked the wind and said to the waves, "Quiet! Be still!" Then the wind died down and it was completely calm. He said to his disciples, "Why are you so afraid? Do you still have no faith?" They were terrified and asked each other, "Who is this? Even the wind and the waves obey him!"*
   *Mark 4:35 - 41*

I have been a parent close to eight years. This is not a long time, but I do know that I am a parent for life. In good faith, I pray that's a long time. When Desiree and I left the hospital with Brooklyn, we were not handed a mission statement for parents from the nurse that escorted us to our vehicle. Desiree read some books during her pregnancy and we talked to people who already had children. We knew that we had to have an infant's car seat properly strapped into the backseat of the family car. At home, we knew enough to have Brooklyn's bedroom set to go, painted yellow, with a changing table, plenty of diapers, a crib, and a mobile. We felt like we had a good handle on this whole new experience of being parents, piece of cake! Once all three of us were strapped safely in the car we were on our own. A life's worth of lessons and adjustments to be learned.

Parenting may be the most challenging role we will have in our lifetimes. Without a doubt, parenting is the most important responsibility of our lives. If there were such a set of rules that existed to help give parents the absolute answers to raising children, I am sure it would include characteristics such as love, compassion, and support. There is no perfect mission statement for the parent of the high school athlete; situations and circumstances are different for everybody. In defining success for the parent of a high school athlete, I would suggest five gifts parents can give their children. A parent can be successful at helping their high school athlete be successful if, when given the opportunity, they believe in and apply the objectives which lie outside the lines of the volleyball court, softball diamond, or football field.

## Objective One: The Gift of Support

As the foundation of all families, parents, by nature, support their children. I know that no matter what happens to me, good or bad, that my parents will be there to support me. I know I have done some disappointing things, made some poor choices, and my parents caught me before I fell or helped me back on my feet. However, they never stopped loving me. Their consistent encouragement helped me stand on my own. Through their affirmation I became a loving, sensitive husband, father, teacher, and coach.

God created our spirit to love and to be loved. This is at the very root of our existence, the place where our uniqueness dwells. Parents understand that love filling their spirit, maybe to a degree more than anyone else. If your children can feel your love, they can get a glimpse of the grace of God. Furthermore, when children feel the love of their parents they will know they will always have a base of support.

For some, saying "I love you" can be the most difficult thing to say. Maybe this is because we all know the significance of the term and the idea of the commitment. When we love someone we are committing a lifetime of support. When I was a high school athlete, I knew that my performance on the football field or basketball court never changed the love my parents gave to me. It is a genuine, unconditional love that speaks to the inner most depths of our soul. This love will last a lifetime beyond the days of high school.

In addition to the love my parents gave me, I knew they respected the coaches who worked with me. My father didn't always agree with the coaches, but never once, in my ear shot, did I ever hear anything but respect for the men who gave their time to be my coach. Years after high school my father did tell me that, on two occasions, he talked with a coach of mine. First, was in my junior year of basketball. I was a starter on a very average team. We were in practice one day and I was having difficulty in executing the scheme our coach was attempting to teach. I was not having a good day. I have to say that I respected my high school basketball coach. He had been a long time coach, a friend of our family, and had been very successful in terms of wins and losses. More importantly, he had been successful in helping boys become responsible young men.

In the midst of working on a full court press, I kept screwing up my responsibility. The basketball ended up in coach's hands and with the ball under his arm he blew his whistle, challenged me a little, and then told us to set it up again. When I was walking back to reset the defense, I got knocked in the back of the head. In my sweaty, winded state I thought, "What the hell was that?" Then I heard the ball bouncing behind me. It was the ball hitting me in the back of the head. My coach had let his frustration get the best of him and threw the ball at my head.

I was humbled for a moment and really didn't make much of it. In fact, I probably deserved to get knocked in the head; after all, I was being somewhat of a knucklehead. This type of thing wasn't brutal abuse and probably happened to other kids I played with as well. This incident did not cause any bodily injury; there was no blood. The only thing wounded for a moment was my ego. I survived.

Later that night, I was home eating dinner and told my parents about the incident. I was really telling them, matter-of-factly, about the situation that happened at practice. My dad told me, much later in my life, that this really ticked him off. He felt that I hadn't deserved to be hit in the back of the head so he called the coach, his friend, to tell him that. I give my dad credit for standing up for his child. The coach was receptive to my father approaching him. He wasn't complaining about playing time or my role on the team, he just felt that his son didn't deserve to be hit in the back of the head with a basketball.

Another time my dad contacted a coach that I didn't learn about until many years later was in my senior year of high school. I was the starting quarterback of the football team. I had injured my back lifting weights less than two weeks prior to the first game. This injury would lead to major back surgery more than three years after it happened. I played injured all year, at times in a lot of pain.

There was an upcoming sophomore who was a pretty good athlete. He was a little different quarterback than I was. He could run well, and he was a little shiftier than I was. I was at my best as a drop back passer. Later in the season, as we were preparing for our playoff run, the coaching staff thought it would be a good idea to use this sophomore quarterback on occasion as a change of pace. There were opportunities in games that we had many more points than our opponent that he would get playing time. The coaches would utilize different offensive plays to accentuate his strengths.

I did not do such a good job of communicating this new approach at home. Maybe I feared letting my father down or maybe I was in denial. The truth is, in close games, I was going to be "the guy." I really didn't worry about it too much. However, my father was worried. My father was worried about me emotionally and psychologically.

There were two games, late in the year, where our offense would drive the ball the length of the field approaching the goal line. On a few different occasions, when we got close, the coaches decided to utilize the sophomore quarterback as a change of pace. He would enter the game and I would leave the game. This was a great learning opportunity for me. I needed to support the coaches in what they thought was best for the team. For the most part, I agreed with the coach's decision and accepted this transition as helping the team.

After the second week in a row that the coaches tried this, my dad called the head coach. My dad questioned his motivations asking him if he thought this was detrimental to me. I have no idea what the coach told my father, but in the end, my dad and I both agreed to accept it as a learning opportunity. My dad was just looking out for me. Not once, though, did I ever hear anything negative about the coach. I was always encouraged to do what the coaches felt was best, and I did.

My dad was supporting me the way he knew how. The best way my parents knew to support me was through love. When I call them today and tell them that one of my children is sick, their advice is always to just love those children and hold them tight. That's how they tried to raise me and my siblings. In the midst of a chaotic world when everything seems to be going astray, love will bind us together and provide support in times of need.

My parents never stop encouraging me. They have encouraged me as a high school athlete. They encouraged me to get my college education. They encouraged me through some rough times as a teacher and a coach. The encouragement is a part of the foundation of support that they have provided for me. I hope and pray that I can create such a strong base of support for my own children. I believe that, if parents want high school athletics to be a positive experience for their child, it is incumbent for them to provide unconditional support. The support from parents must range from their own children, to the other children involved on the team, all the way to the coaches who work with the children.

So often have I heard about parents bashing other student-athletes or bashing the coaches. How does this provide support? I often wonder why these parents are not helping in making their child's days of high school, "the best years of their lives", a positive experience. Even more, I challenge the parents who are supporting everyone involved to be role models of support.

In my final year of being the head coach of girls basketball, I had come to be aware of a situation that had happened in the gym after a game. We had just lost a game to arguably the best team in the conference. The seven sophomores playing on the varsity team struggled a bit against the senior laden team that we competed against. There was a group of fathers of a few of these "super sophomores" standing midway up the bleachers discussing the game. The discussion became heated and they were harshly criticizing me, loudly. They were contemplating what to do to get me "fixed" or removed from my position. People could hear them from the gym floor as they decided that "someone" needed to talk to the Athletic Director because there needed to be a change.

A parent of one of our senior captains heard this. This family had been part of the program for about eight years. They had two daughters come through the program. The older daughter was a major contributor to our team. However, the youngest daughter, now a part of this team, did not see much playing time. The parents always supported the coaching staff, the other players on the team, and their daughters. In fact, the parents had been graduates of the same high school. There was a large contingent of their family members in support at most games. When the eldest daughter started and played for huge chunks of time, they cheered and supported the team. When the youngest daughter sat the bench, they still cheered and supported the team.

Upon hearing this heated discussion midway up the bleachers, the father of this family decided enough was enough. He walked up the bleachers and told the other fathers to shut their mouths. If they had a problem with me, they should talk to me or else keep their mouths shut and support the kids on the team. A living example of support and courage, this father finally came to the conclusion that these parents were completely unrealistic. They were unable to appreciate all of the success they had just witnessed as our young team hung with a more experienced and highly successful team. Similarly, they failed to celebrate the perseverance and heart they just witnessed from their own children; they couldn't see beyond the scoreboard.

My suggestion to all parents who support the high school athletic experience, when faced with a similar situation, is to step in and, metaphorically, punch them in the face with the reality of high school athletics. The reality is to learn lessons that will help the student-athletes be successful post high school. Parents are not exempt from teaching their children lessons. In fact, it all begins and ends with them by fully supporting the experience.

## Objective Two: The Gift of Acceptance

In supporting the experience of the high school athlete, parents must understand the idea of acceptance. In helping their children gain the most from the high school athletic experience, in other words, receiving the education of the whole person, parents need to have an understanding of acceptance. Acknowledging that we have to live with the choices we make and their consequences is a valuable lesson for any young person to learn. Finally, it is important to love and appreciate our children for who they are, not what we, as parents, think they should be.

When we choose not to accept something we are creating conflict within our minds. The conflict turns to finding blame with others and a sense of shame with self. Acceptance involves forgiving ourselves for the past and not applying pressure for a perceived future. The earlier in life that we can learn to accept the moment we are in now, the sooner we will be able to develop a positive sense of self-worth.

Acceptance of where we are in our lives as adults means that we have accepted the results of the choices we made. Maybe we chose to go to college after high school or maybe we chose to get into the work force. Maybe we chose a life partner who we had fallen in love with and continue to share life with. Maybe we chose to be in a relationship with a life partner for the wrong reasons and it ended. In any case, we must come to some acceptance of how we got to where we are in our lives.

Acceptance of being in the moment means that we are not pressing to be something tomorrow other than who we are. We must know our own strengths and weaknesses and how to apply them to uncover our true spirit. The practice of acceptance can occur naturally, but often times results from a disastrous or destructive episode in our lives. The sad and lonely moments of our lives often bring us closer to God. In knowing God, we know ourselves and can fully accept and appreciate our own beauty.

In order to gain this acceptance it is essential that God is the focus. By putting God at the center of our lives, we give ourselves the best chance at acceptance. Knowing God has created uniqueness within us, and knowing that God is walking with us through our journeys will give us peace. We know that God has intended something great for all of us. He created, with His own hand, that greatness. The journey of our life is to find that purpose and passion and share it with others.

When we come to accept God, we accept ourselves. Parents of high school athletes that have learned to accept themselves in God can help their children learn the same and apply it to their own lives. Acceptance does not mean we want less. Acceptance is simply the idea that we embrace God's gift to us in each moment and personify that gift in all that we do.

High school athletes have to accept their roles. The roles they have on a team are based on their strengths. Parents, void of ego, will have the best capacity to help their children in this regard. The quarterback of the football team must accept the role of leader. The third string quarterback must accept the role of "scout" quarterback, preparing the defense for the next opponent. All roles are significant to the success of the team.

As I coached high school athletes I initially thought I needed to emphasize the significance of the kid who had the "lesser" role on the team. I fell into the pattern of ego that assumed the only perceived roles that were significant were those of the kids who contributed on game night. I assumed that the player on the team who had the most skill naturally would want to be counted on in crucial game situations. I found out how wrong I was. Accepting the role of "go to player" holds the same weight as accepting the role of practice player; some kids who have the skill maybe are not mentally or emotionally ready to have the weight of the team on their shoulders.

I found this out when, in the final seconds of a tight basketball game, we had drawn up a play in a time-out for our "go to player." She had a disturbing look in her eye that signaled to me that she was a bit insecure in this situation. We did it anyway, and things didn't quite work out in terms of the score. However, a great lesson was learned for me and for this athlete. I knew that I had to help this student-athlete accept her role as "go-to player." From that point on, I understood the significance of helping kids learn their role and challenged them to accept it.

In a completely polarized situation I had an athlete who appreciated her role on the team as practice player. She believed it was her responsibility to make the team better by busting her butt in practice each and every day. I remember a practice when she was playing outstanding defense on our "go to player." The better skilled player got angry with her and said, "Knock it off! Quit trying to make me look bad."

I couldn't pass up this teachable moment. I told the "go to player" to step off the floor. If she wasn't interested in improving, then she really shouldn't be at practice. I told the "practice player" to switch colors and join the "starting five." As the better of the skilled players watched from the sideline, I had a discussion of what it meant to prepare to be the best. I presented to her that she should be thankful that her teammate thought enough of the team to try to make it better even if she knowingly might never see the floor on game night. I then told the entire team that it was the responsibility of the people who contributed on game night to play as hard as these "practice players" were playing in practice. The "practice players" found their purpose in practice for helping the team. It was the purpose of the "starters" and other girls that played regularly to play with passion and to represent the whole team on the court.

I was disappointed one night after a basketball game with the student-athletes who were regular contributors on game night. We were finishing a stretch of games against opponents who we were much better than in terms of wins and losses. We were approaching a critical stretch of games that would determine the conference championship. I wasn't overly concerned with the conference championship. I was more concerned about giving our "practice players" game time experience, the reward for working so hard all season long, emotionally and physically. Plus we were in a position where we could conceivably attain both objectives: the conference championship and important playing time in games for our "practice players."

We had taken a 20 point lead by the end of the first quarter. At halftime, we still had 18 points more than our opponent. I really wanted to get every member of the team meaningful playing time in the second half. To our opponent's credit, they fought back and got the point differential under 10 about midway through the second half. It was a close game, in terms of the score, until the final minute.

I was disappointed that our "regular players" had allowed our opponent to climb back to within striking distance. We finally ended up outscoring our opponent; we celebrated that accomplishment in the locker room after the game. After coming together to celebrate our hard work, I told the whole team that I wanted to talk outside of the locker room to all the players who played in the game. When they met outside of the locker room, I expressed how disappointed I was that they did not accept their role that night. They looked bewildered, and a captain spoke up, "but coach, we won the game." I told them why I was upset and how it was important for them, when given the opportunity, to do their best to show their appreciation to their teammates, the "practice players." The appreciation would come in the form of getting our team in a situation for those players to be successful in a game situation. They understood.

However, my mistake was not saying that in front of the other student-athletes. They felt invisible when I pointed out that I just wanted to talk to the "players that played in the game." That was not smart on my part. Even though my intentions were to support them, it actually made them feel left out. The captains got wind of this immediately in the locker room and squelched the negative talk. I still had to have the conversation with them though, to apologize. We were a team and we, including me, needed to accept our responsibilities and roles among the team.

Parents need to do the same with their children at home. Children need to accept their status, accept the things they have no control over to be successful in all that they do. Parents need to accept their own lives in order for them to help their children accept theirs. The choices we make certainly affect the outcomes of our lives. Once we are able to fully accept those outcomes, we can either maintain our success or improve and learn from previous life choices. This lesson needs to come from home first and built upon in the realm of high school athletics.

## Objective Three: The Gift of Humility

Understanding the concept of humility comes through the acceptance of "self." People who can control their ego and not get lost in the fleeting perceptions of form can begin to fully appreciate the gift of humility. I suppose it could be argued that humility is not a gift but rather a curse. The presence of humility is the awareness that we are all just as important as someone else. Humility means that we share our gifts and talents that God has crafted within us. Thankfulness and appreciation for opportunities presented to us is humility. The gift of humility gives each one of us the presence to accept ourselves and others.

Allowing our egos to triumph over the moment disengages us from humility. If, at any given time, we allow our egos to falsely lead us to believe that we are superior in any way, shape, or form to anyone else, we lack the capacity to be humble. At times, the media plays a significant role in feeding a person's ego. This is not the media's problem, it is the issue for the individuals who allow their identity to be created and attached to the ego. Humility is the presence of mind to understand the importance of the role we play.

The media also feeds the victim persona that helps feed the ego. The people, whether it be high school athletes or their parents, who believe they deserve attention over someone else based on performance or any other inconsequential factor are feeding their egos by claiming superiority over the people who are getting the attention. They are the victims. They perceive mistreatment from others. Someone else is getting what they deserve. The gift of humility will help these people appreciate their own relevancy based on their own talents. In this case, humility will squash the victim persona and bring forth a positive sense of self-worth.

The other persona the media helps to maintain is the one who survives off of the positive affirmation. By seeing their name in print or by hearing the good word about themselves creates a perceived sense of superiority over others. The public often likes to view high school athletes as quasi rock stars, especially in small communities. This happens within communities and within the fabric of the school, thus creating a false identity while controlling the dynamics of relationships.

As a result, some of these high school athletes and their parents begin to display a sense of entitlement. It becomes acceptable behavior to miss half a school day because of a game the night before. It becomes acceptable to not do homework or to even request no homework on the night of a

**Parents: Pivotal Players in Healthy Development of Child**

| | | |
|---|---|---|
| 1. **Support** | encouragement, constructive criticism, healthy dialog |
| 2. **Accept** | live with choices, accept their consequences |
| 3. **Humility** | model humility, work cooperatively, appreciate talents |
| 4. **Believe** | the greatest gift we can give our children is belief |
| 5. **Faith** | share faith with children, help them grow in spirituality |

big game. There is a nasty myth that the faculty, staff, and administration of schools value athletics more than academics. I have experienced parents at parent-teacher conferences wanting to just talk about their child as athlete rather than student. I have experienced parents giving lip service to academics when their child is struggling, but their actions are in pursuit of athletic attention and prowess.

The media is not to blame. There is a public interest in high school sports. Writing feature articles on student-athletes and the teams they play on helps the newspaper make money. Highlighting the success of high school athletes and their coaches on television helps those stations make money. The more attention they can create, the more people will want their product. Parents have to give the gift of humility to their children. Keeping success and failure in perspective will help children create a real sense of who they are deep inside. I am no greater than you; you are no greater than me. We have all been crafted by the same Hand. It is our biggest responsibility to share that uniqueness.

We have all been gifted talents. I have a talent for music. I have a talent to write. It is my responsibility to share my talents with the world. I have played my guitar and sang in church and in my classroom. I write poetry and share it with my family, colleagues, and students. Humility allows us the capacity to share rather than to hoard.

The majority of high school athletes have talents that surpass athletic ability. Some have musical talent, some artistic talent, some conceptual talent, and so on. Our children have to accept the idea that there is a need for them to identify their talents. It is then important that they learn to share those talents. They will learn these things from their parents. The gift of humility includes modeling the sharing of our own uniqueness.

I have coached several student-athletes that were well on their way to identifying their strengths and sharing them with the world. One of a few four-year starters I had the opportunity to coach provides a great example of someone who was gifted many talents beyond athletics. This child, as a high school athlete was involved in three varsity sports all four years of high school. She earned 12 athletic letters, the most a student-athlete can earn in the school where I teach. She was also an active member of 4-H. Furthermore, she was also an active member of the school band, flute choir, and pep band. Finally, she was also a talented member of the school chorus.

In fact, she earned many awards for her performances in solo and ensemble competitions. Between her junior and senior year, she was invited to Washington D.C. to give a historical presentation that she had created in her U.S. History class. She had many friends, from many different groups in the school. She knew she had musical talent. One night, on senior night, the last regular season high school basketball game of her career, she sang a duet with her mother before the game. It was an outstanding performance of "The Star Spangled Banner." The team was successful that night as well, beating a team that, in post season play that year, qualified for the state tournament finals. The success that night though, was the model this young lady gave to all of her peers in sharing her talent.

Basketball was a hobby for this young lady; a hobby that she loved. She gave everything she had to her team. As a three year starter, she came into her senior year hoping to be a four year starter and have a grand finale to her organized basketball playing days since she wasn't going to play basketball beyond high school. However, she was confronted with a huge challenge her senior year because she was asked by the coaching staff to be the backup point guard. She was asked to come off the bench to provide depth for her team and to help her team in a way that she was not used to.

The conversation I had with her was not easy, and I knew she was going to take it hard. I also knew, deep in my heart, that this student-athlete would accept the new role because it meant doing what was best for the team and because she was grounded. She always put the team in front of her own needs, her own ego. She did have an outstanding year playing basketball and meant more to our team that year than any other player. She worked hard in practice every single day, and, when called upon in games, made the absolute most of her opportunities.

We need to look no further than this example when attempting to identify which parents have been successful in supporting their children in their role as high school athletes. This child's parents allowed their daughter to explore many different interests. In that exploration, this child found many talents that would serve her well into the future that were beyond athletic ability. Her parents also instilled strength in humility that allowed this young lady to accept a new role, trust the coaching staff, and fulfill her role to the best of her ability each and every day. She is a great example for all high school athletes and their parents.

## Objective Four: The Gift of Belief

Jim Valvano talked about the greatest gift his father gave him was the gift of belief. Parents who believe in their children no matter what the circumstances, create a positive sense of self-worth. Believing in our children and instilling that belief is essential to the maturation of student-athletes. In turn, this belief transforms into a growing confidence that helps to form the true identity in each person. Knowing that someone believes in us provides a net of support when we entertain new ideas and when we approach uncharted waters in our journey of life.

Recently, I had a former player walk into my classroom after school one day. In my final year of coaching she was a sophomore and continues to play on the team. She was a varsity starter when I had the opportunity to be her coach. I had not talked with her since my resignation in the spring. It was now fall of the following school year.

She asked if I had a minute to talk. I did not hesitate because her demeanor seemed to be serious and I really didn't have anything I needed to be doing at that moment. She sat down in front of me and asked me plainly, "Did you ever doubt me?" My response, without hesitation, was, "Absolutely not. I never doubted you." She was referring to the circumstances surrounding my resignation as head coach of the girls basketball team. There was some pressure from outside sources that wanted a change in the direction of the program. There was some sense that a few of the student-athletes wanted that change as well. It is amazing how kids will believe what their parents have them believe. Parents are the most influential people in a child's life.

She was asking me if I believed in her, if I believed in her as a person. She wanted me to know that she always respected me as her coach and wished that things wouldn't have gone down as they did in the final months of my tenure. I told her that I understood how she felt about me. I also told her that I did believe in her and I still do believe in her. Her demeanor changed. I sensed that she was completely relieved. It appeared as though a tremendous weight had been lifted from her shoulders. Our conversation turned to other things as we laughed about a few light hearted, fond memories we had. I wished her the best of luck in her upcoming basketball season.

Just before school let out for Christmas break, I found a handmade card on my desk. It is not surprising to find cards of this sort at this time of year. I read the card and was filled with a sense of pride in what it said. The card described someone of integrity, someone of substance. Finally, the card described someone who always believed. The card was signed by the player who had come to talk to me after school some two months earlier. I was humbled in knowing that I could share the gift of belief with this student-athlete. I was proud of her courage to step up in the midst of perceived peer pressure, and I was thankful for that moment.

Student-athletes who receive the gift of belief from their parents or any other influential person in their life will continue to grow stronger in their ability to take risks. Risk taking leads these children to areas of their lives that maybe they were unwilling to explore. This new found hope and support will lead directly to children having the capacity to find their true uniqueness, to find their true talents. Teachers, coaches, and parents have the obligation to push children to their maximum potential. Children who have a safety net of belief will have the greatest opportunity for reaching that potential.

The student-athlete that came to visit me and left me a well thought out Christmas card has an inner beauty of leadership. She comes from an interesting home where both of her parents are remarried. This type of situation can be difficult for children. This student-athlete is a stubborn, hard working young lady loyal to her teammates and coaches. As a freshmen and sophomore, understandably so, she was not yet ready to accept the role of leader. On the court as a sophomore, I remember her being the first in line for all the drills. I remember her sprinting through every drill, forcing her teammates to work hard.

I understand that as a junior she has taken on the role of vocal leader as well. I understand that she is a presence in the locker room that continues to hold her teammates accountable for their actions. Not only does she bust her butt in practice every single day, she now demands it verbally from her teammates. Her inner beauty is beginning to emerge. She is beginning to accept her role. All of this comes from belief. If someone along her journey did not believe that she could be such a leader, her uniqueness never would have been stimulated to reach that potential.

Confidence grows when fertilized with belief. Under the blossom of confidence lie the roots of our inner beauty, our uniqueness. When we believe in someone, we allow them to reach to the depths of their hearts to give us their pure self. Parents have the obligation to share belief with their children. Show them you believe in them through support. Tell them you believe in them. Most of all, *just believe in them*. Children will excel our greatest expectations when, in fact, someone believes in who they are and what they do.

I know that I have reached the point of success in my career due to the belief my parents had in me. I have reached success as a father because of the belief I received from my parents. I have reached success as husband because of the belief my parents gave as a gift. Throughout the journey of my life, the confidence I have in myself is a direct result of someone else believing in me. That confidence has allowed me to find God in my journey and to glorify what it means to have God at the center. What greater gift can we give each other than the gift of belief?

## Objective Five: The Gift of Faith

The most important gift a parent can give their child is that of faith. The strength in spirituality grows over time when the seed is planted early in the life of a child. Keeping focus on God as center of the entire universe will allow for the proper perspective on life's successes and failures. Transcending the world as we know its' form will allow for the emergence of self. I know that wherever I go my faith will be with me. Faith is as constant as the sun's rising and setting each day; as long as we accept God, in faith, and completely acknowledge His presence in the spirit of every living thing we will be at peace with who we are and in sharing our uniqueness.

The concepts of faith, religion, and spirituality are weaved into the fabric of our communities; these are significant components to the moral standards of our society. Recently I opened a local newspaper, *The Green Bay Press-Gazette*, and noticed an entire section entitled "Faith". The section included upcoming events in the community, op/ed pieces, and feature articles. This not a Christian based newspaper; it is a medium that publishes stories of interest to sell its product. The editors of this paper felt that a section on Faith was worthy enough for news and would help sell papers. Faith is a moral compass for all. It is as much a part of who we are in our communities as the biggest employer, the school district, and the city council.

As a child, I was inundated with Catholicism. My parents were devout Christians. We had paintings of Christ around the house along with Biblical passages sprinkled here and there. There was always a large Bible on a coffee table. Depending upon the time of year, you might find the bible open to a particular story from one of the four Gospels.

We had two priests who I remember as a child at our church. Both of them were friends with my parents because my parents were so involved with the church. It would not be a surprise to get a visit from one or both of them on occasion.

They might stop by for a birthday, an anniversary, a holiday, or maybe for no real reason at all other than being moved by the Spirit. We were regular church goers, my parents in their Sunday best and all five kids lined up minding their P's and Q's.

My family was active in the church. My mother would read and sing at church once a month. My brother David and I were altar boys. I remember a few times I partnered with him, but because I am eight years younger than he, I was usually paired with other boys my age. My parents were active in getting a Catholic high school up and running in our community. All five of us children attended that catholic high school, even though there was a public school not four blocks from our home.

I learned, early on, the significance of faith and spirituality. I remember my confirmation in the latter years of high school. I had a dream the night before my confirmation. It was an intense dream. There was a spirit with a stern, booming voice telling me that I would be filled with the Holy Spirit. Through the influence of my parents, I was immersed in spirituality and faith. Prayers at the dinner table and before bed were part of the daily routine. My parents taught me how to pray too. Not just reciting prayers, memorizing words, but they taught me how to give thanks and to bring to mind others that may have been challenged with some sort of life circumstance.

I know that I have a strong spiritual connection. As an adult, when I have been faced with trying times I have turned to my faith and spirituality. This gift was given to me by my parents as a child. I now turn to faith in good times and in bad. God is the good and He will be there to help us through the bad. It is peaceful knowing that each and every moment of our lives is filled with the glory of God.

Winning or losing a high school athletic contest means very little in the scheme of the universe. The presence of faith allows us to keep in perspective what truly is important. The Spirit will guide us, when we allow it, to free ourselves from the material of the world. The "surface stuff", namely our appearance, the cars we drive, the homes we live in, the amount of toys we own, will not identify who we are. What is important dwells deep within our soul. That which God created for each of us is embedded into our Spiritual DNA that we must awaken to share with others.

The awareness of what truly is important will offer us a life of peace, void of our ego. Faith will allow us to transcend the anxieties we encounter in our lives. Seeing beyond the judgmental eyes of others, capturing our inner uniqueness, and releasing our talents will make us transparent to the world, giving of our whole self as God had intended.

When we give this gift of faith to our children, we can expect them to always have that gift. It is a gift of a lifetime. When parents successfully instill in their children the proper perspective, they will be able to transcend the fleeting thoughts and emotions of this world as they mature into adulthood. This gift of faith must come from the most important church in our lives. That church is located within our homes. Parents and family promote, first, the magnificence of spirituality. Any time outside of the home that children get spirituality is icing on the cake.

As a teacher and a coach I believe that I have subtly brought spirituality into my work. I do work in a public school and there has been a conflict of interest in regards to the separation of church and state. I believe my work is a calling from God. Therefore, the way I treat students and athletes is guided by the Spirit. The way in which I approach my job each and every day is influenced by the Spirit. On game nights before the start of the game, our basketball team would form a circle, coaches and players, and hold hands. I would talk about giving thanks for the opportunity to be a high school athlete and coach, and I would bring to mind the ideas of good sportsmanship.

There are many ways in which parents can provide the gift of faith. This gift is greater than any other gift we could give our children. Our faith will be with us every moment of our lives here on this earth. Having faith, a true connection to spirituality, guides our perspective and leads us to the truly important aspects of our lives. We must find our uniqueness through the presence of the Holy Spirit. We are called to share that uniqueness with others. The gift of faith will bring forth the beauty in ourselves and the beauty we see in others.

One of the best times of the day for me is when Desiree and I sit down for dinner with Brooklyn and Dawson. Nearly every night we make the time to do this. Sitting down at the table provides many opportunities for discussion without judgment. I remember as a child the significant impact sitting down at table with my parents and siblings had on my development. This family time presents parents with the time to provide the many gifts children need.

In my short time as a father I have learned many things in regards to my role as parent. I do know that I will be a parent until I die. I will never be able to retire from being a parent, but the benefits are worth more than any life insurance plan, health insurance plan, or dental plan. The pension is in the glory of creating a legacy. I know I will be a parent long after I die as well. The gifts I give my children will live on through them. As I have done, hopefully my children will share the gifts they have received from Desiree and me with their own children and others who cross their paths.

There is no perfect mission statement for any of us who are parents. We do the best we can with what we know. I know that God loves me and all of His people with greater love than Desiree and I have for own children. That is an amazing amount of love. All the books we read, and all the people we talk to about our children, it all comes down to the gifts we are willing to share with our children. When God is our focus, the Spirit will guide us in all of our endeavors to raise our children.

Parenting is the most important responsibility of our lives. The least we can do for our children is give them the gifts of support, acceptance, humility, belief, faith, and love. All parents have the capacity to give these gifts in some form. There is no doubt that parents can consider themselves a success if they can offer these gifts to their children. All of these ideas go well beyond the lines of high school athletics. These gifts will help children prepare to be independent and will create the ultimate positive sense of self-worth. What more could we ask for as parents?

# THE FOUNDATION OF SUCCESSFUL COACHES

*To be nobody but yourself in a world that's doing its best to make you somebody else, is to fight the hardest battle you are ever going to fight. Never stop fighting.*
   *E. E. Cummings*

    The premise behind my mission statement as a head coach in high school athletics was to help build a sense of self-worth within the individual student-athletes who I coached. I was not successful in all cases for multiple reasons. The reasons some of those student-athletes may have not have felt an increasing sense of self-worth or built upon the base of self-worth they already had at home was a result of the child's own development and degree of acceptance modeled by their parents. In the end, though, the decisions I made in regards to the team and the student-athletes that made up the teams that I coached began and ended with the idea of building a sense of self-worth in each and every one of the student-athletes I have been privileged enough to teach and coach.

    I have identified five standard objectives that should define the success of a high school coach. First, it is imperative to understand that these objectives are beyond the scope of winning and losing. Winning is certainly a part of what defines success for a coach. However, these objectives are far more significant benchmarks than simply outscoring an opponent. The immediacy of looking to a scoreboard to define success is shortsighted when it comes to the purity of high school athletics and the meaning of its intended purpose. There are a myriad of ways to teach these skills and, even more, there are ample opportunities for teachable moments with these skills. Successful high school coaches simply take advantage of these opportunities to help student-athletes build a sense of self worth.

## Objective One: Relationships

In every coaches mission statement there must be an emphasis on building relationships. This idea seems broad in its scope, but is fundamental in its purpose. A coach has the responsibility to build relationships with parents and the student-athletes. A coach also must foster opportunities for student-athletes to build relationships amongst themselves as well. Building positive relationships with others is a nutrient for our proper growth as people. In healthy relationships we all have the opportunity to share our talents. It is in relationships with others that we can discover who we are; we discover our sense of self. Conversely, by nature, all relationships are reciprocal; we all have the opportunity to help others discover their sense of self. We can give others the opportunity to discover the special talent God has gifted them by participating in a mutual relationship.

Being connected with others and having a shared emotional passion is needed and presents the opportunity for growth as human beings. This can be, if emphasized, done within the framework of high school athletics. As I have matured, I have found that positive relationships with others are important for two reasons. First, in most things that we want to accomplish in our lives, whether it is professionally or personally, we must count on other people. Secondly, we build relationships out of mutual respect and admiration: spending time with others in entertainment, faith sharing, or any other kind of personal enrichment.

Throughout my professional career, I have had many opportunities to collaborate on projects with fellow colleagues. In the presence of the athletes I coached, God always presented opportunities during my coaching career to model healthy relationships. I believed it was important for me to model the responsibility I had in my adult relationships for the student-athletes I coached as well as the students in my classroom. I was always sure to treat my peers with respect when I addressed them, especially in the presence of influential young boys and girls.

When God had allowed me to be present during phone conversations my student-athletes had with their parents calling for a ride home or informing them of some other details, I always reminded those student-athletes to say "please" and "thank you" to whomever was on the other end of the phone conversation. That was something I learned from my high school coaches. Believe it or not, reminding young people of proper manners and modeling appropriate relationships does not stop after the children reach third grade. It is a lifelong lesson that successful coaches continue.

On three occasions while coaching girls basketball, I remember three separate young ladies coming to practice with a mark on their necks often called hickies. I felt like I needed to take the opportunity to talk to the kids about appropriate relationships. Any intimate relationship, namely boyfriend and girlfriend, should not require either one of the two to "mark" their territory. I wanted the girls to take pride in their appearance and believe they were important enough to have a positive self-image. I also wanted these young ladies to understand that they were representing themselves, their family, their school, and their team when they played basketball. Having such "marks" weren't representing any of those groups in a positive manner.

Modeling and demanding appropriate communication skills is quintessential to relationship building. As students learn in their language arts classes, in communication there has to be two things in place for it to be effective. There must be a sender and receiver. The "sender," or speaker, must address the "receiver" with respect. In proper communication there must be mutual respect between sender and receiver. The speaker cannot be condescending and the listener must listen with an open mind.

Interestingly, we live in a world where our teenagers identify with the terms "send" and "receive" in texting and emailing. Modern communication has allowed people to escape face to face relationships. It is a bit discerning that some people are much more comfortable communicating behind a computer screen. The use of blogs, even in the high school setting, is growing in popularity. In all of these cases, messages can be misinterpreted and lead to a breakdown in the relationship.

In my fifth year of being head girls basketball coach, I had two student-athletes who had been lifelong friends. They were friends primarily because their fathers worked together and their families had spent a lot of time together. One was much more mature than the other and as high school wore on, they began to somewhat separate socially. There was tension between the two almost daily. Both were good basketball players, one better than the other. Ironically, the one who was maturing faster, emotionally, was limited in her basketball skills. She did have a high basketball IQ, but was limited physically. The more emotionally immature student-athlete was an outstanding basketball player who received a lot of attention for basketball. Her friend was feeling the tension of her ego not being fed anymore because the other young lady was getting more attention.

The better of the two players believed in me and my message. She couldn't convince the other young lady to fully buy in. I felt like the other student-athlete was bucking me because of the attention her lifelong friend was getting. It was somewhat out of my control. I had a difficult time building a relationship with her parents in the beginning, but was successful through consistently making the effort to communicate with them. I finally confronted them on their child's lack of self-esteem and her stubbornness when it came to basketball. I, somewhat surprisingly, found out that they were concerned too. We were on the same page and a healthy relationship was conceived.

About one third of the way into their senior season, the better athlete of the two was so frustrated with her friend that she was not practicing well, not playing well, and not communicating with me effectively. I had made many attempts to connect the two of them again. I had consistently made the effort to give them the same amount of attention. I even did my best to talk to them about how important the relationship was between them. I told them that nothing, especially high school athletics, should come in between a healthy relationship.

I finally encouraged the better of the two athletes to confront her issues with her friend. She needed to clear the air and let things fall out as they would. I told both of them that they needed to get things worked out so it would no longer affect their team. After practice one night, there was a blow out between the two of them in the locker room. The more distant one, the one lacking the self-confidence, even though she was more mature, wanted to walk away and avoid the confrontation. The less mature of the two would not allow that to happen. She said her peace and they went their separate ways.

Later that night, I talked with the father of the despondent student-athlete. He told me that his daughter was feeling badly about what happened, but it needed to happen. The family had invited the lifelong friend over after dinner. They talked and cried and talked some more. They got to a point of agreement on some issues and agreed to disagree on some other issues. From that point on, both of them continued their relationships and it had even grown to a greater depth. It was a learning experience for both of them in building and maintaining relationships.

It is important for teachers and coaches to continue to advance with 21st Century vehicles of communication. Cell phones, email, blogs, and internet communication are all ways our student-athletes are receiving information. It is important to make use of these technological advances while, at the same time, communicating the old fashioned way, face to face.

The idea, in helping student-athletes build relationships, is to give them opportunities to feel good about themselves within the relationships they develop with their peers as well as to build life-long interpersonal skills. It is also essential that they see appropriate communication and relationship building from their teachers and coaches. I enjoyed having the student-athletes I coached, as a team, into my home for a meal once a year as well. I always felt it a great opportunity to model family relationships. I always sensed that the young ladies I coached appreciated Desiree and I opening our home to them. Desiree always did her best to have food the kids liked and we always did it over the holiday season. Our house was warm with holiday peace, joy, and love. My parents would also be invited. I always thought it was important to show that, even beyond high school, the relationships we have with our family last forever.

My parents made many relationships with the student-athletes I coached as well as their parents. Not every teenage kid I coached was comfortable enough to get to know my parents, but some certainly did make the effort. I was so proud of the student-athletes I coached when I would see them giving my mom and dad a hug or a high-five after a game. The warmth I felt in my heart from these types of exchanges went way deeper than the result of the game the team had just played. I was even amazed that my parents thought this was all worthy enough to take the time to do especially since they lived over an hour's drive out of town. They continued to make me feel valued as a person in my profession. Even today I have many people ask me about the well-being of my parents or that I should pass along a salutation of some kind or another.

I wanted to have as many team activities include students' parents and other family members. We had a meal at the beginning of the year with all involved, we would stop for pizza or a meal of some kind on the way home from long road trips, we would have a holiday gathering after a game, we would celebrate the final regular season home game for the seniors, and we would have an end of the year awards banquet. In all of these situations, I wanted as many family members there as could be there to promote the importance of family and the significance of life-long relationships. Accepting others and celebrating the successes of each other is an important lesson in building relationships that can be accommodated through coach's role in high school athletics.

In most high school athletics today, there are many assistant coaches involved depending upon how many student-athletes are involved in the activity. In my younger years I was not as good at developing great relationships with my assistant coaches. I was not as good at delegating. I know this was the result of my overactive ego; I believed that the actions and results of the program were mine to own. This characterizes an unhealthy relationship but sure is typical of a young head-strong coach. I had even learned under two terrific coaches the art of delegation, but had not mastered it in my early years.

High school coaches have an excellent opportunity to display appropriate cooperation in relationships. Being cooperative with a group of people helps develop positive, healthy relationships. Head coaches and their assistants must work cooperatively at building upon the objectives I address here to help student-athletes experience the most out of their high school education. Team sports are naturally set up to develop and maintain cooperative skills.

The skill of cooperation goes far beyond the walls of high school. In nearly every job there are situations in which people must work with people. Whether it is working with customers, clients, or colleagues all of us have, at some point or another, have to work with others. High school athletics is a perfect environment for this skill to be learned. Granted, this skill is worked on in the classroom in virtually every school in America. The arena of high school athletics provides an opportunity for a coach to extend this lesson into athletics.

There are a plethora of team building activities that can promote cooperation. When I coached football, the emphasis to the student-athletes each and every day at practice included working together to create successful opportunities. I have always taken advantage of situations that would allow the student-athletes I coached to extend their cooperation even outside of the arena of high school athletics. Any time an experience presented itself in terms of helping someone out at school or in the community that needed a group of people; I would volunteer the student-athletes on the teams I coached for whatever assistance was required. I also promoted team decision making. Whenever concerns arose amid the team, there was an opportunity for collaboration to make appropriate decisions. I always believed that discussions of this nature should take place outside the company of the coaches. The kids needed to have the discussion, come to a consensus, and communicate through the captains to the coaches.

The respect shared in these relationships is amazing. To be able to respect people's ideas and philosophies across generations is an awesome model of healthy relationships. Kids' learning to respect coaches and their parents is important. To earn that respect, coaches, parents, and athletes all must show a level of respect that begins with honesty and trust. As adults know, the characteristic of honesty and the security of trust are extremely valuable characteristics.

The discussions kids would have and their decision or input needed to be relayed to the coaching staff honestly. In all healthy relationships there is an unwavering element of trust. I was always told by my parents that I wouldn't be punished for telling the truth. That is not a cop out or justification for making bad decisions. It is a lesson in trust. When we make poor decisions, it's important to own up to it, learn from it, and move on. Even though my parents told me I wouldn't be punished for telling the truth, it was known that I would have to face the consequences of my actions.

I have stressed this point with my students and athletes. Tell me the truth as to why the homework is late. In knowing the truth, maybe I can help. As for my athletes, tell me the truth about why you're late to practice. In knowing the truth, maybe we can work together to prevent it from happening again. Certainly, the student is going to face late penalties for the missing assignment and the student-athlete is going to have to run extra sprints for being late to practice, but as long as the truth is known, then we can work to improve upon the mistake. Trust is the most fundamental element in creating and maintaining any healthy, working relationship. In every relationship, the trust must be reciprocal. Head coaches must trust assistant coaches, colleagues must trust each other, a spouse must trust the other spouse, parents must trust their children, and children must trust adults. Honesty is the key.

We often get caught up in little lies. The little lies, though, add up to significant mistrust and the outcome is a dissolving, dysfunctional relationship. Teaching the importance of being honest is a crucial skill for high school coaches to model and teach. Many kids may get this lesson enforced at home, but not all have that opportunity. Furthermore, learning the acceptance of the truth in being honest will lead kids to understand the concept of accountability.

As student-athletes learn the lessons of proper communication and honesty, they can begin to stand up for something they believe in on their own. Their degree of self-worth rises and, naturally, they become people of integrity. The more children are exposed to the meaning of spirituality and the significance of relationships, the more they will understand the concept of being morally good, willing to make a positive difference in the world. When coaches value the idea of building relationships with people and then modeling that healthy lifestyle for their student-athletes, they can consider themselves a success. Building people of high moral character through honest communication and respect is more than we could expect for our children. When my children meet this objective, it won't matter how many wins the teams they participated on achieved. All that will matter is the ability they have to apply these lessons in their own lives as adults.

## Objective Two: Preparation

In every coach's mission statement there must be an emphasis on preparation. Under the rushing rapids of preparation trickle many valuable life-long lessons. Preparing to compete encompasses the characteristics of responsibility, accountability, and work ethic. Coaches who do achieve this objective will, without doubt, be successful. Before children graduate from high school they, hopefully, will have had many opportunities to have learned the valuable traits of preparation. It is no secret that being organized in our preparation in the post high school world will make us more efficient in our jobs and our relationships. When the chains of winning and losing are broken to free up the soul to learn things that can actually be applied later in life, the better chance our student-athletes will have at succeeding.

As an English teacher for 14 years, I have heard time and time again comments like "Why do we have to read this?" or "When will I ever have to use this in the future?" or "This doesn't matter because I am going to be a zoo keeper." The fact is that the lessons a coach should teach can provide easy answers to these questions. Why should people learn to prepare? Why should people learn to build effective, healthy relationships? The answers to these questions are obvious. We need to learn these things because they are life. God wants us to prepare ourselves for life after death by living a lifestyle of integrity. We build relationships because God implanted love in all of us with His Hand. There are no greater lessons to be taught. Can we learn these things in outscoring our opponent? Maybe, but I wouldn't want to take the chance that they might be learned that way and miss the opportunity to teach or to learn the important lessons of growing from the inside out.

The trait of responsibility is one that must be learned for each and every person to be fully successful. It also is a trait that helps to fend off the controlling destruction of the ego. If a person is responsible, then the person is exhibiting trust. Anyone who is responsible will answer for their own actions. In responsibility, there is a justification of the actions committed by a person for the common good of all.

In my time in coaching, there were many teachable moments of responsibility. In football, each player on the offensive line has the responsibility to block the first person in the area the play is designed to run. Each player on that offensive line must trust the other to take care of his responsibility. Furthermore, the running back carrying the ball must take care of his responsibility to run in the general direction the play is designed to run: an individual taking appropriate action for the common good of all.

In the preparation of a student-athlete in any given sport, responsibility comes in the form of each individual meeting the required expectation. For proper preparation to occur it is the responsibility of each student-athlete to effectively communicate, fully understand personal expectations and the expectations of the team, positively represent the team, and be prompt. When these criteria are met, then the preparation to compete can begin.

Completely understanding the expectations a coach has of an athlete comes from a positive rapport and effective communication. At the beginning of each basketball season, I would ask the players to rank themselves. At first I explained that if they ranked themselves one through five, then they thought they were a starter. If they ranked themselves six through nine, then they believed they were going to earn many minutes of playing time. This provided me with interesting information. First of all, I could get a true sense of each player's self-worth in the explanation of their ranking. Secondly, it provided me insight to whether or not the thoughts of the coaching staff and the thoughts of the individual players were on the same page.

If I sensed negative self talk in their explanation I would immediately address that issue with the individual player. Then I would continue to provide positive feedback for that particular student-athlete, to a point. It is important to build the child up through affirmation as long as the shower of compliments is not feeding the ego. In other words, if the player is just looking for attention by shrouding themselves in negativity, then the affirmation was not going to be effective. It was my job to help that child understand the inner spirit, void of ego, and the true role they were responsible for within the framework of the team. I never used the term "ego" with student-athletes. I would often discuss the motivation behind their actions to uncover the reason they felt invisible.

If the ranking of the coaching staff and the personal ranking of a player were polar opposites, we would have to properly communicate the differences. It was then impor-

## THE FOUNDATION OF SUCCESSFUL COACHES

tant to strategize ways to get the two ends closer together. It was my responsibility to help each player understand the coaching staff's expectations of her. It was her responsibility to follow through with the plan to meet those expectations.

The notion of accountability follows closely to responsibility. The idea of holding someone accountable simply means that the person can answer, justifiably, for the actions committed. Accountability implies an understanding of what is expected. In high school athletics, coaches must hold student-athletes to a high degree of accountability. This is yet another skill or character trait that is emphasized in the classroom. High school athletics provides an extension of the academic classroom to promote accountability in yet another situation.

There is a certain expectation that each player will understand the role he has on the team. When I was coaching football, there were times a player would get hurt and have to leave the game. His backup was held accountable for his preparation by being able to enter the game and perform to the best of his ability. The player was able to step in and justify his actions because he took the responsibility to prepare. Ultimately, he held himself accountable to his teammates.

The difference between responsibility and accountability in learning to prepare is subtle. Being responsible is being trustworthy to others. Trust is a trait within itself, but being trustworthy means that others can count on you. There are requirements that are expected of each individual to make the "whole" effective. Accountability is the complete understanding of what is expected and the capability of justifying the actions.

Once the concepts of responsibility and accountability are established in preparation, a true work ethic must be modeled and demanded. In everything we do, if we want it done right, we must work hard. Work ethic requires hard work, but our work must be smart. Why should we try to chip our way through a brick wall when we can walk through the door ten feet away? I remember Jim Valvano once suggesting in a motivational speech that hard work doesn't always equal success, but there is no chance for success if a person doesn't work hard.

Work ethic also means being consistent and not being complacent. In preparing to do anything, to be successful, we must be consistent. Once we have established ourselves in the action plan to achieve our goals, we can't get complacent. We have to face each and every day with the same enthusiasm we did the day before. We must prepare with positive energy consistently in order for it to pay off. High school athletics provides a great opportunity for work ethic to be developed and strengthened.

As student-athletes learn the lessons of proper preparation, they will understand the significance of responsibility and accountability. They will recognize the difference between the two and will be able to act for the better of the "whole." Being responsible and holding each other accountable will lead to the separation of the ego and the inner spirit and strength each of us has been gifted. Furthermore, the work ethic gained in learning to prepare is a lifelong skill that will help develop a sense of pride and strong sense of self-worth. The power of spirituality becomes much more clear and dominant when people decide to be responsible and work hard in their preparation. We become closer to what it is that God has intended for us and we become aware of the same in others. Building people who are accountable, have a high degree of work ethic, and ultimately preparing to compete in a very competitive world is more than we could expect for our children. When my child meets this objective, it won't matter how many wins the teams they participated on achieved. All that will matter is the ability they have to apply these lessons in their own lives as adults.

## Objective Three: Discipline

A mission statement would be incomplete without the acknowledgement of the significance of discipline. High school athletics provides a golden opportunity for discipline to be emphasized and nurtured. In its fundamental meaning, discipline simply implies proper, purposeful preparation. The effect of discipline is the improvement of self-control; having self-control leads to an increased level of self-worth. To be disciplined means to be able to abide by a set of rules given by an authoritative figure. It is also the fuel of internal motivation. It has been proven that the presence of internal motivators leads to much more success than external motivators. Being disciplined will help every individual be successful beyond high school.

In their preparation, student-athletes are conditioned to react in mostly unpredictable situations. Learning to be disciplined in their responsibilities and being committed to the methods of the system will help student-athletes become more marketable as students beyond high school and effective in the work force. Discipline guides people when faced with adversity. Overcoming obstacles helps people mature and makes them emotionally stronger.

In the fourth year of my head coaching career, we were competing at the sectional level in the semi-final game. It was an amazing game between two evenly matched teams. Each team had one outstanding player with an exceptional supporting cast. Our team was just two wins away from the state final four, a feat that the girls program had never accomplished in the history of the school. We were playing this particular game on our home floor. The gym was jam-packed; the bleachers were full on each side of the court along with the sets of bleachers on either end. Both schools had their pep bands in attendance with large student-body sections. Our game was the first of two games in that gym that night. The winners of each game would move on to play each other the next night.

### Coaches: Mentors and Role Models for Student-Athletes

| | |
|---|---|
| 1. **Relationships** | model appropriate relationship building |
| 2. **Preparation** | proper preparation allows opportunity to succeed |
| 3. **Discipline** | purposeful preparation, emphasize self-control |
| 4. **Leadership** | value leaders and their talents |
| 5. **Self-Worth** | respect for self, parents, teachers, coaches, peers |

# BEYOND THE SCOREBOARD

The team I was fortunate enough to coach that year was extremely disciplined, from the very best player on the team to the player that saw the majority of her court time in practice. They believed in the system and trusted what they had learned. They were disciplined.

Given the adversity the team faced that night, they remained focused on the things they were taught as a team. They supported each other, trusted each other, and helped each other

achieve success. The game was close in score for all four quarters. Our team was fortunate enough to play the game with the lead most of the night. Late in the fourth quarter our opponent fought back to tie the game. We had the last possession and got a shot off that missed the mark. The game went to overtime.

With the crowd of nearly 1,000 people waiting in the lobby for the second game of the night to begin, in the gym the crowd of nearly 2,000 people had to cheer on their teams for four more minutes. It was loud. It was hot. Communication between players on the floor and between coaches and players was almost impossible unless hand signals were used. The players on both teams had to rely on their instincts and their preparation for this moment which included the discipline they learned throughout the season, throughout their lives.

The overtime period was no different than the previous four quarters. It was a close score the entire time. Our team eventually prevailed, outscoring our opponent earning the right to advance to the sectional final game. One more win and we would be in the state final four. I have never experienced a game in which both teams had to rely solely on discipline to react in unpredictable situations. As I reflect on the girls who made up the team I coached and even the girls who I knew on the other team, I know now that most of these young ladies have gone on to college, graduated, and are beginning their own professional careers. All of these kids, now young women of the world, learned to be disciplined in adverse situations. This skill has helped them to be successful adults and will continue to serve them well for years to come.

It takes courage to be disciplined. It is hard work to make a commitment to achieve success. It is hard work to abide by a set of rules given by someone else, especially as teenagers. It is a credit to coaches that can teach the art of being disciplined to high school student-athletes. Learning to get up each and every day with a purpose, knowing that being prompt is important, and believing in a unified vision are situations in which discipline is required. If student-athletes are exposed to this concept and can master it, they will be successful in anything they attempt.

## Objective Four: Leadership

Each and every basketball season, as part of the mission statement I had a section I entitled "Set the Tone." This was the leadership portion of our mission statement as a basketball program. Coaches share a responsibility with teachers and parents to teach the value of leadership. Furthermore, it is important to teach the skills of leadership. Coaches, teachers, and parents have the obligation to model appropriate leadership skills.

As the head coach, I expected the student-athletes on the varsity team to set the tone for the entire program. It is their team and their program. I believed the success of the team was dependent on fundamental, positive leadership. From the top down, including all coaches, leadership had to be modeled. I always told the student-athletes I coached the old cliché, "actions speak louder than words." If a player wanted to be captain, the coaching staff asked them to apply. The application process was easy. All they had to do was respond to two questions about leadership: 1) Can you promise to be the Captain the team is looking for?, and 2) What leadership qualities do you feel are your strengths?

The response to the second question was intended to come from a list of leadership qualities that was included on the captain application. The responses to these questions would go a long way for the coaching staff in determining which player or players would be best suited to lead the team. The leaders chosen would need to accept their role and the conditions of their role as leaders. In some cases it was an easy decision, in some years it was extremely difficult. All teams, athletic or otherwise, need good leaders.

So often, on teams that accumulated more wins than losses, I sensed an expectation of entitlement. The whole idea that someone deserves something just because it is assumed their "right" bothers me. None of us have the "right" to harm anyone else, physically or emotionally. When a group of high school athletes accumulate more wins than another group they are competing against in the same sport or even another group of athletes within the same school, that does not make them superior people. The leadership of the school and the team must teach and practice humility.

Remember, we are all created by the same hand, God's hand. We are all gifted unique talents which make us all different. This does not imply that any one of us is better than another. We must share our gifts with each other. If we fail to do that, we are not fulfilling our purpose. Humility recognizes that there is something greater in the universe and that we are just doing our part, what is expected of us. In teaching leadership, it is important to stress the use of leadership as a gift and to utilize that talent for the improvement of others.

As children grow, leaders emerge from the group. Some have the gift to lead, others need to be led. Both concepts are important to understand the effects each role has in the world. Leaders must be taught to lead in constructive ways. Followers must be taught to follow with discipline and belief. Again, high school athletics provides many teachable moments in leadership.

I always felt it important that leaders understood, believed in, and put into practice the mission statement of the team. The success of the team, meaning the health of the relationships on the team, depended upon how well the guidelines of the mission statement were enforced. The leaders also had to set a good example for the followers, and all other players. Finally, I believed it was important to teach and model constant encouragement by promoting enthusiasm, intensity, work ethic, and cooperation.

# THE FOUNDATION OF SUCCESSFUL COACHES

When I was the starting quarterback of my high school football team, I learned an extremely valuable lesson in leadership as a junior from my football coach. I was the quarterback of a team that was dominated by seniors who had high expectations of winning. They had been successful as a group for several years. I actually earned the starting quarterback position over the head coach's son who was part of that senior group.

I had developed a unique bond with the offensive coordinator of the football team. This particular coach was also the junior varsity basketball coach who I had played for as a freshmen and a sophomore. He and I had developed a close relationship. He was not always easy on me; in fact, he challenged me daily. I am thankful for the life lessons I learned from this man. Outside of my father, this coach was the biggest influence on my life as a young man.

I remember walking off the practice field with the offensive coordinator one day after practice about mid-season. We had just come off of a butt whooping, our first loss of the season, at the hands of the best team in the conference. I confided in him that I was feeling pressure from the seniors. I felt that they didn't believe in me and really wanted their friend, the head coach's son who was playing running back, to be the quarterback. What he told me that day resonates with me in every moment I feel the same kind of pressure. He simply said, "You're the quarterback. When things go well, people love you, your name is in the headlines of the newspaper, and your teammates will carry you off the field. When your team loses, you will get the blame and sometimes teammates might point the finger. You need to be a leader and accept that role."

He put it all into perspective for me that day. Take the good with the bad and accept it. That lesson learned made me a stronger, better person. I apply that lesson in my adult life all the time. I have also applied that lesson to kids I have taught and coached. Leadership is believing in self and in others. Leadership is accepting constructive criticism and making the necessary adjustments to actions and behaviors. Finally, leadership is having pride: using appropriate language, maintaining healthy personal hygiene, and practicing and conveying a positive attitude always.

A coach's success will be measured by wins and losses by the public. That is the culture of sports all over the world. However, teaching skills that go beyond the scope of winning and losing, beyond the scoreboard, are valuable to the success of each individual. A coach will be considered successful when he helps student-athletes learn the skills needed to survive in the world. Learning how to lead and learning how to follow leaders is a skill that should not be underestimated in the realm of education.

## Objective Five: Positive Sense of Self-Worth

I believe the student-athletes in any high school program must be respected as people. Reciprocally, the athletes must respect their parents, teachers, coaches, teammates and officials at all times; respect breeds respect. The lasting impression we, as coaches, want the student-athletes that come through our programs to have is one of pride, accomplishment, and strength in self-worth. The coaching staff and all others associated with the program must promote a positive attitude, high expectations of character, honesty, and integrity.

Every student-athlete must commit, wholeheartedly, to the team concept – physically, mentally, and emotionally – if the team is going to reach its highest potential and succeed. It only takes one misplaced ego to wreck the fragile trust that exists between players and coaches and player to player. Lack of commitment and effort begins to tear apart the fabric of team work, which, in turn, brings on total failure during practice and games. It only takes one person – coach, student-athlete, parent, or athletic director – with misaligned values to ruin the delicate balance of trust. From the most dominant player to the least dominant player, each must believe they are unified and not one is more superior to another. We must strive for unity, chemistry, and loyalty.

Successful people who have a positive sense of self-worth have attitudes that generate thoughts like, *"What can I con-*

*tribute to the team?, What can I do to get better?, What needs to be done where I can be of assistance?"* These thoughts contribute to positive attitudes which, in turn, bring on cooperation towards a common goal. Coaches that teach these lessons, model them, and apply them each and every day are successful. Kids that exit a program feeling a positive sense of self, are ready to take on more challenges post high school.

Student-athletes who learn, through high school athletics, to conduct themselves in an acceptable, appropriate manner at all times have learned a valuable lesson. Coaches who emphasize the importance of maximizing each student-athlete's potential in the classroom are successful. The life lessons learned through high school athletics may be learned in winning or losing, but the coaches that stress these lessons each and every day are the best coaches in our schools.

Student-athletes need to be ready to learn these life-long lessons. Some are not quite ready as much as others. Parents can help their children be ready for these lessons by supporting teachers and coaches that guide the kids. When coaches reach the five benchmarks I have laid out here, consider them a success. There is nothing wrong with taking opportunities to learn things that will be helpful as students graduate from high school and move out into the world. I know I am the product of many good lessons taught to me by coaches I respected.

# THE INTEGRITY OF SUCCESSFUL ATHLETIC DIRECTORS

*The supreme quality for leadership is unquestionably integrity. Without it, no real success is possible, no matter whether it is on a section gang, a football field, in an army, or in an office.*
   Dwight D. Eisenhower

   I have a tremendous amount of respect for Athletic Directors. Their jobs are not easy. Balancing an enormous amount of responsibility in scheduling co-curricular activities, attending events outside of the school day nearly five nights a week on average, and serving as liaisons between coaches, students, and the public takes a special person. In recent years, some school districts have even changed the title of this important position to Activities Director. The person in this position is in charge of most, if not all, activities that occur outside the normal hours of the school day.
   Activities outside of the school day can include, but are not limited to, athletics, school musicals, forensic competitions, student senate sponsored events, jazz band, spirit assemblies, student clubs, booster club meetings, or any other activity that involves any portion of the student body. In addition to scheduling these events, making sure that there is proper supervision for such activities, and maintaining equity in opportunities for all school groups, an Activities Director may

have other responsibilities. In our school district, our Activities Director is also in charge of student attendance concerns. Truancy and habitual tardy issues are common disciplinary situations our Activities Director has to take care of during the school day. When I first began my tenure as a head coach, the Athletic Director that was nearing retirement at the time, also had teaching responsibilities during the school day beyond the athletic obligations.

It is no secret that, given all the responsibilities that Activities Directors are faced with, this person needs to be highly motivated and organized. I have had the pleasure of working for two Athletic Directors in my tenure as head coach. In addition, I have met many Athletic Directors over the years in my job as head basketball coach. I am empathetic about the unique challenges posed to Athletic Directors on a daily basis. However, I am convinced that there are successful ways of directing athletics that can be the most beneficial to coaches, parents, and, most of all, the student-athletes of high school athletics.

I can only comment on the Activities Director as Athletic Director because that is the capacity in which I worked with these men. The Athletic Director who hired me was only in position for two more years before he retired. He had been an Athletic Director for many years and did his job effectively. The Athletic Director who succeeded the man who hired me was, and still is, a work in progress. The observations I outline here are mostly based on the experiences I had for eight years with the second Athletic Director. In some cases, the observations might seem to be overly critical, but in a changing landscape of high school athletics, there are many elements that need to be examined with a critical lens including the direction of athletics. The reflections of my experiences throughout eight years of collaborating with the current Athletic Director are the foundation for the following outline of success. The critical analysis has led me to five objectives that define the success of effective Athletic Directors as administrators of coaches.

## Objective One: Be Supportive

Athletic Directors can have an overwhelming duty to be supportive. It can be overwhelming because of the various groups that he must support. In the framework of athletics, an Athletic Director must support parents, coaches, and student-athletes. A daunting task considering each group just might have its own agenda. A well organized Athletic Director can and will efficiently manage all three groups in an effective manner creating outstanding opportunities to learn in a safe, productive environment.

For an Athletic Director, the first action to take in developing support for parents, coaches, and student-athletes is to create and maintain a mission statement. This living document needs to exist beyond the parameters of the athletic code. The mission statement must give examples of appropriate expectations of parents, coaches, and student-athletes. Furthermore, the Athletic Director must be the living model of this mission statement.

In the final weeks of the last season of my head coaching tenure, I had come to the conclusion that something was wrong. Specifically, something was wrong with the leadership of our athletic department. This final season began with my Athletic Director on my doorstep with a six pack of beer telling me that I needed to get my program to the next level. There is nothing wrong with encouraging success in terms of winning, but it was certainly out of character for him. He was always supportive of me as a head coach and wasn't someone who regularly showed up at a coach's house. In fact, what he was telling me weren't thoughts born of his own imagination; he had to be feeling pressure from outside influences. I knew that parents had been bending his ear, even though, to his credit, he never fully admitted it to me.

The group of student-athletes I was coaching that particular season had some ego driven parents. One in particular had some influence with the Athletic Director. Innocently, this parent talked to the Athletic Director making general observations about the management of the team as well as the direction of the team. In fact, this parent contacted me within days of this unexpected visit by the Athletic Director and confirmed that he had shared his concerns in regards to the ability of my coaching staff. Like any good administrator would, my Athletic Director listened. However, this influential parent strategically planted a seed of doubt with the Athletic Director that a change would be welcome. This parent was suggesting immediate, all-encompassing change, but perhaps underestimated the inherent power to influence the Athletic Director.

I believe it is important to point out that during my 10 seasons as head coach of the girls varsity basketball team, the athletes I had the opportunity to coach, compiled 124 wins against just 100 losses. The first season of my tenure, our team only outscored our opponent twice, while being on the other end 19 times. Needless to say, things drastically improved in terms of winning in subsequent years.

Nevertheless, I started to believe that our school district had begun to lose perspective as to what was truly important in the realm of high school athletics. I began to wonder to myself and question out loud to my administration about the benchmarks of athletics. I wondered what our district considered a standard of success for our coaches and student-athletes. I questioned the Athletic Director's philosophy in this regard.

In my meanderings and questioning I received no answers. Why didn't I receive answers? No one had answers because there was no mission statement. I suppose there is no mission statement so that administrators don't get themselves stuck in a corner, especially in addition to the structure and consequences of the athletic code.

In order for the structure of proper support to be in place, there must be a developed mission statement. When there is no mission statement, then there is no consistency in how coaches are treated or in how concerns from parents are handled. Thoughts and ideologies then become as inconsistent as the wind. Athletic Directors must support the coach publicly and privately.

In my final season as head coach, as parent pressure began to mount for the Athletic Director despite having a winning season, I decided to meet with all three of our building administrators, the Principal, Vice Principal, and the Athletic Director. I was in this meeting as a basketball coach not an English teacher. I was under the assumption that the Athletic Director would run the meeting while the other two were there to witness the interaction. I was wrong. The Vice Principal ran the entire meeting while the Athletic Director contributed very little.

I could sense a couple of things happening. First, the Athletic Director was beginning to feel trapped with the onset of parent pressure. Secondly, the other two administrators seemed to be in support of my position and were doing their best to alleviate the stress and pressure in any way they could. In the end, however, the entire situation was the responsibility of the Athletic Director as administrator of all co-curricular activities.

I was overly frustrated when I left that meeting because I knew that the Athletic Director was not in full support of me in my position. I wanted to know why. In fact, during that meeting I demanded to know what it is that I had done wrong, what the benchmarks of success were, and what just cause there was for the lack of support. There were no answers from any of the administrators. In fact, I was told that I had done nothing wrong, just that "people" wanted to see change.

The Athletic Director, some weeks later, wanted to follow up with me alone. In this follow up meeting, that lasted all of 10 minutes, my Athletic Director said, "You should resign; I see no other way around it...you are on an island all by yourself." Are these words of support? I completely understand his point that a group of parents were targeting me with ungrounded criticism. A few parents believed my leadership style was ineffective. After some thought and in his attempt to continue to support me as he always had, my Athletic Director followed the previous statement by saying, "...but I support you and will continue to support you if you choose to continue coaching."

I was stunned at the paradoxical comments my Athletic Director was making. I was speechless. My thoughts swirled. " Why isn't he on the island with me?" I thought, "Why isn't there a definition or outline of what I have violated or done wrong?"

The point is, Athletic Directors have to be supportive of their coaches in the midst of parent pressure. All parents look out for the best interest of their own children, rightfully so. I do the same thing. However, the Athletic Director must act as the mediator between coaches and parents. Athletic Directors must advocate for the coaches they hire. More importantly, they are advocates of student-athletes. With that said, isn't it important then to fully support, through actions and words, those coaches who are best for student-athletes?

I believe there is something wrong with the Athletic Director being critical of coaches who have not gotten their programs to the sectional level in the state tournament on a consistent basis. Is that really what high school sports are all about? Are we failures if we haven't accomplished that consistently? Have we lost our perspective? And *if* that is the main objective, then why weren't all of the other coaches being held to that standard? A well developed mission statement will help alleviate such problems and allow Athletic Directors to support and nourish all coaches in their district to the benefit of all student-athletes.

## Objective Two:
## Personal Observations Equal Good Decisions

Amidst the mountain of responsibilities faced by an Athletic Director there lies a personal relationship with each coach he is directing. As teachers must develop rapport with their students, so too do Athletic Directors have to make the same connection with their coaches. I believe that it is malpractice to make decisions about coaches based on hearsay or checking the local newspaper for scores and comments. Athletic Directors must develop an intimate relationship by *frequently* talking with coaches, observing practices, and attending games.

Athletic Directors will have a difficult time making their own decisions about a coach's effectiveness or lack thereof if he infrequently observes his work. In fact, an Athletic Director will have the capacity to address parental concerns if he truly understands how the coach works with the student-athletes. Ultimately, the Athletic Director will build a foundation of support through his frequent observations. The more interaction an Athletic Director can have with all the coaches, the better he will understand the objectives and mission of each coach and their programs.

I suppose it could be argued that the coaches who have teams that win on a regular basis never hit the radar of the Athletic Director. Just like teachers who never have any discipline problems; aren't those the teachers that the administrators love the best? I am sure it is the same way with some Athletic Directors. They want coaches who can stay off the radar. When the red light on the radar screen begins to blink, then there is a problem that the Athletic Director has to address, sometimes publicly.

There are two ways to avoid the humiliation of publicly addressing coaches or concerns within a particular athletic program. First, all coaches should be on the radar. Every coach should be observed, frequently, in the various elements of his job. Second, all Athletic Directors must adhere to an athletic mission statement.

In my final season as head basketball coach, my Athletic Director frequently made comments about my coaching staff. In his defense, my Athletic Director engaged in this type of discussion with me every year; it seemed as though he genuinely wanted to help me out by looking for opportunities to hire quality assistant coaches. During the final season of my head coaching gig, I thought these comments were interesting because he had not frequently observed the coaching staff in action or had meaningful, professional discourse with them on a regular basis. He, at best, remotely made connections with the coaches on my staff. Our Athletic Director never attended a road game of ours so I knew that comments made in relationship to games that weren't played at our school were coming from observations made by others. If he was concerned with the production of the coaching staff, he could have traveled, even to our own gym, more frequently to make his own observations. Furthermore, if he would have observed more frequently, he would have had the capacity to make objective, educated decisions regarding me and my coaching staff.

I believe there is something wrong with the Athletic Director questioning a coaching staff without having proper knowledge of the intimate details of the coaching interactions with student-athletes. This begs the question, "What are you basing your observations on?" Furthermore, I demand of Athletic Directors who make decisions about coaches and programs that they must be present. Have they seen enough to make appropriate judgments and decisions?

Following a game in my final season as head coach in which we were outscored by a formidable opponent by just a few points in overtime, my Athletic Director met me as I headed out of the gym. He shook my hand and told me, "Nice game coach." That was nice; this was his honest effort at providing visible, public support.

My response to him was not so favorable. During this season there were several moments in which the parents of our student-athletes loudly, in public, voiced their opinions of the coaching staff, the play of the team, and, most often, the officiating. This particular game was no exception.

The parents of our opponent provided a wonderful example of a group of people that supported the student-athletes, coaches, and officials. As I walked out of the door of the gym that night, moments after the game had ended, while my Athletic Director shook my hand, I told him that the way the parents of our opponent acted was a great example to everyone. I was recognizing the power of positive energy within the world of high school athletics.

Apparently, shortly after my interaction with my Athletic Director a member of our coaching staff approached him. He made mention of the quality of officiating during that game. My Athletic Director, in a later meeting, made the judgment that our coaching staff had lost focus at the end of that game. He based that decision on the two comments made by me and another member of the coaching staff. I don't believe our coaching staff lost focus. What I do believe is that both of us took the opportunity to make a timely observation to our Athletic Director about significant outcomes during a situation that he witnessed. Because these moments were few and far between, we felt the need to take advantage of the opportunity.

My point in mentioning the parents of our opponent was that they were a great model for the positive side of high school athletics. It made me wonder who was supposed to serve as a model, outside of me, for the parents of our student-athletes. Outside of our coaching staff, I wondered whose responsibility it was to encourage the parents of our student-athletes to support their children and the coaches.

The more often an Athletic Director is present for games, practices, and individual meetings with coaches, the better he will be in making decisions in regards to the effectiveness of the coaching staff. God provides us with an abundance of abilities and places us in situations that help define who we are. I had a colleague once tell me that there is no way that I could be judged based on one mistake or even two. When appropriate relationships are developed each person develops a "credit" to make mistakes. It is imperative that Athletic Directors provide many opportunities to be involved with their coaches to give support and proper feedback. Relying on frequent personal observations gives Athletic Directors the opportunity to provide the best experience possible for student-athletes.

## Objective Three: Equity in Visibility

Athletic Directors have an enormous responsibility to be present at many events outside of the school day. It is probably one of the most challenging aspects of the job. However, the Athletic Director gets paid a salary to take on these obligations. All Athletic Directors, I am sure, understand this part of the job when they apply for the position and, ultimately, sign the contract. No matter the success of a particular program, the Athletic Director must be equally available for all athletic teams and events.

I suppose it can be argued that it is impossible to be present at ALL events. I am not suggesting that an Athletic

Director be present all the time. This is where a highly organized individual effectively manages his time to handle all of the obligations. I am not naïve enough to claim that the sport I coached didn't receive attention from the Athletic Director. In fact, I know that the sport I coached received more attention from the Athletic Director than some others. However, that just solidifies my argument that Athletic Directors must learn to balance their time to show equity.

In the most turbulent season I coached, my final season, the Athletic Director was more noticeable, but not to the point where he could make informed decisions about me, the assistant coaches, or the program. A perfect example of this was the last game in which our team participated in that season. We had traveled just 15 minutes from our school to take on one of the top ranked teams in the state. We were outscored in that game by just two points to the eventual state champion runner-up. Our Athletic Director did not make the short trip.

Maybe he had other obligations with his family that night. I accept that. Maybe he was ill or tired. I accept that too. What is unacceptable is that he later made observations about that game that he did not even witness. I believe that an Athletic Director that is effectively doing his job will be willing to be present at major contests for each sport, like the one we were in that evening. Being present allows the Athletic Director to make observations based on personal experience.

To further illustrate this point, during parent-teacher conferences one evening in February of that same basketball season, our Athletic Director admitted to me that he was going to cut out early to watch the boys basketball team play a road game some 40 minutes away. I remember seeing our Athletic Director at no more than five road games over the course of eight years.

Certainly he may have been at more that I didn't notice, but he was never short on telling me when he was present when we participated on the road. In fact, he would often make observations about the games we played on the road based on the blurbs he would read in the newspaper. The

**Athletic Directors: Five Keys for Gate Keeper of High School Athletics**

| | |
|---|---|
| 1. **Support** | be an advocate for all student-athletes |
| 2. **Observe** | frequent, personal observations equal good decisions |
| 3. **Be Visible** | be equitable, albeit difficult, for all teams and events |
| 4. **Be Organized** | collaborate with all coaches |
| 5. **Be Honest** | the truth is liberating |

game summaries provided in the newspaper do not do justice to the real story of the game. It's like looking at major league baseball box scores and noticing that a player had two hits in four plate appearances. What the box score doesn't tell is whether the hit was a solid single to center field or if it was a dribbler hit to the second baseman off the end of the bat. Being present at the game itself or even reading a complete description of the game from a quality beat sports reporter can be insightful.

Critical analysis from the Athletic Director can be very helpful to the success of a coach. The critical analysis should be made through many avenues. Those avenues include meetings with coaches, listening with an open mind to parents, talking with student-athletes, and observation. All of these avenues are helpful in the implementation of a positive experience for student-athletes which will create a positive sense of self-worth. Make plenty of observations to make wise, educated decisions.

# Objective Four:
# Leadership and Collaboration with All Coaches

Modeling leadership skills for coaches is another element of the Athletic Director's job description. In order for this to take place there needs to be meetings between Athletic Directors and coaches. The meetings can be presented in three ways: one on one, individual meetings, or group meetings with head coaches and their assistants, or, finally, group meetings with all head coaches.

A good leader senses when there might be dissention and controversy among the subordinates. Even Odysseus from the classic *The Odyssey* understood that his men were questioning his authority and decision making. Nevertheless, he motivated them and kept them focused on their goals. The bottom line is Odysseus needed his men and his men needed Odysseus. The same holds true for Athletic Directors and the coaches who work under him.

Frequent meetings to discuss goals, challenges, and morale need to take place between the head coach and the Athletic Director. With intimate meetings between the two a trust develops. Furthermore, a unified vision is developed for the best interest and success of the student-athletes. A positive dialogue that develops between coach and Athletic Director only leads to productive, learning opportunities for student-athletes.

I had several meetings of this type throughout my tenure as head coach. I was always honest with my Athletic Director, and I believed he was always honest with me. I always believed that there was a mutual respect between the two of us. He had even told me many times that I was the best advocate in our school for women's athletics. I believed in him.

Another effective way of keeping morale high and maintaining proper leadership is to have a meeting between the Athletic Director, the head coach, and his subordinates. This meeting presents the Athletic Director as one with the athletic programs. It also prevents a perception of mistrust between assistants and the head coaches. A good leader makes his goals and message known to all involved and doesn't rely on his message to be translated by others. This prevents any ugly misunderstandings. Furthermore, it develops a strong sense of security, trust, and support.

Unfortunately, a meeting of this sort never took place in my years as coach. I believe this was a missing ingredient in terms of my Athletic Director completely understanding and appreciating the dynamics and chemistry of my coaching staff. There were too many blind observations made without having this much needed connection between the Athletic Director and all coaching staffs.

Finally, a meeting between Athletic Director and all head coaches has a tremendous impact on the direction of the athletic program. The mission statement of the athletic program can be acknowledged and enforced. In this scenario there is sharing of ideas and a common vision that all head coaches are involved in their positions on behalf of the best interest of all student-athletes involved. All egos are set aside and a genuine desire for each program to succeed in teaching life lessons which leads to winning. A common interest and a unified vision amongst all head coaches provide the ultimate environment for success.

This type of meeting happened once in my ten year stint as head coach. It happened shortly after school let out for the summer. Only a handful of head coaches were present. Apparently the meeting was not mandatory for all head coaches. If it had been expected that all should attend, then an appropriate time when all coaches could meet would have been set up. Furthermore, the ideas discussed in meetings like this must be carried through; important meetings that address the needs and concerns of a group of highly interested, vested people must be more than just a formality, not something to just cross off the list.

## Objective Five: Honesty

In my deliberations to resign my position as head girls basketball coach, a defining moment occurred about a month after the season ended. A sophomore student-athlete approached me midway through the last period of the school day. It was my prep period and I was available for her. She pulled out her phone to show me a text message she had received from one of her sophomore teammates. This student-athlete was visibly upset; she was in tears and looked pale.

She told me she had just received this text message from one of her teammates and that she was so bothered by it in class that she needed to make me aware of the situation right now. She loaded the text message for me to view. It read, "_____(last name of Athletic Director) told us to get a list of stuff together if we want Steltz out. Got any ideas?" The text was sent to all of the other sophomore teammates; there were seven in all.

I was completely floored by what I read in that text message. I felt completely betrayed by my Athletic Director. Just days prior to this incident, he told me he supported me, even though I was on an island all by myself. I felt that any trust I had in my Athletic Director shattered like thin ice on a springtime lake. I felt as though I was now drowning in the coldest of waters.

Maybe that was the intention, to get me to cave. I guess I wasn't strong enough to handle the situation because it had finally gotten to my heart: the student-athletes I was coaching. Every part of this was now wrong. The permeation of the real problem was eating like acid at the very core of what I believed in. I needed to respond to this young lady who told me she didn't know what to do about the text.

I told her that there was nothing wrong with being honest with the other girls. She could never feel bad about being honest. I told her that she didn't have to do anything on my behalf; I wanted her to feel comfortable amidst the worst form of peer pressure. If she felt strongly that these girls were wrong or that the Athletic Director was wrong, there would be nothing wrong with telling the truth. I also told her that I would understand if she didn't say anything at all.

Athletic Directors must be honest with themselves and with their subordinates, the coaches. My Athletic Director never met with me to tell me that he had requested that the student-athletes who had concerns were asked to write them down. I knew this was a practice of his administration strategies. I understood that. In fact, I really wasn't bothered that maybe he did ask for a list.

Asking for a list from parents, adults, is one thing, but from student-athletes? That is a completely separate issue. I thought, at the time, that this could invite complete fabrications of anyone's wildest imaginations. At what point was this going to end? I even wondered to what extent people would go to get what they wanted. I knew that I had the power to put a stop to the nonsense that pointed to me.

I knew, as well, that I wasn't the problem. There were much bigger problems surrounding this situation that wouldn't go away with my resignation. I just knew that my life would become more peaceful and the lives of some of the student-athletes as well, like the girl who approached me with the text message.

The girl who shared the text message with me shared it with her parents that same evening. Her father was upset. He contacted the Athletic Director. I have no idea what resulted from this conversation other than the fact that my Athletic Director knew I was aware of the text message. My Athletic Director never addressed the issue with me; in fact, we never met about this issue before I handed in my resignation.

I handed my resignation in very early on a Monday morning. About mid morning, my Athletic Director bumped into me in our school's library. He stated that he was taken by surprise when he read my letter of resignation. I think I was more surprised by that comment when just weeks prior he suggested I do just that.

Later that day, in a meeting that lasted all of ten minutes, he asked, "What would you like me to tell people when they ask about your decision?" I looked at him somewhat dumbfounded and told him that the ideas presented in my letter of resignation could be restated. It appeared to me that he had not read it very thoroughly or maybe misunderstood it; however, this could have been just my perception; I have no proof that he didn't read it.

I know that my Athletic Director really did his best to be honest with me. He had told me that he believed that the demeanor of the parents in regards to me was only going to get worse and gain momentum. He told me that he thought there were going to be letters to the editor in the local paper and letters to the school district's superintendent and possibly the school board. In his defense he said he felt that these things were quite a possibility. He also told me that he thought there was a petition being passed and signed by some that indicated their displeasure in the success and direction of the girls basketball program.

I give him credit for being honest with me. However, there was no just cause to support an argument against the direction of the program. The Athletic Director has the responsibility to be honest, not only with the coach but, with parents and student-athletes as well. If there is a well written mission statement done collaboratively with parents, administration, and coaches, the truth is an obvious outcome. The practice of telling one group what they want to hear, then telling another group what they want to hear is ineffective and wrong. I am not suggesting that is what my Athletic Director did; I just know that many coaches throughout the district were closely following my situation and were concerned.

As I told the student-athlete in regards to the text message and the ideas behind it, there is nothing wrong with honesty. In 99% of all situations a person can never go wrong being honest. Because of the multiple responsibilities and the mountain of obligation that an Athletic Director must balance, the best practice is to be consistent and honest.

The five objectives I have outlined here clearly define success for Athletic Directors. People in this highly taxing position must be highly motivated and organized. I am truly empathetic about the unique challenges posed to Athletic Directors. I am convinced that Athletic Directors that are supportive, present, personify leadership, and are honest are the most beneficial to coaches, parents, and, most of all, the student-athletes of high school athletics.

My commentary is based solely on my experience as a coach under two Athletic Directors. I am not an expert in terms of administrators, but I do know how it feels to be supported at times then, at other times, to be left on an island all by myself. Furthermore, I have witnessed how dissenters can gain power when administrators are easily influenced. I intellectually understand the obligations of each Athletic Director. The reflections of my experiences can provide insight for coaches and Athletic Directors as to the importance for a mission statement and a successful unified vision between coaches and their Athletic Directors.

# THE VISIBILITY, VALUE, AND VALIDATION OF SUCCESSFUL STUDENT-ATHLETES

*This above all: to thine own self be true,
And it must follow, as the night the day,
Thou canst not then be false to any man.*
    *William Shakespeare*

Once success has been defined for coaches and parents, the definition of success for student-athletes is easy. Because of the many pressures facing teenagers today, having a clear vision of success for high school student-athletes is quintessential in their maturation and development of a positive sense of self-worth. The foundation of the student-athlete's success is in the objectives both of the coaches and parents. When coaches and parents meet their objectives, their burden of responsibility, along with the student-athletes buying in to the objectives, then those children will begin to feel visible, valued, and validated as people.

It is important to recall the evolution of the athlete when defining success. In the beginning, way back when children are in pre-school, athletes are formed because they love to play. There is a genuine desire to play with peers and even, in some cases, to compete. As part of the definition of high school student-athletes it is important to bring to mind what brought them there to begin with: to have fun and the love to play. Brooklyn thoroughly enjoys recess and gym class more than anything in elementary school. She longs for snow days and holidays to have the time to play, just play.

As part of the foundation of success, student-athletes who enjoy their experience within themselves will be successful. The last component to this definition is to use high school athletics as a learning tool to prepare for the future. I believe it is appropriate in this section to write about the student-athletes that I have crossed paths with who have been successful. With the success stories it is easy to understand how these student-athletes met the first four target objectives and why they were successful.

## Objective One: Athletics as Learning Tool

In my first year as head girls basketball coach I was delighted to cross paths with a young lady who was mature beyond her years. She was a junior in high school and understood the gift of faith. She had been through an extremely challenging situation some years earlier. Her mother had died, literally in front of her eyes, after a long bout with cancer. This young girl was in middle school at the time, the baby of the family. She had an older brother and sister. Both of her parents had been teachers, her father also was a coach.

This young lady understood the importance of high school athletics. As she was an exceptional athlete in three high school sports, she knew that athletics was just a small part of who she was. She had learned much from her mother before her mom left this world to be in the presence of God. Once, this student-athlete shared a video montage she had created in the memory of her mother. As a rookie head coach, she had accepted me and my approach to coaching. She listened to my message and personified the goodness of high school athletics.

Some years after she had graduated, I received a phone call from this young lady. She was in her third year of college and home for winter break. She had continued to play softball, her favorite sport, in college and was only home for a short time due to her college athletic responsibilities. She had wanted to see me because she had something for me.

She gave me a Christmas present. I am not much for receiving anything from the student-athletes I have coached. I have always felt that I was just doing my job meeting the expectations required of me and didn't need any recognition. I did tell the players I coached from time to time when it came to the end of the year awards banquet that the greatest gift they could ever give me was to have learned something throughout their high school basketball experience that they would apply to their own life, something that would help them in their future successes.

Nevertheless, this young lady, after not having spoken in years, gave me a present. Upon opening the package I found a framed picture of a basketball sneaker on a gym floor. The picture was a side view from the floor, implying that there was a foot in the shoe. Under the photograph there were words written. Before reading the words, I read the card she included with the package. In the card she wrote, "Some people teach us lessons that help us throughout our lives. Thank you for being that someone and giving me the gift of the lessons you taught. I now know what it means to 'get on the line.'" Above the picture are the words "A Coach's Words."

"Getting on the line" in athletics implies that there will be some form of running. The running will require strength, endurance, and will involve pain. A phrase this young lady pointed to within the words under the picture were, "…the line is the beginning of the journey – to potential greatness." She understood what it meant to apply discipline to her own life. She understood that by enduring the lessons she learned from "getting on the line" she would be successful in the game of life.

The gift she had given me was more important to me than any one win or loss. It wasn't the framed picture and the subsequent words. It was the idea. She was able to make the connection between the work ethic she learned in athletics, as an extension of the classroom, and how those lessons had helped her become successful post high school. She was now independent and knew how to push herself, internally, to achieve her goals. She had learned the valuable lesson that high school athletics helps to educate the whole person. Her sense of self-worth would continue to grow to help her reach her full potential.

Later on, well into the middle of my tenure as a head coach, the teams I was coaching had developed a reputation of being successful in terms of wins and losses. These teams also had a reputation for being tough, always playing hard no matter what the circumstances were. Upon my resignation, I received an email from a former student-athlete who was a part of the basketball program four years prior.

She commented to me that she didn't believe high school basketball was about how many wins our teams had accumulated by the end of the season. She thanked me for what I and the coaching staff had taught her team. She mentioned things like character and integrity. She also mentioned how important it was to me that all student-athletes represented themselves and the team with honor and respect. She believed that one of the most important lessons she learned was that the good of the group always came first.

She ended by commenting that these were "lessons that we'd [her and her teammates] remember throughout our life to be successful." As a coach, it is so important to emphasize the importance of academics first. Then, it is important to stress the idea that there are life lessons to be learned in participating in high school athletics. Using athletics as an opportunity to learn beyond the scope and sequence of the classroom invites the education of the whole person. Student-athletes can consider themselves a success if they can learn a lesson or two from participating in athletics that will help them to be successful throughout their lives; gaining as many tools as they can will help them in building their adult lives into something special. Furthermore, it will help them to uncover their inner uniqueness to share with the world.

## Objective Two: Meet Coach's Objectives

Each year I coached the coaching staff would create a poster for the locker room. The poster highlighted team goals for each game that we believed were necessary for our team to be successful. The poster was placed in a very visible area of the locker room. I would also make reference to the goal chart in our pre-game chalk talk and in our post-game reflections.

Prior to the season beginning, the coaching staff also had the student-athletes create two goals. One goal was a personal goal while the other goal was a team goal for that season. After the student-athletes articulated their goals in writing they had to provide an action plan, explaining how they were going to achieve those goals. The coaching staff would then create individual goal posters for each member of the team. On that goal chart was listed several individual game goals we asked our student-athletes to achieve. Also on those individual goal charts were listed the goals the players wanted, themselves, to achieve in that season. For each goal that was achieved, both on the team chart in the locker room and on the individual charts posted on their lockers, there was a sticker placed next to that goal for the particular game we played.

Student-athletes must know the objectives of the coaching staff in order to meet the desired objective. The power of goal setting and the impact of seeing those goals each and every day before practice or a game kept those goals at the center of their consciousness when stepping into the locker room. Goal setting is a powerful tool in achieving and maintaining success. The coaching staff always emphasized that the action plan, or their actions, spoke much louder than the words or ideas.

In my final year coaching girls basketball our team had a starting lineup of five sophomores. From that team, I recall many individuals who worked hard at meeting the objectives of the coaching staff. As part of our discipline and proper preparation objectives, the coaching staff consistently expected student-athletes to sprint from drill to drill, to sprint before and after water breaks, and to sprint on and off the court when checking into and coming out of a game.

This objective was worked on each year with every student-athlete we coached. During this final season, maybe the message had gotten old or maybe student-athletes were not getting the results they perceived they should have been getting through such objectives. As a result, from time to time, a few student-athletes would forget to sprint or just choose not to. There were two athletes however, both sophomores, who did meet this objective every day.

One of these two players was extremely valuable to her team. She had many skills that would help her team be successful. She worked hard in every drill we had, even when she was so tired she would have rather fallen over. She was first in line for each drill, always pushing her teammates to the point of exhaustion. She never minded the idea that her teammates would get frustrated with her because she worked so hard. In fact, she always set the tone in practice.

She always listened with her ears and her eyes. I could always read in her eyes the commitment she had to her team. During games she played extremely hard. She would play until we had to drag her off the floor. She understood work ethic, discipline, and preparation. I have no doubt in my mind that this particular student-athlete will be successful in her future as a result of her willingness to meet the objectives the coaching staff had laid out in front of the team.

The other example of a student-athlete being willing to meet the objectives of the coaching staff came from another sophomore. She was not a starter all year, but worked her way into that starting role. She was a player who the coaching staff knew they could rely on, both off and on the court. She was a quiet, unassuming young lady that truly led by example. She did everything the coaches asked of her.

Shortly after the coaching staff concluded the season ending meeting and conducted the exit interviews with the underclassmen it was time to start organizing inventory and putting things away for the off-season. The season ending meeting and exit interviews were done in my classroom. The coaching staff had left the room as we prepared our next plan of action. We separated and got to work.

I was headed back to my classroom to organize the practice jerseys and basketballs the players had turned in at our meeting. To my surprise, one of the players had come back to my room and was sitting in a chair. It was the quiet student-athlete who did all that we asked of her on and off the floor. I asked her if she needed something. Her simple response was, "no." I asked her if she had something on her mind or wanted to talk. Her only response was to shake her head no and sort of smile.

I then began to just make small talk about the season. I reiterated what the coaching staff had told her in our exit interview. We were proud of her efforts during the season. We were thankful for her commitment and willingness to do what was in the best interest of the team. I tried to talk about some memorable moments from the season that included her and the team. I was doing my best to build a relationship and to make a connection.

As I was attempting to make small talk, she listened intently with her ears and her eyes. She followed me with her eyes as I worked at organizing jerseys and basketballs. Finally, I sat down across the table from where she was sitting and I genuinely thanked her again for a great season. I encouraged her to continue to work hard and do all the little things that she did well already. Then a question popped into my head as I was really trying to carry this conversation, which, by the way, I had no problem doing. She stayed because she wanted to talk, or to listen, or maybe because she just didn't want the basketball season to end. In any case, God had called her to stay.

Maybe God called her to stay for my benefit as well as for hers. The Spirit moved me to ask this question. "Why, when a lot of your teammates struggled in doing things we asked them to do, did you always do everything we asked of you?" She looked at me, smiled, and shrugged her shoulders. The thought then came to me that I needed to be more specific in my question to elicit a verbal response. The Spirit then moved me to ask the next question.

"For instance, during games, you always sprinted on to the court when checking into the game, and when summoned out of the game by a substitute, you always sprinted off the floor. In the midst of the peer pressure, why did you always do this?" To this question she finally had an answer. The teacher in me finally asked the right question.

Her response was simple but truthful and genuine. "Coach, because you told us to." That response blew me out of the water. I know I shouldn't be so surprised when a student-athlete complies with the objectives of the coaching staff. But the trend in coaching high school athletics has become somewhat disturbing. In an age when we see many student-athletes and their parents owning a sense of entitlement in all that they do; in a time when so many kids are just looking out for themselves because that is what they have been taught at home; in a time when student-athletes choose not to follow direction from teachers, coaches, or parents because they feel that there is no immediate impact on their success; this child simply stated that she did what was asked of her because I "told her to."

First of all, this is a real credit to her parents. Apparently, her parents have instilled an honest work ethic and a faith that their daughter be respectful to adults, particularly teachers and coaches. Furthermore, she has been encouraged by her parents to do the things, within the parameters of being appropriate, that coaches and teachers ask of her. This child's response came amidst a season of turbulence with some student-athletes not responding the same way to the knowledge and expectations of coaches and teachers.

Secondly, she avoided the constant draw of peer pressure to not listen or to not believe in the best interest of the team. She rose above the muck of some poor attitudes emanating from her friends and teammates. This student-athlete is a model of how a team member conducts herself on a team. Her actions spoke much louder than her words. She was a genuine young lady. All of these qualities and skills she harbors within her spirit will open the doors for a successful future.

Finally, I have had the opportunity to coach many student-athletes with this same attitude. However, I have noticed that these types of attitudes are becoming rarer. The norm seems to be leading to entitlement and selfish thoughts and actions. That is the part of the culture of high school athletics that needs to be re-aligned. The values are misplaced which leads to chaos and hurtful actions. Meeting the objectives of the coach, believing that those objectives will aide in a successful future, and helping to lead in such a way will certainly benefit all student-athletes. Furthermore, meeting objectives of the coach will lend itself to building upon a solid foundation of trust, work ethic, and confidence. This will, in turn, continue to build the positive sense of self-worth in all student-athletes.

## Objective Three: Meet Parent's Objectives

Parents have the most important role in the life of their child. When they satisfy the objectives of giving the gifts of support, acceptance, humility, belief and faith it is up to the child to utilize these gifts. Upon receiving these gifts from their parents, the children must apply them to their own lives. The first gift the child must apply to allow all others to make sense is the gift of acceptance. Student-athletes must be willing to accept the gifts from their parents. When there is acceptance with an open heart and an open mind, the student-athletes will then have the capacity to meet this particular objective.

The student-athletes that have accepted the gift of support from their parents already enter high school with a solid base to build upon. The foundation that is created within them is built upon confidence and self-worth. The student-athletes who I have worked with that carry themselves with confidence and radiate a positive sense of self-worth are the ones that have been given support by their parents.

I suppose there is a maturity level that needs to be reached before the children have the capacity to accept these gifts. However, the parents who are consistent in their support will allow for the most growth in their children. These parents are genuine in their support and their children thrive in the high school setting. These are the children who will receive the most out of their high school experience. With the safety net of support, children will have the opportunity to receive an education of their whole self.

In accepting the gift of support, student-athletes must learn to accept the importance of humility as well. Not all student-athletes have the same foundation of confidence and sense of self-worth. In F. Scott Fitzgerald's opening to

# THE VISIBILITY, VALUE, AND VALIDATION
## OF SUCCESSFUL STUDENT-ATHLETES

*The Great Gatsby*, the narrator, Nick Carraway, points out, "In my younger and more vulnerable years my father gave me some advice that I've been turning over in my mind ever since. 'Whenever you feel like criticizing any one,' he told me, 'just remember that all the people in this world haven't had the advantages that you've had.'"

I have always felt that the insight provided by Fitzgerald through his narrator encompassed the idea of humility. Having the awareness that God has gifted each and every one of us in different ways provides us the opportunity to be humble in our own achievements. Even though I might have had parents who were supportive, that doesn't make me any better or worse than my spouse, co-worker, or teammate. All it means is that I may have had different opportunities to that point in my life.

Student-athletes who can apply humility to their own lives will learn the significance each one of us has in the universe more efficiently than their non-humble peers. Having humility allows us to help others find their inner uniqueness to better serve the world. As God as our focus, the center of our life, we need look no further for humility. I am humbled by the greatness and grace of our God. His love for us reaches beyond anything we could imagine. The sooner we understand this concept and accept it, the sooner we will be on our path to finding our true talents.

The love God has for us is similar to the love parents have for their children. God believes in us as parents believe in their own children; accepting that belief will allow us to believe in others as well as ourselves. Furthermore, accepting that

**High School Student-Athletes: Visibility, Personal Value, Self-Validation**

- Learn through Athletics
- Respect and Respond to Teachers and Coaches
- Listen and Learn from Parents
- Participate in Athletics for Fun, for The Love of The Game
- Apply, to Life, All Lessons Learned

belief means we feel valued. Knowing that we have those who believe in us certainly leads to a positive sense of self-worth. This positive sense of self-worth allows us to look in the mirror and see God's image reflected. Believing is not seeing, rather it is an intangible part of the love we all share.

The greatest gift we can receive is the gift of faith and spirituality. This gift provides us the opportunity to love and to be loved. Student-athletes who can recognize the importance of faith, even if it is only to a small degree, will have a lifetime of support and belief. Spending a moment in prayer each day will create a calming peace. Faith provides the proper perspective on our lives. It continually reminds us that we are all created by the same Hand, all with a uniqueness to be shared with the world.

As parents meet their own objectives and as student-athletes accept the gifts from their parents, they will continue to grow and succeed. In these objectives, the success rate is not measured by how many points are scored, how many pins are had, or how many tackles are made. These objectives help student-athletes grow, in faith, on the inside. These objectives, ultimately, will give these young people the best chance at being successful beyond high school.

## Objective Four:
## Have Fun for the Love of the Game

In my second season as head basketball coach I was graced with a student-athlete who personified the love of the game. As a freshman, it was decided by the coaching staff that she would be a member of the varsity team. She didn't start right away, but played extensive minutes. After the sixth game of that season, she was inserted into the starting lineup. She became the school's all-time leading scorer, earned a scholarship that paid for her undergraduate degree and a major portion of her master's degree.

As she matured, she reminded me daily, yes daily, to have fun. Basketball is supposed to be fun. She had a love for the game. This particular student-athlete did not let the pressure of her peers or her community affect her love of the game.

# THE VISIBILITY, VALUE, AND VALIDATION
## OF SUCCESSFUL STUDENT-ATHLETES

That love carried her all the way through college. As she kept in contact with me over the years, through her words and actions she reminded me to always have fun.

I was talking with another former student-athlete during my ninth season as head girls basketball coach. This player had been an outstanding athlete in our high school, excelling in three sports, volleyball, basketball and track. Excelling might be an understatement. She was voted the conference player of the year in volleyball her senior year, she was the captain of her basketball team as well as a three year starter, and she still holds several track records at our school.

I was telling her how challenged the coaching staff was at combining the current student-athletes on the team. There were some head strong kids and the team was made up of student-athletes from all four grades, freshmen through seniors. The freshmen were exceptional, but not quite ready to take it to the next level. I had two exceptional seniors who had high expectations for their final year. It was a challenging mix we had to deal with as a coaching staff.

She just looked at me, smiled, and told me that all of it was just for fun. I was shocked at the simplicity and truth of her statement. This coming from the most competitive kid I had the opportunity to coach. Her new found perspective, now some five years removed from high school was surprising but refreshing. At that moment in time, she really put coaching into perspective for me. I needed to take a step back and look at my purpose for being involved in athletics. Way back in the beginning, in my youth, I did it because it was fun and I was driven by competition.

At the time I was finding it a challenge to deal with personalities that were in conflict by nature. Even more, the opinions of the parents were polarized as well. There were parents who wanted to be over involved with me. I probably allowed that a little too much over the course of my coaching career and probably listened too much because I cared.

This former student-athlete reminded me that playing the game and coaching the game was meant to be fun. If it was no longer fun, then a change needed to take place. I needed to change my perspective. One of my assistants and closest friends once told me that if I feel tired, then the kids probably feel the same way. I applied it to this situation. If I wasn't having fun, the kids probably weren't either. I needed to change my approach.

One afternoon I was having a conversation with one of my students, and I posed a question to him. As a non-athlete, I asked him how he perceived high school athletics. I thought his response interesting. He first said, "The only reason to play a game is for the love of it." This boy, a junior in high school at the time I posed the question, had participated in high school athletics as a freshmen and a sophomore. I asked him why he no longer participated in high school athletics. He told me that he had other interests and he had begun to lose touch with having fun because of the fierce competitive nature of high school athletics.

I posed another question to him. I wondered if he felt pressure from anyone or anywhere else to continue to compete. He admitted that there was peer pressure, to be among the "in-crowd," a student needed to be an athlete. That is where the attention was gained. He followed that thought with this next comment. "If you [the student-athlete] are not playing for the love of the game, and you are only playing for winning results, then you are abusing the game." Wow. He used the word "abusing." This young man had the proper perspective on what high school athletics was all about. Interestingly, this child with the appropriate perspective felt forced out due to the fierce peer pressure there was to win at all costs. We all could learn from this perspective; remember to keep the fun in game. We are playing, coaching, and being fans for the love of the game.

All of us, parents, coaches, and student-athletes, must remember why we are involved in the game. Whatever game it is, it is important to remember that the one thing that attracted us to it in the beginning was the idea that it was fun. We laughed, we played, and we developed relationships that provided a life time of memories. Maintaining the perspective that game is meant for fun and our purpose for being involved, inherently, is because we have a genuine love for playing. Maybe it keeps us young. Maybe it keeps us physically fit. But, in the end, we enjoy it and receive a sense of satisfaction because of the fun we have playing.

## Objective Five: Visibility, Value, and Validation

By the time of graduation a high school student will have met certain academic criteria set by the state and the local school district. Meeting these criteria means that the high school student is prepared for a future in the work force, a community college, or a four year university. Meeting these criteria also means that each child who crosses the stage at graduation and receives a signed high school diploma has reached a certain level of success. Some students have met the standards of success to different degrees. This is why we have valedictorians, salutatorians, etc. Some students are distinguished in other ways such as being included in the National Honor Society, graduating with honors or high honors. All in all, there are varying degrees of success for the high school student.

The participation in athletics for a high school student provides another arena in which to learn valuable life lessons. The criteria for success are ambiguous for the high school student-athlete. Depending upon the expectations of all involved, namely parents, coaches, and student –athletes, success can be defined in many different ways. In order to avoid chaos and conflicting views of success, it is mandatory that school districts define exactly what it is they would want their high school athletes to gain from their experience.

I believe the best place to start to measure the success of high school athletes is with the Three V's: visibility, value, and validation. All three of these concepts inherently develop a positive sense of self-worth and reach far beyond the fleeting definition of success defined by winning and losing. People want to be noticed: they want to feel important. People want to know that their contribution is welcomed and worthwhile. Finally, people want to know that they have found their inner uniqueness and are sharing it with the world. High school athletics provides the framework for all of this to flourish.

Some teenagers may act as though they want to be left alone. Some may seem as though they are content in going through life without drawing attention to themselves. By nature, we all want to feel visible. For those quiet kids in my classroom, maybe it is just a mention of a piece of clothing or a written comment on an assignment. However, everyone has the desire to be visible.

Consider the alternative. A child from a large family, maybe the middle child, may be able to get away with anything and no one notices. That same child, maturing into adulthood, may want to express something within a family debate, but no one listens with an open heart or open mind. High school athletics provides an opportunity for student-athletes from all sorts of different backgrounds to be visible.

Some student-athletes become much more visible than others. However, these are not the ones who need the attention. The students, who aren't recognized in the newspaper, aren't on prom court, or not class officers need to feel visible. Small gestures by influential adults like teachers, coaches, and parents, will help kids feel visible. A smile, a handshake, a "thattaboy" or "thattagirl," a congratulatory card all are small ways to help students feel visible.

The high school I teach at did an experiment a few years ago. As we walked into a room for a staff meeting, on the walls hung large post-it posters with the name of every student in the school. All staff members were given multi-colored stickers in the shape of a circle. The staff was then asked to place a sticker by every student with which they had a connection. When the exercise was finished, we quickly realized that there were several students who had no dots by their names.

The point of this activity was to show that, while some students had developed some unique relationships with faculty and staff, there were some "out there" that did not hit anyone's radar. These students were clearly not visible. It made us all wonder, if school is supposed to be a safe environment for children, how could it be that we allowed some children to slip by unnoticed? Even more, it made us wonder if these children had any support at all in their lives. In other words, did these children feel visible at any point in their lives? Did

## THE VISIBILITY, VALUE, AND VALIDATION
## OF SUCCESSFUL STUDENT-ATHLETES

anyone love these children, simply, for who they were? We decided that, as a group, we would reach out to these students to help them find their inner uniqueness. Therefore, staff members signed up to make connections with the various "dotless" students.

As adults trained in helping the maturation of children, we decided that our students needed to feel visible to help in their growth of success. Studies showed that students who felt connected to someone were much more likely to succeed. These kids tended to own their responsibilities and hold themselves accountable more often. The student-athletes that can exit their high school athletic careers feeling visible have a better chance of succeeding in life.

The individual goal charts that our coaching staff had the student-athletes put on their lockers had a column for each game entitled "spotlight." After each game, or at the end of each week, we met as a team to hand out "spotlight" stickers. Each member of the team had the opportunity to "spotlight" one of their teammates for whatever reason they wanted to. It didn't even have to do anything with basketball ability. It could be random acts of kindness being recognized, or homework help, or simply friendship. In any case, this was a technique designed for two reasons. One was to force kids to speak up and show appreciation of their teammates. The other was to give everyone the opportunity to be visible, if only for a moment. The student-athletes being spotlighted were then given a sticker to place on their poster in the appropriate column, a moment of visibility they would remember for the rest of the season. During quiet times, I was able to walk around the locker room, checking those posters to make sure everyone had been visible at some point or another. If someone hadn't been, I made sure that someone would find a reason to "spotlight" that person or the coaching staff would make it a priority to shine the "spotlight."

Once student-athletes feel visible, it is important that they feel valued. Value comes from the recognition that who they are, their talents, their uniqueness, are important to the world. Each member of a team has value, and good coaches understand this best. Identifying the value of each student-athlete on a team is imperative. The most important ingredient to this idea of value is the ability of a coach to articulate that value to the student-athlete.

The definition of value for each person comes directly from within. The importance of discovering our inner uniqueness, our talent cannot be overestimated. Once we understand what God has intended for us, our value emerges effortlessly, void of ego. Finding peace in acceptance and sharing our gifts with others allows us to celebrate who we are. This new found value, a feeling that is not fleeting but cemented for all time, will support a positive sense of self-worth. Student-athletes that find their value from within are well on their way to a successful future.

As value is found from within, so goes the notion of validation. We need to look no further than the Spirit that dwells within each of us for validation of who we are and who we are meant to be. Spending time validating ourselves through the perceptions of others creates a false sense of security. Validation through form, material things, and attention creates an identity that is not who we truly are.

Who we are lies deep beneath the surface of the material world. Who we are lies even deeper below the surface of our egos. Examining what makes us passionate and in what ways we can help others, is where we find our validation. It is from within that we must see our value. It is from within that we must believe in who we are and that God has created us with masterful strokes of genius. It is from within that we find peace with God.

Nothing matters more than the relationship we have with God. There is no relationship on earth that is more important, there is no "thing" on Earth that is more important, and there is no purpose on earth greater than what the Spirit moves us to do in His name. Helping our student-athletes understand the depths of their soul will guide them to a fulfilling, successful future.

The success of a high school athlete can be measured with exit interviews that pose the following questions. *Do you feel visible? Explain why or why not. Do you believe you have value? Explain why or why not. Do you believe there is vali-*

*dation for who you are and what you are doing? Explain why or why not.* As with the circled sticker exercise conducted by myself and my co-workers some years ago, so too can we identify which student-athletes have gotten the most out of their high school education. The purpose of high school athletics reaches far beyond winning and losing, far beyond the scoreboard.

*Part Five*
# EFFECT OF YOUTH SPORTS

# A HOPEFUL BEGINNING

*It is paradoxical that many educators and parents still differentiate between a time for learning and a time for play without seeing the vital connection between them.*
    Leo Buscaglia

    The examination of youth sports and its relationship to high school sports is intriguing. There is a direct correlation between the two. In fact, it is the foundation to any mission statement of a youth sports program directly linked to a high school athletic program: preparing elementary and middle school aged athletes to participate in the high school program. Independent programs, such as those supported by the YMCA, reflect their own values and not those of any affiliate. In any case, the benefits of youth sports are many. In contrast, especially in the last 20 years, we have seen the drawbacks youth sports can have in the development of a positive sense of self-worth.
    The lasting negative effects of participation in youth sports are many. They range from adults overemphasizing its importance to the divisive competition that arises amongst peer groups. At one point in the history of athletics the values were properly aligned with the expectations. But as athletics has evolved into being fiercely competitive at all levels, from professional sports right down to elementary youth programs,

there has been an increasingly underestimated misalignment of values. The development of these misaligned values begins as early as 5$^{th}$ grade for both athletes and parents.

The importance of youth sports for many parents and athletes can be lasting as well. Positive outcomes of involvement in youth sports include learning effective collaboration strategies and the value of sportsmanship. At its fundamental purpose, athletics, throughout history, have been a vehicle for teaching and learning skills in adverse situations that cannot be simulated in any type of classroom setting. Furthermore, character building has always been a trait of athletics. There is a need in our society to get back to identifying what is truly important about participation in youth sports. The realignment of values is necessary for the mental health of both parents and children. Youth sports have their place in our society, but only with healthy and proper motivation by the adults overseeing such activities.

There are two distinctive groups at very different developmental stages of youth sports. Children in grades pre-k through fourth grade and their parents are involved for several different reasons. For the most part, the children who fall into this category are motivated by healthy reasons. Children in grades five through eight and their parents begin to be drawn by the poisons of youth sports. At this stage of development, there are increasingly fewer kids participating because of the negative sense of self-worth that begins to emerge in youth sports.

Directly correlated to these two distinctive groups is the development of the brain. Certainly the surge of hormones children experience in grades five through eight plays a large part in their sense of self-worth. The emotional development of each child of this particular age group coupled with their emerging identity can be a telling sign as to why some kids choose other activities outside of youth sports. The younger of the two groups is not consciously aware of the impact of identity and the inner uniqueness each has within. If and when they do become aware that they are "different" in terms of their skill level set in youth sports, they don't often

## A HOPEFUL BEGINNING

associate that with failure or being "outed" from their social group.

I have volunteered to coach both Brooklyn and Dawson. I have coached both of my children in soccer at the pre-K and Kindergarten levels. I have recently volunteered to coach Brooklyn in a basketball program sponsored by the YMCA. The dynamics of my experiences with my children in these settings are quite interesting. I have learned a lot about the various idiosyncrasies of coaching very young children; this in stark contrast to my tenure as a varsity head coach at the high school level working with young adults ages 14 – 18. These experiences, juxtaposed, provide wonderful insights in developing a sense of what values are important at all levels of development and, furthermore, how misaligned our values have become.

Yes, I have been an accomplice in the misalignment of values. Maybe I am a product of believing in what society deems important in terms of youth sports and high school athletics. The general public simply understands the scoreboard, the difference between winning and losing. Championships, trophies, and attention, all of which are perceived to be important by teams, players, coaches, schools, and communities, are the beginning of the misaligned values. However, I have a much better perspective now. I do understand that what we are seeing as a society is a disturbing trend of selfish acts that cause emotional and developmental damage to our children.

I have had the opportunity to both oversee a youth program and be a volunteer coach in a youth program. In coaching Brooklyn and Dawson in soccer I have grown to appreciate the innocence in which these kids approach sport. It is fun. It is a game. They don't have insecurities about their talents, they don't have expectations in regards to their own ability or the ability of their teammates, and the amount of time committed to the sport at this age is very limited. I know that my children have enjoyed being with the team, practicing a little, and competing a little. The early stages of learning commitment, work ethic, and teamwork begin to take form.

In youth sport, pre-K through fourth grade, all of the children participate in the games. Some kids are interested while some others would rather chase butterflies or stomp their feet in a mud hole. There is a genuine opportunity for volunteer coaches to model the celebration of hard work. Giving high fives to each other and showing genuine excitement to each other when a task is completed are both good ways in which coaches can begin to develop a positive sense of self-worth for the children participating. In any case, this is where the purest form of the purpose of athletics can be captured. It's maintaining this purpose that begins to fade with time.

The basketball program sponsored by the YMCA that Brooklyn and Dawson are involved in has done its best at maintaining a culture of appropriate athletic values when it comes to youth sports. I have volunteered to coach both Brooklyn's team and Dawson's team. All of the children participating in this program are between the ages of five and ten. The directive given by the leaders of the local YMCA have emphasized a value/idea of the day. Each value is identified by a word that the coaches must emphasize to the children. The five points of emphasis in the YMCA's program are sportsmanship, caring, honesty, respect, and responsibility. My hope is that each parent coach who has volunteered promotes these ideas. However, my fear is that there are other agendas on the minds of some parents.

**Emphasis of Youth Sports:**
*Sportsmanship*
*Caring*
*Honesty*
*Respect*
*Responsibility*

The values promoted by the YMCA are fundamental to emotional and psychological development of all kids. Because the YMCA is not affiliated with any high school sports program, it can stand on its own behind a shield of principles that protects children from the bombardment of fleeting ideologies that promote winning. Learning is not in the winning; learning is in the preparation. As a head varsity basketball coach, our coaching staff always prepared our teams to win, but we believed we would win under similar principles emphasized by the YMCA youth program. When parents, athletes, and coaches are willing to stand on such principles, winning is an attainable goal. Proper values must be in place early on and emphasized for children who participate to get the most out of their experience.

There is a general belief among some parents that if their children don't start participating at a very young age, they will be left out when they get to high school. They feel that their children will be too far behind if they first get started in sixth grade. The hardest part of this insecurity is the admission that they are right. If kids first begin to take an interest in basketball in sixth grade, it is quite possible that they will be five years behind the other children participating. Given the amount of camps, leagues, and youth tournaments that have occurred in those five to seven years the children first attempting the sport in sixth grade have a slim chance at competing with other kids at their grade level.

The pressure that parents feel to get their kids involved early because of something that may or may not happen some 10 years into the future is then projected onto the children. Some children are wired to flourish under this pressure. But, what if they fail early in elementary school? What then becomes of their positive sense of self-worth? On the other hand, what if they experience a tremendous amount of success early in elementary school? What then becomes of their ego and the search for their inner uniqueness?

It is easy to understand the distinct connection between youth sports programs and high school athletic programs. It actually presents quite an interesting riddle. What energy force needs the influx of youth and excitement channeled into honing skills to create excellence; and what energy force needs a greater purpose, a highly valued, visible commodity to feed its growth? The energy force in the first part of the riddle is high school athletics, and in the second part of the riddle the energy force is youth sports programs. It is the quintessential conundrum. What keeps the high school athletic program alive and thriving is the youth program feeding it. What keeps the youth program alive and thriving is the high school athletic program it feeds.

To a person, high school head coaches will answer, when asked what the most important part of success is, that building a foundation of skill sets through a youth program is a priority. A coach who does not put his time into supporting a youth program is not helping the high school athletic program. The head coach of a high school athletic program should be considered the expert in that school district for that sport. It is the responsibility of the head coach to recruit volunteer coaches and train them to act in accordance to the program's mission statement. It is also the responsibility of the head coach to interact with all of those youth participants whenever possible. This is a difficult task and the very reason why there needs to be volunteer coaches and a mission statement to keep everyone in the program on the same page.

The evolution of youth sports has drastically altered the landscape of high school athletics. The expectations for winning are greater, the pressure to succeed continues to mount, and the values are becoming increasingly misaligned. The pressurized expectations are affecting coaches, student-athletes, and parents. At one point in time the benefits of youth sports far outweighed the negative effects. However, due to the distorted expectations, there has been a shift in the outcomes of children who participate in youth sports.

Our vision needs to be adjusted and the reins pulled in, to truly help our youth find their passion, to strengthen their weaknesses and accentuate their strengths. Youth sports must be the opportunity adults take to help children mature, with the ability to problem solve and make good decisions about their lives. It is time to realign our values with what youth sports is essentially about: developing a positive sense of self-worth in a committed collaboration among peers with adults, void of ego, as the guides. It is time to tip the scales away from the drawbacks of youth sports in favor of the benefits youth sports can provide.

# BUILDING A STRONG FOUNDATION

*Love yourself—accept yourself—forgive yourself—and be good to yourself, because without you the rest of us are without a source of many wonderful things.*
    Leo Buscaglia

    The evolution of organized youth sports is a growing phenomenon. Today, youth sports are at an all time high in regards to participation. According to a CNN.com report by Laura Hilgers in June of 2006, there were "an estimated 41 million American kids playing competitive youth sports." The Centers of Disease Control and Prevention promote active lifestyles for the enhancement of youth health. In fact, the CDC makes recommendations for communities to increase activity among children to prevent childhood obesity hoping to limit the increasing number of young diabetics being diagnosed in America. The popularity of youth sports provides adults a great opportunity to teach lifelong lessons, and to prepare kids emotionally and physically for their futures.
    Benefits of youth sports are many. Along with being a positive activity to promote a healthy lifestyle, youth sports are an opportunity for children to understand the dynamics of socialization, sportsmanship, commitment, as well as to begin the discovery of their inner passion. Children who participate in multiple activities, in which youth sports are just a portion

of these activities, will have the best chance at a balanced, healthy lifestyle. This balance provides an understanding of one's uniqueness, strengths, and weaknesses. Children will have the capacity to share their talents much better when they know, through involvement in an array of activities, God's beauty within.

Children in elementary school need to be exposed to a variety of activities. The exposure will help them better understand themselves and their role within the world. At a very fundamental level, youth sports are an opportunity for socialization. I know that when Brooklyn gets to her activity, whether it is dance class, YMCA basketball, youth soccer, Girl Scouts, or youth softball her first priority is to figure out which friends are present with her.

Youth sports provide opportunities to build on friendships already established as well as create a safe environment for children to meet new friends. The dynamics of this socialization has a tremendous impact on how children will learn to work cooperatively. Furthermore, the connections created with adults and peers in an environment that promotes healthy relationships will lend children the power of confidence. This acquired confidence will also give children the tools to react to adversity properly. Adults have the opportunity and obligation to model appropriate behavior in regards to positive relationships and reacting appropriately to disagreements. Building a network of positive relationships when children are young will provide them with support as they are faced with tough choices later on in the adolescent stage of development.

As children build relationships in youth sports, they will undoubtedly have fun, the root of all games and play. In elementary school, children enjoy gym class, recess, and games within the classroom because they all provide a form of play. Playing is fun. There are days when Brooklyn's favorite part of school is coming home so she can play with her little brother. Building positive relationships in healthy environments, such as we see in our schools, gives kids another opportunity to have fun. When children find that a certain activity is no longer fun, they begin to withdraw from that particular activity. Youth sports can be, and should be, fun.

Adults can mask teaching lessons when children are having fun. As a coach of high school student-athletes, I used a similar idea. Conditioning isn't always fun, so the coaching staff would "hide" the conditioning within the skill drills. There was a purpose, then, according to the student-athletes, to the increase in their cardio activity. They didn't just have to run and run and run as a separate drill. They were conditioning throughout the entire practice.

The lessons of commitment and sportsmanship can have long lasting affects for children. These lessons can be learned within the parameters of youth sports. When children are having fun, adults can take such moments to teach valuable strategies for success. Commitment provides children with an attitude of seeing something through to its end. It also provides a measure of accountability to coaches and peers. This accountability adds to the social framework of building relationships. Sportsmanship provides an internal respect for others, a respect for the game, and displays value in self and others.

My father always told me that when I started something I had to finish it. The implications of this rule are infinite. For example, I remember in the Pinewood Derby in Cub Scouts, I was working on my derby car and was really excited about the idea, initially. Knowing the amount of work involved and that I wasn't getting immediate results, I wanted my father to just finish it for me. That was unacceptable. This applied to youth sports as well. Any time I started something, I was expected to finish it. That is commitment.

Commitment also means that I am responsible to myself and to others. In my job, I am responsible to the students I teach, my colleagues, and the community. Youth sports can begin the foundation of commitment by teaching the importance of roles. Children don't really appreciate the idea of roles until third grade; they don't necessarily grasp the idea that a team counts on all of its members to do certain parts. It is never too early to start emphasizing this component, because some children are ready for it sooner than others.

Commitment to self, by being present and seeing an activity through to its end, and commitment to others, by accepting and fulfilling a certain role, is an important lesson to learn. Youth sports provide the opportunity for adults to model and teach commitment.

Equally important is the modeling of sportsmanship. Learning that everyone is equally important is valuable. Remember, it is under one hand that we were all created. God has

**Benefits of Youth Sports**

- Promote Healthy, Active Lifestyle
- Build Positive Relationships
- Valuing Self and Others
- Commitment to Self and Others
- The Roots of an Emerging Positive Sense of Self-Worth

provided us the model of sportsmanship by accepting and loving all of us equally. It is inherent in each of us that we have the capacity to respect others as we respect ourselves. A major benefit of youth sports is teaching sportsmanship.

Early on in elementary school, sportsmanship is in the form of respecting the importance of each individual. There is a genuine care for the success of each person in the activity. Thus begins the conception of positive sense of self-worth. Anytime a person can care for someone else there is value for each person. In coaching youth soccer and youth basketball, it is important that each child has equal opportunities in drills and in games. Therefore, one child does not get preference over another child. Equal opportunity promotes a respect for each other early in elementary aged participants.

As children grow into the latter stages of elementary school, middle school, and high school there are lessons to be learned in sportsmanship in terms of winning and losing. Our competitive drive, our ego, does not like to lose. However, in sport there is always a winner and a loser. Brooklyn told me once, when participating in bowling at a friend's birthday party, that she was the third winner. I really like that terminology, rather than loser. Truthfully, there are lessons to be learned in winning and losing.

I know that, as a high school coach for many years, it is the ultimate goal to win, to outscore our opponent. However, there were times when, even in winning, maybe we weren't gracious winners, or we lacked confidence, or we felt sorry for ourselves for various reasons. Everything is not always perfect in winning. I believe that in most youth competitions, children are putting forth what they know to be their best effort. If that is the case, then there really is no "losing." Sure, maybe we didn't outscore our opponent, but if we did the things we set out to do with our best effort, then we certainly did accomplish something.

As winners it is important to recognize the effort of everybody. It is just a game. There are much more important victories in life. For instance, the woman who has defeated breast cancer or the relationships that have survived the test of time and have been connected on a deep emotional level are greater victories than any soccer game in fifth grade. Even more, we can look at the person who is the first in the family to attend college and earn a college degree as a much greater accomplishment than winning a conference championship in high school.

If the lessons of youth sports contributed in any way to the victories of life, then youth sports is a viable, much needed, component of youth development. Sportsmanship can pave the way for genuine respect. It can then add to a positive sense of self-worth which should be at its fundamental purpose. Respect of self and others is an important ingredient in working collaboratively with others. In making contributions to the group, a positive sense of self-worth is created and resonates throughout life.

The most important element of youth sports that is beneficial in a child's development and hinges upon the recognition of a positive sense of self-worth is finding the passion that God created for each of us. Upon our creation, God had an intended purpose for each of us. We all have a role to play in the universe and there are many ways to uncover this inner uniqueness.  First, children must be exposed to a plethora of activities and opportunities that highlight their strengths and weaknesses.  Second, we must control the ego's pollution of our identity.

In order for children to understand their purpose they need to be involved in many activities.  Brooklyn has been involved in dance, music, Girl Scouts, and various youth sports.  In observing her interest, or lack thereof, in any of these areas, Desiree and I are able to help guide her.  Through prayer and reflection, we are able to help process her greatest interests.  Her strengths might not yet be her favorite interests.

Brooklyn has a wonderfully creative, imaginative mind.  She is also sensitive to the needs of others, sometimes more than her own.  My daughter is also at a point of enjoying the social elements of school and other organized activities.  She is exceptional in drawing, coloring, and pretending.  She has an intrigue to plunk around on the piano, strum a guitar, and bang on drums.  Brooklyn is highly in tune to the emotional swings of her peers and attempts to make them comfortable and also has an interest, so far, in softball, soccer, and basketball.  Her interest in these sports is not for the sport alone, it is for the social dynamics; it is another opportunity to be with her friends on a very different level.

There is no saying if and when all of this might shift for Brooklyn.  However, as parents, we wouldn't know what we know about her if she wasn't involved in a variety of activities.  For our children to find their passion, it is important to expose them to a multitude of activities in many different arenas of life.  Some people don't figure this stuff out until later on in life.  The sooner we can help our children find their inner uniqueness, the sooner our children will develop confidence and internal motivation to succeed.  In sharing their talents, our children will develop and maintain a positive sense of self.

Youth sports must provide children an opportunity to explore themselves.  The amount of children participating in youth sports and the parents working with them must help kids recognize the life lessons to be learned.  Youth sports provide positive activities for children that promote an active, healthy lifestyle.  There are lessons to be gained in commitment, sportsmanship and the dynamics of cooperation. Mostly, children have the opportunity to explore who they are, determine their strengths and weaknesses, and share their talents as God intended. When applied correctly, valued appropriately, and kept in perspective youth sports is a benefit to every child.

# POTENTIAL DESTRUCTION

*Our prime purpose in this life is to help others. And if you can't help them, at least don't hurt them.*
   *Dalai Lama*

    As youth sports has evolved from activities designed to just keep young boys out of trouble in the early part of the 20th century to an all encompassing, competitive beast of the ego, the drawbacks have increased. At one time, the benefits were that children had a safe place to hang out, be competitive, and stay out of trouble. Many adults then saw the positive impact youth sports were having on children in terms of their character development. An increased demand for more sports and more participants ensued.
    The after school programs then turned into intramural programs which then led to the interscholastic programs we see in high schools today. In constructing my own ideas on these topics I have consulted several high school student-athletes. I asked them about both the benefits and drawbacks of youth sports. All of them included one or more of the ideas I had already presumed as the benefits to youth sports. In addition to what I have outlined as benefits, a couple of them responded that youth sports provided a knowledge base to what was expected in the high school sports program. These student-athletes listed many more drawbacks than benefits.

# POTENTIAL DESTRUCTION

This is a disturbing observation knowing the number of children involved in youth sports today.

I believe that many adults give lip service to the benefits of youth sports, but the pressure adults put on children to "be the best" is concerning. The modeling of commitment, sportsmanship, and collaboration is decreasing, while high stakes competition, deceit, and win at all cost is increasing. We have lost touch with the roots of organized youth sports. Today, there is organization to a fault. Parents believe that youth sports are a vehicle to high school success, recognition, and even money (i.e., athletic scholarships, etc).

In talking with friends that have children in the latter stages of elementary school and middle school that are involved in youth sports, it makes my stomach turn to hear of the pressure parents and children feel. I truly believe that parents feel it much more than the children. However, the children can sense the pressure, and eventually will act out as a result. Our values need to be reestablished to properly promote growth, emotionally and physically, among our children.

Youth sports provide many opportunities for adults to teach life lessons. The drawback to this is that parents become overly involved. Children become dependent upon the adults to organize play. What is lost in all of this is the creativity for children to make rules themselves, abide by the rules of the group, and play. There is too much organization from adults.

Certainly adults can provide a safe, healthy environment for children to participate in youth sports. But, when parents make it more about them and not the children there is a problem. In talking with several high school student-athletes a common response when asked about the drawbacks of youth sports was that parents often forced them to play. As result of this applied pressure, children begin to hate the sport and withdraw. All of us have in common the need to make our parents proud. If we feel as though we are failing our parents, one of the coping mechanisms is to withdraw. This only creates bitterness and resentment in the important relationship between parent and child. It does not build a positive sense of self-worth.

Parents do need to expose their children to many activities. There is a fine line between teaching kids the life lesson of commitment and forcing them to participate when they really are not moved to do so. Parents need to embrace their children's interests for the sake of their children, not for themselves. In contrast, parents need to steer their children away from things that perpetuate a negative self image. The only way to do either of these things is to expose children to many opportunities.

Along the line of thinking that children do need to be exposed to many activities, when asked about drawbacks of youth sports, many high school student-athletes admit that the time commitment is challenging. When I was a child, there were not as many programs readily available for youth as there are today because the expectations were very different. Summer time was my own time. That is, until I got to high school. I never felt the pressure of time. Today's children are burdened with the time constraints that youth sports presents. Parents must be aware of the possibility of burn out in their children.

Parents that become too involved with their children in youth sports become obsessed with the success and failure of their child. These parents teach the wrong lesson to their children. When success is accomplished, parents gloat in the glow of the accomplishment. When failure occurs, instead of looking within and helping the child to look within, parents model finger pointing. It becomes the coach's fault, or worse, the fault of the other members of the team. Any time we can deflect responsibility for our actions on others, we feel much safer. This does not make it right. We have to control our ego to learn from our own mistakes, own them, and make ourselves better people.

> Parents:
> Embrace your children's interests for the sake of your children.

The overzealous parent who then coaches their children in youth sports creates an absolute disaster. There is a need for volunteer coaches in youth sports. Most often these volunteer coaches are parents of the children involved. It is important that volunteer coaches are given the appropriate tools to be successful and to act void of ego. The National Alliance for Youth Sports has compiled a plethora of information for parents, youth coaches, and athletes to properly guide all involved in youth sports in their report entitled *National Standards for Youth Sports, 2008 edition*. This resource, along with proper guidance from trained high school coaches, can provide the proper perspective for youth coaches to establish a healthy, learning environment for children.

As children grow into the middle school stage and on into high school, they begin to sense divisions based on athletic ability, academic ability, and socio-economic status. In my discussions with high school athletes, more than one expressed the idea of "politics" in youth sports. Children who didn't have a parent volunteer as coach felt that the children who did have a parent volunteer received preferential treatment. Furthermore, when pushed to define politics, most student-athletes responded by saying there were hidden agendas or plans by parents and that parents influence the high school coach. Ugh....politics. Children understanding the concept of rhetoric and hidden plans within the framework of youth sports that is supposed to be fun.

The politics and belief that there is something hidden, beyond the control of performance, that dictates who plays and who doesn't play does begin to take the fun out of sport. It also perpetuates a sense of dishonesty. In fact, it promotes what some might consider "sucking up" to the coach. All of it, in its summation, leads to divisive competition among peers. Children begin to view each other differently based on their own parent's perceptions and expectations.

The children that are forced to play youth sports by overzealous parents begin to hate their sport. The unfortunate result of this is a growing apathy in regards to athletics. Because they are forced to play something they don't want to play, they lose interest, don't care, then begin to be questioned by their peers. The kids who are passionate about the sport become disgruntled with the kids who don't care. Added to the pressure from home, these children then experience peer pressure. There is no development of self-worth. In fact, in cases like these there may even develop a negative sense of self-worth. The worst part of all this might be the fact that these children lose the opportunity to learn life lessons through participating in athletics.

The pressure from peers can be relentless. Some children may want to participate in youth sports because their friends are involved. It is possible that, in order to feel important and accepted, children will participate in activities that are not interesting. Some children find themselves getting sucked into participating from peers and parents. There are even cases when children feel pressure from siblings that have gone before them. Living in the shadow of siblings that were talented in athletics can be detrimental to emotional development. If an older sibling has set a high standard in athletics, some children feel the pressure to live up to that standard.

I have seen children handle the pressure from home better than peer pressure. I have observed student-athletes that were best friends through elementary school and when it came time to compete athletically with their best friend, a gigantic wedge was placed in the middle of the friendship. A bitter, divisive relationship emerged. The competition between teams and teammates so often accepted and encouraged in youth sports can present problems in relationship development. Learning how to develop appropriate relationships is then inhibited.

The development of "A" teams and "B" teams, while it does give more children the opportunity to participate, it also perpetuates an unhealthy divisiveness between peers. I suppose it might be argued that, academically, students should be challenged to reach their maximum potential. If they need to be in an accelerated class to reach their potential, then that is where they should be placed. Children should be placed in groups where they can achieve the maximum amount of success. The idea in youth sports, however, can be explosive. Parents and coaches need to help children process who they are, what their role is, and how to react to such situations. When not processed out appropriately, children develop a poor sense of self on one end, on the other end is the child who inflates his ego and attaches his identity to attention that is, at best, fleeting.

All of these drawbacks lead to the misaligned values that youth sports have come to embrace. The focus of youth organizations such as the YMCA and the National Alliance for Youth Sports is to promote what is in the best interest of the children. The outlines provided by such groups are useful. However, appropriate action must take place in order for the proper values to be personified. Many adults will articulate that the benefits of youth sports are character development and learning life lessons. The real benefits, though, as perceived by some of these same adults include winning, performance in high school, and possibly athletic scholarships to Division 1 or Division 2 Universities.

The misguided perception that winning in youth sports will equal similar results in high school is utterly ridiculous. Ultimately, there is no correlation between youth teams that win and the high school program. Winning comes from developing a spiritual connectedness to self. Helping our children identify what their true talents are will help them succeed, win. Teams that are made up of participants that completely understand their role will find the most success. Understanding and accepting the role are two very different concepts. The winning comes with acceptance.

In no way, shape, or form should any coach, volunteer or paid, youth coach or high school coach, accept winning over learning. I would much rather have the players on teams I have coached be better prepared for the world, than win. Can both exist together? Absolutely! The best teams I have had the opportunity to coach were made up of individuals that maybe weren't the most skilled student-athletes, but they understood their role.

Coaches:
Always promote learning over winning...always.

I once had the opportunity to be the head coach of an All-Star team. The team was made up of "the best" skilled players in our Division in our part of the state. I had watched these All-Star teams play against each other in previous years and noticed that the teams that were the most successful, that won the games between the North and the South, were the teams that understood their roles. Even amongst elite players, roles need to be defined. As a coaching staff, in less than a week, we were able to help our elite athletes understand their role to maximize the team's potential. As a result, we won the game. More importantly, we were able to help these kids develop positive working relationships with complete strangers.

Learning is, by far, the most important objective of any sports program, youth or otherwise. Giving children the tools to recognize their egos and control it is priceless. Knowing what is important in athletics will help our children develop a positive sense of self-worth. The value of youth sports is not in winning or fielding a winning team. The value in youth sports must go way back to its roots. Give children the opportunity to be a part of a positive experience that encourages growth as people. Accentuate the strengths of each other and help build up the weaknesses.

With high expectations and unrealistic standards, it is no wonder young children begin to withdraw from sports. It is no wonder there is no progress made in building a positive sense of self-worth. The apathy that children begin to develop toward sports coupled with the emotional withdrawing from friends and other activities should be a red flag to all adults. We need to reestablish values that promote a spiritual connectedness with the universe. This might seem overwhelming, but it's not. As adults, when we can let go of our own insecurities, check our ego to allow our inner uniqueness to shine a spirit of compassion on our children, then we can really help to develop the leaders of tomorrow in a world that needs more selfless people. If properly managed and applied, youth sports can be a valuable tool in this development.

*Part Six*
# BUILDING A MISSION STATEMENT

# THE MISSION

*Management must speak with one voice. When it doesn't management itself becomes a peripheral opponent to the team's mission.*
   *Pat Riley*

Every high school athletic department must have a mission statement to serve as a compass. The mission statement can be used as a guide for the application of policy and procedure. The expectations of the coaches, student-athletes, and parents must be outlined within the mission statement. When concerns among coaches, parents, and athletic directors are raised, referring to sound guidelines can save many people a lot of grief. The creation of a mission statement is a proactive approach to administering and managing high school athletic programs.

Using the athletic department's mission statement as a model, each high school athletic program must have its own guidelines. All mission statements, athletic departments as a whole or specific high school athletic programs, must reflect the vision of a collaborative group of people. The group must be comprised of parents, student-athletes, coaches, and athletic directors. A collective vision for the expected outcome of each athletic program will formulate a healthy relationship between schools and communities

# THE MISSION

Heading into my second year as a head coach I knew I needed a mission statement to serve as a guide for the vision of the program. I had gotten the idea from a dear friend of mine who had been a varsity girls basketball coach at another school in our conference. I used her mission statement as the basis for creating one for our program. Along with my coaching staff and a few parents in the program, using my friend's mission statement as a resource, we created one for our program.

I handed out the mission statement each year to all varsity basketball players and their parents. I also worked with the junior varsity coach to create a mission for the junior varsity portion of the program. Parents often referred to the mission statement in regards to the programs beliefs, values, and procedures. The ideas that follow here are taken directly from the mission statement created for our basketball program.

Our mission statement began with a statement of intention. It is the intent of the program to teach life skills and basketball skills which provide opportunities for success. As a team, the coaching staff will always model and encourage the following four objectives:

1. **We are going to play hard.** Anything less than 100% cheats the team and the individual.
2. **We are going to play smart.** We must play within the team structure and recognize individual abilities and limitations. We must understand team objectives and carry out the plan of the coach.
3. **We are going to play together.** We will celebrate all team victories, large or small, and we will celebrate the success of the team, always. The success of the team is the greatest feat in team sports.
4. **We will have fun.** Basketball is a game to be enjoyed. However, fun is the result of hard work!

I believe the student-athletes in our program must be respected as people. Reciprocally, the athletes must respect their parents, teachers, coaches, teammates and officials at all times; respect breeds respect. The lasting impression we, as a coaching staff, want the athletes that come through this program to have is one of pride, accomplishment, and strength in self-worth. The coaching staff and all others associated with the program will promote a positive attitude, high expectations of character, honesty, and integrity.

The next section of the mission statement addresses the significance of being a team player. Effective collaboration is one of the most important life skills that can be modeled and taught through high school team sports. Every student-athlete must commit herself, wholeheartedly, to the team concept – physically, mentally, and emotionally – if the team is going to reach its highest potential and succeed. It only takes one person with her own selfish interests to ruin the delicate balance of trust. From the most dominant player to the least dominant player, each must not believe they deserve more awards, recognition, or playing time. We must strive for a unified vision through team chemistry and loyalty.

All players must understand that the varsity level is highly competitive. Each player must understand and accept the role she has on the team. The coaching staff will be straightforward regarding team issues. Not all players can start. Not all players will play in every game. However, all players are key ingredients to molding a strong team. It is the responsibility of the coaching staff to explain team roles to each player. I believe that good things will happen for our program during our season if we believe in and work with each other.

The practice of discussing roles with student-athletes then led into the longest section of the mission statement: *communication*. Communication only occurs when a message is sent and that message is received. You can send all you want but, until the message is received, understood, and acted upon, communication has not taken place. If any team function is to be successful, it must have constant communication, which will avoid misunderstandings and hurt feelings.

I will be straightforward concerning team issues. I will discuss situations with players that may need improvement, change, or encouragement. I believe in communication as a vital ingredient to success and human development. I will communicate with all student-athletes when appropriate and necessary; remember, communication is a two way process (sender and receiver).

## THE MISSION

As a coach I must look out for the best interest of the team. Since players do not always like what they hear and share these thoughts at home, mixed messages develop along with a false sense of reality and a false sense of self. Players might respond to questions by family members with, "I don't know, the coach won't talk to me." This chain of events sets into motion powerful feelings of anger and resentment toward the coach. Often times this leads the parent to coaching his/her daughter which is to the detriment of the team, not to mention the student-athlete. This creates divided loyalties, cliques, drives wedges between the student-athletes, and destroys team chemistry.

How much better would it be if parents reserved comment to themselves and told their child to fix the problem with the coach? Remember it is part of our mission to teach life skills – communication is an extremely important life skill. When adults have problems or concerns with their boss, they must address it with the boss. How much better would it be if parents said to me, "Coach, can we talk about the expectations we have for my child?" The coaching staff does not expect our student-athletes to be looking in the bleachers for guidance during any game. As a coaching staff, it is our job to coach. In order to do that we must have the undivided attention of each and every one of the student-athletes at all times.

Furthermore, the coaching staff is always willing to discuss issues with both the players and their parents. If parents have a concern at any time throughout the season, they should contact the coach to set up an appointment to meet. We might not agree on the solution, but we can agree to disagree, and still work together to accomplish success for the student-athletes within the framework of the program. Anything can be discussed as long as it is done in an attitude of mutual respect. Good communication between player/coach and parent/coach must be modeled and can proactively eliminate problems. When issues arise, I request that the player accompany the parents. The coaching staff will be honest with the players and their parents. I do not want the players or parents to feel that there is something going on behind their backs.

Communication between a player and a coach can consist of praise, instruction, and information. All of these messages can be conveyed in a friendly tone or as constructive criticism. Oddly enough, it seems that players only remember the criticism. The coaching staff will always encourage the student-athletes, concerning criticism, to listen to what is being said and not how it is being said. Players often times think of it as an adversarial relationship instead of speaking the truth from the heart -- a comment or criticism actually designed to help the student-athlete learn a life lesson or, simply, to improve. The relationship that is developed is professional and, therefore, the criticism is not personal.

Positive feelings about one's ability and the desire to earn more playing time are admirable qualities; however, it is part of the coaching staff's job to define roles for players and determine who should play -- why and when. On game nights, we will play the players who give our team the best opportunity to be competitive and successful.

Often times players work hard in practice and make significant contributions to the team's success but hardly get the opportunities in games because of another player's ability or the talent of the opponent. I firmly believe that these players are just as important to the team's success because, in practice every day, they push the players that see the most playing time. It is also highly unjust of me to "throw" a player into a game situation if I feel it is a situation that will limit her success. Playing in a game where the competition is ahead of a player's ability does more to damage a player's confidence than build a positive sense of self-worth.

There are many reasons that factor into the decision-making process of who plays and why. When in doubt of such decisions please reflect on the following guidelines:

- Give the benefit of the doubt to the coaching staff; avoid prejudging the situation.
- Keep any personal, negative comments to yourself. Address the issue in private with the coaching staff.
- Encourage your child to talk to the coaching staff to work

## THE MISSION

it out. Give your child a chance to grow and learn a valuable life-lesson from the situation.
- Be Patient. Give it time.
- Do not "bad-mouth" a player, the coaching staff, or the program in the stands. If we are all not a part of finding solutions to resolve conflict, we are a part of the problem

If at any time parents make derogatory or negative comments about the coaching staff, one of the players, the team, or the program children are learning the wrong lesson on how to handle a concern or a conflict. As a result, the student-athlete will question teammates and the coaching staff. What will happen is the very thing parents are trying to avoid; parents can and will affect the student-athlete's performance because of a negative attitude and negative mind set.

Following the section on communication in our mission statement was an outline for ethical behavior. We entitled this section our *Code of Ethics* for the program. We had identified five specific elements to emphasize in our code of ethics. These are not an exhaustive list of ethics by any means. This list reflects the ethics that the coaching staff believed were essential to address with the student-athletes and parents in our program.

First, all student-athletes are to conduct their behavior in an acceptable, appropriate manner at all times. If you think you are doing something wrong, you probably are. Ask yourself, "Is this the right thing to do?" Second, strive for your maximum potential in the classroom. All athletes are students first. All student-athletes are enrolled in school to get an education. Use this opportunity to be educated in the classroom and on the basketball floor. Third, be punctual; being on time sets a great example. As we mature into adulthood time is an expectation for all of us; people are counting on us daily and it is our responsibility to meet our deadlines and to be present when we are expected. Fourth, be respectful. It is essential that we always display positive sportsmanship. We must respect ourselves, officials, coaches, parents, teammates, and our opponent. Finally, celebrate hard work. Share in the success of others with enthusiasm. Be genuine in your desire for your teammates to succeed. Stand to cheer on your teammates after a score or great defensive play.

**Code of Ethics for Student-Athletes**

| | |
|---|---|
| 1. **Behavior** | appropriate at all times in all situations |
| 2. **Max Potential** | make best effort in classroom and on court |
| 3. **Punctuality** | know that people are counting on you |
| 4. **Respect** | respect everyone, including self |
| 5. **Celebrate Hard Work** | acknowledge the successes of all people |

After defining the code of ethics in our mission statement, the ensuing sections outlined the expectations of the players during practice, on bus trips, activity prior to a game, during the game itself, and the conduct of the players on the bench. A few of the highlights from this section included things like being courteous to opponents, officials, and fans at all times; never verbally or physically respond if provoked; use appropriate language at all times; and, never express verbal, facial, or bodily displeasure with an official or coach. There was also an emphasis on student-athletes accepting the coaching staff's decisions in regards to game situations or substitutions. Student-athletes were always encouraged to hold comments and questions for the coaching staff in regards to substitutions and the like until after the game.

Practice expectations really set the tone for the entire program. If our teams are well prepared, they certainly have a much better chance at being successful. Proper preparation is a key ingredient to success and a well learned life lesson. We must take advantage of the practice time we have planned. The attitudes and work ethic of our practice sessions set the groundwork for our season.

Our section of the mission statement for practice expectations included five targets of emphasis. Punctuality is an absolute must. Whatever the starting time all players are to be dressed and ready to go five minutes prior to practice. Players who need to be late, for school or family reasons, must clear it with the coach prior to practice. Secondly, when players take the floor for practice, all non-basketball related conversations must come to a close. Basketball is the only topic of conversation during practice time. Next, all players must be in appropriate practice gear. All players must have their previously issued practice jersey. The entire team will enter practice wearing the same colored practice jersey. We are a team. Our fourth target emphasized that every player must perform every drill with the same effort and intensity that she would put into the most important game. Finally, the coaching staff emphasized to all student-athletes that if we are to perform our best at all times, then we must strive to execute perfectly during our practices.

**Practice Emphasis: Five Targets**

1. Punctuality
2. Focus
3. Appropriate Attire
4. Intensity
5. Purposeful Execution

All of these ideas had to be emphasized by all coaches at all levels of the program. I believed that we all did have a unified vision of success. Because of this unity, I believed it was important that all players were treated equally in development of their positive sense of self-worth. There were several examples of this emphasis in our mission statement. Two stand out more than others. First, falling under the category of *bus conduct*, the coaching staff required all players at the Varsity and Junior Varsity levels to ride the player bus to and from games. Being together when we win and when we lose teaches us to be strong and unite in exciting and adverse times. The second example was independent of any other section. The heading read *Loyalty to Your Teammates*. No member of our program will publicly criticize another member of the program. As a member of the team, your first loyalty is to your teammates and your coaches.

In fact, I believe that a mission statement has to have a few clear cut disciplinary procedures outlined that address concerns. A mission statement needs to hold some weight. I suppose it is easy to describe what a program should be and how members of the program should conduct themselves. Well, what if members of the program aren't conducting themselves in accordance to the mission statement? In what we developed as our guidelines, we added a small section that explained disciplinary procedure.

Our mission statement identified five situations of conduct and poor decision making that could result in temporary, and in extreme cases, permanent suspension from the team. First, and foremost, was an athletic code violation. Use of tobacco, alcohol, or any other illegal substances would fall into this category. Appropriate academic standing was also included in the expectations of the athletic code. Second, and maybe the most important concern, was a suspension from a classroom, habitual tardiness, or frequent absences. Poor efforts on class work that could jeopardize eligibility and any lack of respect for teachers was our third target. Fourth, any unsportsmanlike conduct toward coaches, players, officials, or opponents was absolutely not acceptable. Finally, unexcused absences from practices or games would result in disciplinary behavior.

Having expectations like these outlined for student-athletes and parents allows for coaches to give student-athletes the best opportunity to be successful. Any time people know what is expected they have a much better chance at being successful. Furthermore, when they know the consequences of not meeting those expectations it presents opportunities to make good decisions. Finally, if people fail to meet expectations, having consequences outlined in advance makes students and parents more accepting of the punishment. Setting high expectations makes everyone accountable for their own actions.

The coaching staff expected the student-athletes in the program to hold each other accountable to the mission

## THE MISSION

statement because the mission statement wasn't effective if it didn't mean anything to the student-athletes involved. As the head coach, I would challenge the varsity student-athletes. I reminded them that the coaching staff expected the Varsity to set the tone for the entire program. We reminded them that it is their team and their program. We told them that the success of the team is dependent on the following factors:

1. How well they enforced these guidelines for all other players.
2. How well they would abide by these guidelines and set a good example for the other players.
3. How well they demonstrated leadership. The older student-athletes must constantly encourage their teammates by promoting enthusiasm, intensity, work ethic, and teamwork.

The mission statement ended with a few key points that the coaching staff believed were significant to emphasize. It was important that the student-athletes used appropriate language always. We wanted to make sure the players thought about what they were going to say. Their actions and words would be scrutinized, good or bad. We wanted to be sure that the players continued to believe in themselves and to always do what they knew was right. The coaching staff reminded the student-athletes that the entire school looked up to them; they had a tremendous opportunity to be leaders within their community. We wanted them to make a difference. It is important for all student-athletes to learn to accept constructive criticism so they could make the necessary adjustments to behavior and move on. Finally, we reminded the student-athletes to take pride in who they are as people. Maintaining their appearance, personal hygiene, and attitude go a long way in establishing a positive sense of self-worth.

The closing comments of the mission statement were directly from me. I, as the head coach of the program, want to build and maintain a program that our athletes, student-body, faculty, and community are proud to be associated with for the rest of their lives. We want to find value in who we are at a very deep level. It is our passion that drives us to do extraordinary things. When we discover our passion we will feel comfortable and confident sharing it with our world. When our student-athletes put the uniform on it will mean something to them...to everybody, beyond winning and losing. We will be successful!

Having a mission statement for the high school athletic department and a separate mission statement for every athletic program in the school is fundamental to the whole success of the program. The mission statement is a guideline to apply policies and outline expectations of everyone involved. The creation of a mission statement is critical in maintaining a proactive approach to administering and managing high school athletic programs.

# CONCLUSION

# THE SPIRIT WITHIN

*Give the world the best you have,*
  *and it may never be enough;*
*Give the world the best you've got anyway.*

*You see, in the final analysis,*
  *it is between you and God;*

*It was never between you and them anyway*

  Mother Teresa

    My experiences as a high school athlete have helped mold me into the man I am today. It wasn't so much the winning and the losing as it was the life lessons taught by the coaches who were so willing to work with me. The experiences I have had as a high school coach have reinforced the idea that participation in high school athletics can be a vital role in the development of young people. In the lowest moments of my life I have reflected upon all of the positive experiences, many of which have come in the arena of high school athletics.
    All positive experiences I must attribute to the presence of God in my life. The spirit has affected me and influenced me more than any other source. Many of my positive experiences have been with my family which includes my parents, siblings, Desiree, Brooklyn, Dawson, and now Faith and Hope. Many

more of those experiences occurred through my participation in high school athletics. Even more, many positive experiences occurred as a coach of high school student-athletes and as my job as a high school English teacher. In the depths of destruction, I turned to the support of my faith, family, and, in part, the lessons I learned as a high school student-athlete.

Participation in high school athletics provides many opportunities for growing in faith and spirituality. It also provides many opportunities to experience lessons of life. All co-curricular activities in high school must reflect as well as be extensions of the classroom. It is the responsibility of all teachers, coaches, and administrators to provide an environment that educates the whole person. The more experiences students receive in a variety of situations will better prepare them for their future. Athletics is just a part of the vast landscape of education in our high schools.

A portion of athletics that is a significant, long lasting lesson is the importance of physical health. As part of a high school athletic program, student-athletes learn how to take care of their bodies. Furthermore, physical activity generates positive chemical flow in the brain which helps to build a positive self-image. Physical fitness leads to a healthy lifestyle which, in turn is a productive lifestyle.

The most obvious gain in high school athletics in terms of physical health is that of daily exercise. Student-athletes learn to build their muscle mass through weight training. The increase in muscle development leads to the burning of more fat cells within the body. Student-athletes also learn to stretch the muscles of their bodies to generate flexibility. The flexibility allows them to be more agile as adults. Finally, the daily exercise includes cardio fitness. Student-athletes have the opportunity each and every day to build the most important muscle in their entire body, the heart.

In the midst of the daily exercise routine for student-athletes, trained coaches must promote healthy eating. We must remind ourselves and our children that the purpose of eating is to fuel our bodies; so often, people view eating as a form of entertainment. While most of us do enjoy the taste of food and are willing to eat unhealthy foods from time to time, it is important to help children understand the benefits of the good fuel for our bodies.

At some point in time throughout the curriculum in a school district, students have the requirement of taking a health class. These types of classes do teach the importance of eating right and treating our bodies in a healthy way. High school athletics certainly can act as a supplement, or an extension of the classroom, to these classes. The same holds true for physical education classes. While these classes are required for students throughout their educational experience, high school athletics can provide yet another opportunity to practice healthy physical activity and proper choices in eating habits.

Teaching student-athletes the power of good choices is relevant to nearly every situation in their lives. Along with the positive effects of physical activity that high school athletics promotes, there are important lessons to be learned in terms of emotional and mental health as well. Having a healthy mind as well as a healthy self esteem will undoubtedly lead to a positive sense of self-worth. Mental and emotional health can be gained through the experience of high school athletics.

Student-athletes learn the pride of accomplishment through hard work and commitment. Attending practice each day and maintaining a high standard of work ethic will lead to accomplishment. Accomplishment is not defined solely in outscoring an opponent. Accomplishment is defined here as gaining something within the self that will lead to maintaining a positive sense of self-worth, interacting positively with others, and making valuable contributions to society.

Upon achieving set goals, student-athletes learn the valuable lesson of celebrating hard work. In our adult lives, how often do we get excited about achieving a goal in our jobs? It makes us feel good to complete the building of a house, or completing the final tax return, or having a lesson plan that engages all students, or changing the oil in a car, or even cutting the grass. We have moments of internal celebration for a job well done. It is important that student-athletes learn, through high school athletics, this important lesson: to celebrate our successes together.

In order to celebrate our successes, we need to be at peace with who we are. High school student-athletes can begin to understand the negative effects of misplaced egos. Furthermore, they can begin to learn the lesson of acceptance. Accepting wins, accepting losses, and accepting roles are all vital lessons that will resonate well into the future. Accepting where we are and our strengths allows us to strive to reach our maximum potential. Acceptance is one of the most powerful tools we can have to reach success.

High school athletics provides opportunities to sharpen the tools of integrity and honesty. Learning the significance of saying what we mean and meaning what we say will help us earn credibility with others. If we are honest and act with integrity, we can build up sort of a credibility account with those we work with and live with. When we are consistently honest with ourselves and with others, it is acceptable to occasionally be wrong in our perceptions of the world. Others will appreciate our honesty and not judge us so harshly when we do make mistakes. High school athletics is the perfect forum for such lessons to be taught and learned.

As student-athletes grow in their integrity, out of that seed will bud a general respect for self and others. In the growth of all people there are struggles and successes. Each person who becomes aware that struggles and success are not unique to themselves will begin to truly recognize a genuine respect for all people. In achieving respect for self and others, a positive sense of self-worth emerges and continues to grow within.

The arena of high school athletics is one of the most powerful learning environments for our youth. Lessons learned on the field, court, track, wrestling mat, or in the swimming pool are as powerful and significant as anything learned in the classroom. These lessons must be properly delivered by responsible adults, void of ego, who are interested in the success of kids.

High school athletics present opportunities for student-athletes to grow as people. The valuable lessons of acceptance and accountability allow student-athletes to capture their inner uniqueness. Accepting and understanding the inner uniqueness allows people to share their strengths. Our egos will always exist. Nevertheless, we must not allow our egos to haunt us; instead, we must have the control over how our ego affects who we really are.

It is our duty and responsibility to unleash the inner beauty God created for each and every one of us. It is our obligation to share this inner passion with the universe as God has intended. In discovering who we are we can develop a positive sense of self-worth that has long lasting effects on our confidence and our future success. The participation in high school athletics is only a small portion of what helps each person attain a sense of spirituality as well as the ultimate discovery of self, beyond the scoreboard.

# APPENDIX

# APPENDIX A

**Varsity Basketball**

**Mission Statement**

It is the intent of the program to teach life skills and basketball skills which provide opportunities for success. As a team, the coaching staff will always model and encourage the following four objectives:
1. **We are going to play hard.** Anything less than 100% cheats the team and the individual.
2. **We are going to play smart.** We must play within the team structure and recognize individual abilities and limitations. We must understand team objectives and carry out the plan of the coach.
3. **We are going to play together.** We will celebrate all team victories, large or small, and we will celebrate the success of the team, always. The success of the team is the greatest feat in team sports.
4. **We will have fun.** Basketball is a game to be enjoyed. However, fun is the result of hard work!

I believe the student-athletes in the basketball program must be respected as people. Reciprocally, the athletes must respect their parents, teachers, coaches, teammates and officials at all times; respect breeds respect. The lasting impression

# APPENDIX A

we, as a coaching staff, want the athletes that come through this program to have is one of **pride, accomplishment, and strength in self-worth.** The coaching staff and all others associated with the program will promote a **positive attitude, high expectations of character, honesty, and integrity.**

## Be a Team Player

Every player must commit, wholeheartedly, to the team concept – physically, mentally, and emotionally – if the team is going to reach its highest potential and succeed. It only takes one misplaced ego to wreck the fragile trust that exists between players and coaches and player to player. Lack of commitment and effort begins to tear apart the fabric of team work, which, in turn, brings on total failure during practice and games. It only takes one person with selfish interests to ruin the delicate balance of trust. From the most dominant player to the least dominant player, each must not believe they deserve more awards, recognition, or playing time. **We must strive for unity, chemistry, and loyalty.**

Successful people have attitudes that generate thoughts like, *"What can I contribute to the team?, What can I do to get better?, What needs to be done where I can be of assistance?"* These thoughts contribute to positive attitudes which, in turn, bring on cooperation towards a common goal.

All players must understand that the varsity level is highly competitive. Each player must accept their role on the team. The coaching staff will be straightforward regarding team issues. Not all players can start. Not all players will play in every game. However, **all players are key ingredients to molding a strong team.** It is the responsibility of the coaching staff to explain team roles to each player.

I believe that good things will happen for this basketball program this season if we believe in and work with each other.

## Communication

Communication only occurs when a message is sent and that message is received. You can send all you want but, until the message is received, understood, and acted upon, communication has not taken place. If any team function is to be successful, it must have constant communication, which will avoid misunderstandings and hurt feelings.

I will be straightforward concerning team issues. I will discuss situations with players that may need improvement, change, or encouragement. I believe in communication as a vital ingredient to success and human development. **I will communicate with all student-athletes when appropriate and necessary; remember, communication is a two way process (sender and receiver).** As a coach I must look out for the best interest of the team. Since players do not always like what they hear and share these thoughts at home, mixed messages develop along with a false sense of reality. Players might respond to questions by family members with, "I don't know, the coach won't talk to me." This chain of events sets into motion powerful feelings of anger and resentment toward the coach. Often times this leads the parent to coaching their child which is to the detriment of the team, not to mention the athlete. This creates divided loyalties, cliques, drives wedges between the players, and destroys team chemistry.

How much better would it be if parents reserved comment to themselves and told their child to fix the problem with the coach? Remember it is part of our mission to teach life skills – communication is an extremely important life skill. When adults have problems or concerns with their boss, they must address it with the boss. How much better would it be if parents said to me, "Coach, can we talk about _____?" I do not expect the athletes looking to the stands for guidance during any game. It is my job to coach. In order to do that I must have the undivided attention of each and every one of my players at all times.

Furthermore, I am always willing to discuss issues with both the players and their parents. If you have a concern at any time throughout the season please contact me to set up an appointment to meet. We might not agree on the solution, but we can agree to disagree, and still work together to accomplish success within the framework of the program. Anything can be discussed as long as it is done in an attitude of mutual respect. Good communication between player/coach and parent/coach must be modeled and can proactively eliminate problems. I request that the player accompany the parents. I will be honest with the players. I do not want the players to feel that there is something going on behind their backs.

Communication between a player and a coach can consist of praise, instruction, and information. All of these messages can be conveyed in a friendly tone or as constructive criticism. Oddly enough, it seems that players only remember the criticism. I will always encourage players, concerning criticism, to listen to **what** is being said and **not how** it is being said. Players often times think of it as an adversarial relationship instead of speaking the truth from the heart -- a comment or criticism actually designed to help the athlete improve. The relationship that is developed is professional and, therefore, the criticism is not personal.

**Examples of communication lapses by players and coaches:**
*Unrealistic view of a player's talent or ability.
*Expectations of more playing time.
*Breaking into the starting five.
*The fact that a player is a senior and has, therefore, earned the right or expectation to play.

Positive feelings about one's ability and the desire to play more are admirable qualities, however it is part of my job, as the coach, to define roles for players and determine who should play -- why and when. I will play the players who give our team the best opportunity to be competitive and successful.

Often times players work hard in practice and make significant contributions to the team's success but hardly get the opportunities in games because of another player's ability or the talent of the opponent. I firmly believe that these players are just as important to the team's success because they push the players that see the most playing time in practice everyday. It is also highly unjust of me to "throw" a player into a game situation if I feel it is a situation that will limit success for that player. Playing in a game where the competition is ahead of a player's ability does more to damage a player's confidence and ego than anything at all.

There are many reasons that factor into the decision-making process of who plays and why. If you, as a parent, are in doubt please reflect on these guidelines:

- Give me the benefit of the doubt; avoid prejudging the situation.
- Keep any personal comments to yourself.
- Encourage your child to talk to me to work it out. Give your child a chance to grow and learn from the situation.
- Give it time. **Be Patient**.
- Do not "bad-mouth" a player or the program in the stands.

***If at any time you make derogatory or negative comments about me, one of the players, the team, or the program you teach kids how not to handle a concern or a conflict. Your child will question teammates and the coach. What will happen is the very thing you are trying to avoid -- you will affect performance because of a negative attitude and negative mind set.

## Code of Ethics

- **Conduct yourself in an acceptable, appropriate manner at all times**. If you think you are doing something wrong, you probably are. Ask yourself, "is this the right thing to do?"
- Strive for your **maximum potential in the classroom**. You are in school to get an education.
- Be punctual! **You set a great example and impression when you are on time!!**
- **Be respectful.**

# APPENDIX A

- Stand to cheer on your teammates after a score or great defensive play.

## Game Night

1. Varsity players are to report at the time designated by Coach _____. Times will vary due to the site of the game (home or away).
2. **All Varsity players are to sit together during the Junior Varsity game**.
3. Varsity players must report to the locker room no later than the 4:00 mark of the JV third quarter. Players that need to be taped prior to game time should report immediately after the JV half time.
4. **In the locker room, basketball is the only topic of conversation.** This is to help us focus for the game and the responsibilities we have. The coaches should not have to remind you about this focus.
5. Junior Varsity players are expected to stay for the Varsity game whether home or away.

### Pre-Game

The coaching staff will enter the locker room for a pre-game talk during the fourth quarter of the Junior Varsity game. At that time all players are to be dressed in their game uniform and ready to step onto the court.

## On the Court

- Be prompt.
- Be courteous to opponents and officials at all times.
- Play hard. Play clean.
- Do not verbally or physically respond when provoked.
- Use appropriate language at all times.
- Complete attention to the game. You will not visit with anyone while on the court. Your focus is the basketball game. If you are seated on the bench, cheer on your teammates!!

## Bench Conduct

- All players, on the floor or on the bench, will never express verbal, facial, or bodily displeasure with an official or coach. Be respectful. Leave all discussion with officials for the coaches!
- Any action of disgust while on the floor, on the bench, or while coming out of the game will be strongly disciplined – including benching or suspension.
- Players must understand that the coaches do not have time to explain every move at the particular time it occurs during the game. Players should hold comments and questions regarding substitutions until after the game.

## Bus Conduct

Actions on the bus set the tone for the game. It is my expectation that all varsity players, **especially the captains**, take responsibility for seeing that all players adhere to behavior that will prepare us for that evening's game. In order to be mentally prepared for the game and focused, **there will be no talking or music 10 minutes prior to our arrival to a school.** In the event of a loss, the bus will remain quiet for the first 10 minutes of the ride home. The purpose is to allow you to rethink what occurred in the game and assess what you as an individual, and the team as whole, needs to do to improve. I do not anticipate having to address this issue throughout the season.

    **All players at the Varsity and Junior Varsity levels are required to ride the player bus to and from games.** Being together when we win and when we lose teaches us to be strong and unite in exciting and adverse times.

## Post – Game

At the conclusion of each game there will be a brief team meeting in the locker room. The room is only open to members of the team and immediate basketball program.

## Loyalty to Your Teammates

# APPENDIX A

No member of the basketball program is to publicly criticize another member of the program. As a member of the team, your first loyalty is to your teammates and your coaches.

## Disciplinary Procedures

The following conduct can result in temporary, and in extreme cases, permanent suspension from the team.
1. Athletic Code Violation
2. Suspension from class or school or ALC time.
3. Poor effort on class work that could jeopardize eligibility.
4. Unsportsman – like conduct toward coaches, players, or officials.
5. Unexcused absences from practices and/or games. Each practice must be made up prior to game participation. Games missed will result in sitting out the same number of games upon return.

## Practice Expectations

We must take advantage of the practice time we have planned. The attitudes and work ethic of our practice sessions set the groundwork for our season.

- Punctuality is an absolute must!! **Whatever the starting time all players are to be dressed and ready to go five minutes prior to practice.** Players that need to be late, for school or family reasons, must clear it with the coach prior to practice. Unexcused lateness will be handled by appropriate discipline (i.e., 1 lap for every minute late).
- Call my voice mail if you are absent from school. 555-5555 ext. 555
- When you take the floor for practice, all outside conversations stop. Basketball is the only topic of conversation during practice time!
- All players must be in appropriate practice gear. All players must have their previously issued practice jersey.
- **You must perform every drill with the same effort and intensity that you would put into your most important game.**

If we are to perform our best at all times, then we must strive to execute perfectly during our practices.

## Set the Tone

As the head coach, I expect the Varsity to set the tone for the entire program. It is your team and your program. The success of your team is dependent on the following factors:
1. How well you enforce these guidelines for other players.
2. How well you abide by these guidelines and set a good example for the other players.
3. How well you demonstrate leadership. You must constantly encourage your teammates by promoting enthusiasm, intensity, work ethic, and teamwork.
- **Use appropriate language always.** Think about what you are going to say. Others will, always scrutinize your conduct, good or bad.
- **Believe in yourself** and do what is right.
- **Be a leader!!** The entire school looks up to athletes. You have a tremendous opportunity to make a difference.
- **Accept constructive criticism.** Make any necessary adjustments to your actions or behaviors and move on.
- **Take Pride in Yourself.** The maintenance of your appearance, personal hygiene, and attitude go far in defining yourself.

## Program Roots

I, as the head coach, want to build and maintain a program that our athletes, student-body, faculty and community are proud to be associated with for the rest of their lives. When our athletes put the uniform on it will mean something to them...to everybody. We will be successful!

If there are any questions or concerns, please feel free to call me, (w)555 – 5555 ext. 555, (h)555-5555.

# APPENDIX B

## Youth Basketball Mission Statement

It is the intent of the program to teach life skills and basketball skills which provide opportunities for success. As a team, the coaching staff and parents will always model and encourage the following four objectives:

1. **We are going to give all girls in grades 3 – 8 the opportunity to participate.** The importance of participation is the foundation of this program. The youth program is a viable resource to allow kids to participate in a basketball program that is focused on skill development and team work with the intent of being successful in game situations.
2. **We are going to teach basketball skills.** We must teach young athletes the "basics" of the game of basketball. Before the athletes can learn a "motion" offense, they need to sharpen their skills (i.e., dribbling, passing, and shooting).
3. **We are going to play together.** We will celebrate all team and program victories, large or small, and we will celebrate the success of the program, always. The success of the team and, in this case, the program, is the greatest feat in team sports.
4. **We will have fun.** Basketball is a game to be enjoyed. Fun is the result of hard work!

I believe the student-athletes in the youth basketball program must be respected as people. Reciprocally, the athletes must respect their parents, teachers, coaches, teammates and officials at all times; respect breeds respect. The lasting impression we, as a coaching staff, want the athletes that come through this program to have is one of **pride, accomplishment, and strength in self-worth.** The coaching staff and all others associated with the program will promote a **positive attitude, high expectations of character, honesty, and integrity.**

## Participation

Allowing girls in grades 3 – 8 the opportunity to participate in the traveling teams of the youth basketball program is a necessity. The challenge of this aspect of the program is finding people/parents to help as coaches. Furthermore, parents that assist in the coaching need to be qualified, through meetings/clinics with the head coach, and willing to follow with the program's mission statement. Finally, all parents of the student athletes participating must be in support of the coach/coaches of their respective teams and of the program as a whole. It is understandable that not everybody agrees on all decisions being made, but as we build a solid foundation based on the mission statement of the program, all of those decisions will be clearly seen as what is in the best interest of the student athletes participating and the program as a whole.

## Basketball Skills

Teaching the "basics" of the game is essential to the success of all student athletes. For example, a child needs to learn to read in a step by step process. First, a child must recognize letters and the sounds associated with those letters. Then, a child must be able to recognize the words those letters form. Finally, a child has to understand that reading is learning and that, within those letters and sounds, there is information that is being presented. Such is the case with basketball. I want our young players to believe in the importance in being the best dribbler and passer they can be. At the varsity level, if an athlete can dribble and pass effectively it certainly increases that athlete's opportunity to help the team succeed. Every team needs great passers and dribblers. Included in this document are basketball skills standards and benchmarks for each grade level.

## Be a Team Player

Every player and parent must commit, wholeheartedly, to the team concept – physically, mentally, and emotionally – if the team/program is going to reach its highest potential and succeed. It only takes one misplaced ego, player or parent, to wreck the fragile trust that exists between players and coaches and player to player. Lack of commitment and effort begins to tear apart the fabric of team work, which, in turn, brings on total failure during practice and games. It only takes one person with his/her own selfish interests to ruin the delicate balance of trust. From the most dominant player to the least dominant player, each must not believe they deserve more awards, recognition, or playing time. **We must strive for unity, chemistry, and loyalty.**

Successful people have attitudes that generate thoughts like, *"What can I contribute to the team?, What can I do to get better?, What needs to be done where I can be of assistance?"* These thoughts contribute to positive attitudes which, in turn, bring on cooperation towards a common goal.

Each player must accept his/her role on the team. The coaching staff will be straightforward regarding team issues. Not all players can start. Not all players will play in every game. However, **all players are key ingredients to molding a strong team.** It is the responsibility of the coaching staff to explain team roles to each player.

I believe that good things will happen for the youth basketball program if we believe in and work with each other.

## Have Fun

The importance of having fun playing basketball is somewhat underrated. Basketball is a great game that can be enjoyed many different ways. It is imperative that we pass that along to the all student athletes involved in the program. Demonstrate how to celebrate hard work. Fun is the result of working hard and seeing something through. Celebrate all successes, big or small. Encourage student athletes to be fans…become students of the game yourself and share what you learn with your children, their friends, and teammates.

## Coaching Qualifications:

Parents willing to help out and coach must meet the following qualifications:
1. Willing to volunteer time.
2. Willing to objectively support youth basketball program and the team they are coaching.
3. Willing to accept team/teams chosen by Coach Steltz and his staff.
4. Attend coaching clinic presented by Coach Steltz and his staff.
5. Willing to implement drills, offenses, defenses, and philosophy of program.
6. Willing to work with other parents as assistant coaches.
7. Adhere to given benchmarks and standards of each grade level.
8. Willing to positively communicate team status with Coach Steltz and his staff.

## Team Selection

All teams will be selected by Coach Steltz and his staff. Given enough participants and willing coaches, there will be two or more teams in grades three through eight.

There may be A and B teams selected as early as sixth grade and absolutely no later than seventh grade. A and B teams maybe selected earlier than sixth grade depending upon the number of participants and willing coaches. The idea of A and B teams may be different for each grade level. Depending upon the number of participants, willing coaches, and the compatibility of the athletes/coaches, A and B selection is in the sole discretion of Coach Steltz and his staff.

We will have as many teams we can depending upon the number of willing participants and the willingness of coaches. The rosters of each team are subject to change each year based on the discretion of Coach Steltz and his staff.

## Code of Ethics

- **Conduct yourself in an acceptable, appropriate manner at all times**. If you think you are doing something wrong, you probably are. Ask yourself, "is this the right thing to do?"
- Strive for your **maximum potential in the classroom**. You are in school to get an education.
- Be punctual! **You set a great example and impression when you are on time!!**
- **Be respectful.**
- Stand to cheer on your teammates after a score or great defensive play.

## On the Court

- Be prompt.
- Be courteous to opponents and officials at all times.
- Play hard. Play clean.
- Do not verbally or physically respond when provoked.
- Use appropriate language at all times.
- Complete attention to the game. You will not visit with anyone while on the court. Your focus is the basketball game. If you are seated on the bench, cheer on your teammates!!

## Bench Conduct

- All players, on the floor or on the bench, will never express verbal, facial, or bodily displeasure with an official or coach. Be respectful. Leave all discussion with officials for the coaches!
- Any action of disgust while on the floor, on the bench, or while coming out of the game will be strongly disciplined – including benching or suspension.
- Players must understand that the coaches do not have time to explain every move at the particular time it occurs during the game. Players should hold comments and questions regarding substitutions until after the game.

## Loyalty to Your Teammates

No member of the youth basketball program is to publicly criticize another member of the program. As a member of the team, your first loyalty is to your teammates, which includes all teams of the programs, and your coaches.

## Practice Expectations

We must take advantage of the practice time we have planned. The attitudes and work ethic of our practice sessions set the groundwork for our season.

- Punctuality is an absolute must!! **Whatever the starting time all players are to be dressed and ready to go five minutes prior to practice.** Players that need to be late, for school or family reasons, must clear it with the coach prior to practice. Unexcused lateness will be handled by appropriate discipline (i.e., 1 lap for every minute late).
- **You must perform every drill with the same effort and intensity that you would put into your most important game.** If we are to perform our best at all times, then we must strive to execute perfectly during our practices.
- **Use appropriate language always.** Think about what you are going to say. Others will, always scrutinize your conduct, good or bad.

- **Believe in yourself** and do what is right.
- **Be a leader!!** You have a tremendous opportunity to make a difference.
- **Accept constructive criticism.** Make any necessary adjustments to your actions or behaviors and move on.
- **Take Pride in Yourself.** The maintenance of your appearance, personal hygiene, and attitude go far in defining yourself.

## Program Roots

I, as the head coach, want to build and maintain a program that our athletes, student-body, faculty and community are proud to be associated with for the rest of their lives. When our athletes put the uniform on it will mean something to them...to everybody. We will be successful!

If there are any questions or concerns, please feel free to call me, (w)555 – 5555 ext. 555, (h)555-5555

# ACKNOWLEDGEMENTS

*Beyond the Scoreboard* is the product of life-long learning from family, teachers, coaches, students, athletes, parents, colleagues, and friends. I am sure that well over a hundred people fit into any one of these categories that have helped me grow in my profession, personality, faith, and philosophy over my 39 years of life. Thank you, everyone. A few people, however, deserve special mention:

Stacie Kaminski, my vibrant colleague in the English department of Seymour Community High School and trusted friend, spent endless hours editing draft after draft. Her attention to detail is second-to-none; her patience with me is a blessing. Stacie provided valuable feedback and support throughout the editing and revising stages of *Beyond the Scoreboard* all while taking precious time away from her young family.

My oldest sister, Julie Steltz, relentlessly pursued publishing options with me. It was a wonderful learning opportunity for both of us. She became my quasi-agent and never once asked for compensation. Julie spent hours in research to publish *Beyond the Scoreboard*, and she took the time to help her little brother process an overwhelming amount of information to arrive at an educated solution.

Jeff Palmer helped me to uncover my strengths, organize my thoughts, and encourage me to utilize my personal strengths in a very dark time of my life. The numerous hours

# ACKNOWLEDGEMENTS

of dialog with Jeff opened my eyes and my heart to clearly identify the purpose of *Beyond the Scoreboard*.

Many thanks to Cathy Clarksen, William (Bill) Collar, and Duane Rogatzki who helped me mold my coaching philosophies. Duane gave me the opportunity as a college student to begin coaching at the high school level teaching me the simplicity of coaching young adults. The many lessons I learned from Bill seem endless. He made it a point to model how coaches must stand up for what is right...always. Cathy shared with me the mission statement she used in her program, showing me its significance and impact. With this inspiration I was able to create a mission statement for our program and develop a healthy, productive coaching and teaching philosophy.

Curtis Jefson is simply the finest assistant coach and friend I could have ever imagined. He has always been helpful, supportive, and challenged me to give my best for the student-athletes we were coaching. I could not have carried through with my philosophy, expectations, or mission statement without the help and support of all the assistants I have worked with over the years: Joel Cartier, Kerry Danforth, Andrea Gawryleski, Crystal Helm, Gregg Plinska, Angie Quinn, Joy Rogatzki, Jason Setliff, Mark Stanchik, Matthew Timm, Kevin VanVonderen, and Darlene Wesolowski.

The two most influential teachers I had were my sixth grade teacher, Mrs. Casey, and my freshmen High School English teacher, Mr. Jahnke. My love for learning and my desire to become a professional educator and coach began in the comforts of their classrooms. Among the many coaches I have had over my lifetime, I have had three inspirational coaches who have encouraged me and taught me a plethora of valuable life lessons: Greg Jahnke (doubled as my freshmen English teacher), Jim Kersten, and Ron Klestinski.

Thank you to the numerous athletes I had the opportunity to coach. A special thanks to the athletes who were the source of inspiration for many of the anecdotes in *Beyond the Scoreboard*.

Many thanks to my colleagues and friends for providing valuable feedback on the anecdotes, structure, and purpose of *Beyond the Scoreboard*.

Finally, my deepest gratitude goes to my family. My children, Brooklyn and Dawson, who were so patient with their daddy as I spent countless hours writing; they are an endless source of inspiration to me. My two youngest children, Faith and Hope, did not come along until the manuscript was finished, but, in their own way, allowed me to remain faithful in my purpose and continue to hope for good. Desiree graciously allowed me to lock myself away for hours at a time to create *Beyond the Scoreboard*. I thank her for sharing in my dreams and making my dreams come true each and every day; together we will remind each other that all things are possible with God and allow our light to shine bright.

## These Are The Days
Words and Music by Monty Powell and Keith Urban
Copyright c 2004 UNIVERSAL MUSIC CORP., LANARK VILLAGE TUNES and GUITAR MONKEY MUSIC
All Rights for LANARK VILLAGE TUNES Controlled and Administered by UNIVERSAL MUSIC CORP.
All Rights for GUITAR MONKEY MUSIC Controlled and Administered by SONGS OF UNIVERSAL, INC.
All Rights Reserved    Used by Permission
*Reprinted by permission of Hal Leonard Corporation*

# ABOUT THE AUTHOR

**John P. Steltz** is a high school English teacher at Seymour Community High School in Seymour, Wisconsin. With 14 years teaching experience and 20 years coaching at the middle school and high school levels, John has had many experiences with fellow colleagues, student-athletes, their parents, and administrators providing the impetus for *Beyond the Scoreboard*. John has written "The Role of an Assistant Coach" published in *The Point After II* Winter 2000, the official publication of the Wisconsin Football Coaches Association. John was selected an assistant twice and was named head coach once for the Wisconsin Basketball Coaches Association Division 2 North Senior All-Star Girls Basketball team. John lives in Seymour, Wisconsin with his wife and four children.